The Role of Religion in Eastern Europe Today

Julia Gerlach • Jochen Töpfer (Eds.)

The Role of Religion in Eastern Europe Today

Springer VS

Editors
Julia Gerlach
Berlin, Germany

Jochen Töpfer
Magdeburg, Germany

With financial support of Bundesministerium für Bildung und Forschung (BMBF)

ISBN 978-3-658-02440-6 ISBN 978-3-658-02441-3 (eBook)
DOI 10.1007/978-3-658-02441-3

Library of Congress Control Number: 2014955148

Springer VS

Printed on acid-free paper

Springer VS is a brand of Springer Fachmedien Wiesbaden
Springer Fachmedien Wiesbaden is part of Springer Science+Business Media
(www.springer.com)

Preface and Acknowledgements

This book derives from the interdisciplinary symposium titled "Under Construction: The Role of Religion in Eastern Europe Today" which was held in St. Petersburg in September 2012 in the framework of the German Russian Year of Education, Science and Innovation. It was generously funded by the German Federal Ministry of Education and Research (BMBF). The symposium marked the second meeting of researchers and practitioners specialized in the region of Eastern Europe organized by the working group "Religion and Belief in Eastern Europe" at the Institute for East European Studies at Freie Universität Berlin.

The working group was established in fall 2011 and unites junior and senior researchers from different academic disciplines such as Cultural Studies, Economy, Law, Political Science, and Sociology. The aim of the group is to analyze the nexus and tension between religion and the state, religion and society, and religion and economy in Post-Socialist Eastern Europe. These relationships are complex, varied, and intertwined. Interdisciplinary research can contribute to understand them better.

The symposium explored the volatile role of religion – sometimes competing religions – in the heterogeneous region of Eastern Europe, mainly in Russia and the Balkans and was organized in four panels. In their panel "Christianity, Islam, and Eastern Europe: Comparing Russia and the Balkans", Sabine Riedel and Jochen Töpfer analyzed religious communities and religious affiliations and its impact on society and policy in South Eastern Europe and Russia. From the perspective of political economy, Theocharis Grigoriadis suggested in his panel "The Political Economics of Religion: How Russian Orthodoxy Affects Institutions and Policy" that Russian Orthodoxy may affect the country's institutional settings, both the economic nature and transformation of political regimes, supporting his arguments by a political-economic model. The panel "Law, State and Religion in Europe" conducted by Burkhard Breig, Dmitri Dinze and Olga Kudrashova, compared recent discourses on religion and the freedom of religion in Germany and Russia. The panel "The Sacred and the National: Shifting Identities in Russia Today" combined approaches from Architecture, Cultural Studies, and Political Science. Beate Apelt, Julia Gerlach, Nadir Kinossian, Inga Pylypchuk and Heike Winkel interpreted the (re)emergence of religion in contemporary Russia as a process of identity building. The relationship between politics, culture, and religion merges into a new collective identity as part of the state's ideology, visualized in the (re)surrection of state-funded monuments. Recent discourses on religion in Russia including the one on "Pussy Riot" address the amalgamation of religion and politics. This volume presents selected contributions from among those presented in St. Petersburg. The structure of the book follows the symposium.

The working group “Religion and Belief in Eastern Europe” would like to express their thanks to the German Federal Ministry of Education and Research (BMBF) for funding and to the Institute for East European Studies at Freie Universität Berlin and the Faculty for Law at State University of St. Petersburg for the support of the project. During the two workshops, several scholars and practitioners joined and contributed with their insights to the exchange: Dmitri Dintse (Agora), Theocharis Grigoriadis (Centre for European Economic Research), Nadir Kinossian (UiT—The Arctic University of Norway), Olga Kudrashova (St. Petersburg State University), Michael Minkenberg (European University Viadrina), Irina Moroza (Humboldt University), Olga Popova (University of Regensburg), Inga Pylypchuk (Die Welt, Berliner Morgenpost), and Sabine Riedel (German Institute for International und Security Affairs).

As for the working group, the following people affiliated with the Institute for East European Studies at Freie Universität Berlin engaged in the project: Beate Apelt (Political Science), Burkhard Breig (Law), John Eltringham (Cultural Studies), Julia Gerlach (Political Science), Christian Hattendorff (Economics), Blerina Hida (Economics), Jochen Töpfer (Sociology), and Heike Winkel (Cultural Studies).

This volume is an attempt to deepen the interdisciplinary study of the relationship between religion, state, and society in Eastern Europe. Next to presenting the main ideas of selected papers presented and discussed at the workshop, it aims to stimulate for further research in the field.

Berlin, February 2013

Contents

Introduction

Mapping the Role of Religion in Eastern Europe Today—An Interdisciplinary Approach

Julia Gerlach and Jochen Töpfer

The events of 1989/1991 in Europe reshaped the political, economic, and social landscapes. The socialist experiment in Eastern Europe had failed, and the societies of the so-called Eastern Bloc underwent profound changes in almost every respect. The outcomes of the transition, however, are obviously diverse. Some countries chose Western development models and integration into Western organizations as their path. Others adapted Western models selectively, and at the same time introduced new authoritarian measures. A few countries switched from one mode of authoritarian rule to another one.

Nevertheless, 1989/1991 represents a true caesura for all of the former Eastern Bloc countries, because the socialist master narrative became inapplicable. Socialism as a narrative had deeply shaped these countries for decades and had—despite the enormous heterogeneity of the region—resulted in similar patterns of state, economy, and society. This pattern has been reflected in the role of religion in socialist states. In a way, religion was perceived as a competing narrative to that of socialism. Thus, religion had been suppressed in various forms and degrees within Socialist countries, led by the ideal of an atheist society. Closest to this ideal was the People's Republic of Albania under Enver Hoxha. Laws passed in the 1960s literally banned both public and private religion, and the state introduced extreme punishments for any practice of religion. Already in the 1920s, Josef Stalin had started to crack down on religion and religious organizations in the Soviet Union. In many countries of socialist Eastern Europe, churches had been converted into gyms, shopping centers, libraries, or—cynically—into museums of atheism; believers and clerics were persecuted, arrested, and sometimes even murdered.

This top-down approach effectively banned religion from the public sphere. Within the private lives of many people, religion may have still played an important role, sometimes in silent opposition to the state and its doctrine. In the 1980s, when dissident and national movements all over Eastern Europe grew stronger, religion in some countries started to play an important role in identity- and community building. In Poland, the majority of the population identified with the Roman Catholic Church rather than with the socialist government. As an actor, the Roman Catholic

Church tipped the scales during the 'negotiated transition', mediating between the government and the central oppositional player, the *Solidarity* movement.

The years between 1989 and 1991 mark a turning point for the role of religion in Eastern Europe because the atheist doctrine of the socialist period was overcome. Religion was no longer banned from the public sphere. Most of the new constitutions even enshrined 'freedom of religion and belief'. However, today we observe a quite heterogeneous religious landscape in Eastern Europe. There are many different religions and denominations, and the relevance and roles they play for society and state differ quite significantly. This is true, for example, of the degree of societal religiosity; the role that (a specific) religion plays for community and state identity building; and for the organization of *de jure* and *de facto* secularism. This volume explores the current role of religion in Eastern Europe—defined politically as the territory of the former socialist Eastern European countries—from the perspectives of disciplines such as political science, sociology, law, culture, and architecture. The diversity of the field is reflected in the methodological approach of single case studies and comparative case studies. The spatial focus is on the Russian Federation (Russia and Tatarstan) and the Balkans (Bosnia-Herzegovina, Bulgaria, Macedonia, and Slovenia). One chapter on Germany serves as a contrast study.

The overall approach is explicitly not normative in its nature, but aims to understand and explain the current roles that religions play in different societies. The focus is especially on the relationship between religion and politics, respectively state and church—or, precisely, between state and 'organized religion'[1]. Empirical evidence suggests that organized religion underwent a revival in everyday life within most East European countries after 1989/1991. Quite striking is the new visibility of organized religion: renovated or newly erected religious buildings nowadays dominate central public places and sights, aiming to shape regional or national identities. How, then, might we evaluate the efforts that have been put into these building and planning projects? Do they reflect a manifestation of a bottom-up 'religious revival', or do they instead indicate a top-down identity-building process initiated by the state? Is religion just returning to the public space, or has it been instrumentalized by elites for the sake of gaining or accumulating political support?

The contemporary debate on religion in former socialist countries covers various sub-discourses. One is on the forms and degree of religiosity (Pickel and Sammet 2012:7; Müller 2013). Nevertheless, fluctuations in personal religiosity do not necessarily reflect or support the aims, dynamics, and outcomes of constructed collective

1 Here, we use the term 'organized religion' for institutionalized—and therefore nationally and internationally recognized—religious communities, in contrast to other forms of rather diffuse, informally established, and/or temporary spiritual associations that lack a stable hierarchical structure.

identity-building processes initiated by specific political actors. Identity building, conceptualized as the crossing of socialization and life-long learning (Pollack et al. 2003:XV), was a high priority of political elites in its collective form, especially when 22 societies emerged from the nine socialist states in Eastern Europe. Politics of independence was in need of legitimization and hence in search of a collective identity that would establish (imagined) borders between the adjacent neighbors. Indeed, the question is what nature and what kind of identity-building processes took place and are still evolving within the region.

Therefore, we can apply two concepts, which originate from political culture research. The first approach, after Neil Smelser, focuses on the two-dimensional concept of coherence and consensus of a given or postulated political culture of society (Smelser 1992:5/10): First, Smelser asks for the coherence of political culture or identity-building processes, which focuses on the integrity of its elements. Are the ideological elements, in sum, logically coherent enough to enhance the building of collective identity, with the additional task of constructing differences between the neighboring societies? Second, the key word of 'consensus' of the top-down collective identity-building process emphasizes the "degree of sharedness" (Ibid:5) of the newly defined central cultural elements among the societies' populations. Both questions on coherence and consensus guide the disciplinary contributions of the book at hand and hence enable an interdisciplinary integration of the following contributions from the fields of political science, sociology, law, literature studies, and even architecture.

The second theoretical approach that inspired this volume was developed by Mishler and Pollack, termed the "Neo-Cultural Synthesis" (Pollack et al. 2003:237). It can be understood as a response to controversies among social scientists about the concept of political culture, wherein some defend a narrow definition merely encompassing the attitudes of people (following the approach of rational choice) while others prefer a broad understanding that focuses on the core identity of people (culturalist perspective). The approach by Mishler and Pollack integrates both, and focuses on the differentiation of culture within a one-dimensional concept: The continuum begins at *no culture*; progresses via 'thin' culture, encompassing *attitudes* of people towards everyday issues; and ends at the point of 'thick' culture, where the national, religious, ethnic, and ideological *identities* of people become manifest (Ibid:245).

In modern societies, politics tends not to promote a single collective national, ethnic, or religious identity of people. Rather, these ideal-type societies are built up and characterized by plurality (including that of religion) on the macro level, and by the acceptance of multiple identities of people on the micro level. Therefore, ideal modern politics concentrates on aspects of the thin concept of culture:

political attitudes of everyday concern within a democratic, inclusive, and pluralist framework. Politics that promotes an exclusive vision of a single religious, ethnic, or national group is therefore unable (and often not sufficiently stable) to foster long-term societal modernization—neither culturally, politically, nor economically.

Contrasting the focus of the articles in this volume with the above-mentioned synthesis of approaches to political culture and identity, the contributors show that the societies of Eastern Europe in general are ambivalent toward the issue of modernization, toward legitimization after 1989/1991, and the construction of collective identity that often enough includes the relationship between state and organized religion, i.e., religion 'approved' by the state. Having in focus the relationship between state (in particular specific political and administrative actors) and religion, the contributors do not explicitly advocate political modernization in Eastern Europe, but the theme resonates in each of the articles.

The content of the book is presented in three major parts. The first part includes two articles that explain sociological perspectives on the relationship between state and organized religion. In his contribution *'Concepts of Religion and the State: An Application to South-Eastern Europe'*, Jochen Töpfer presents an overview of well-acknowledged concepts in social science, modeling the relationship between religion and state. The comparison uncovers the tendency for Western European social scientists to exclude so-called pre-/non-modern forms of the relationship, although from today's perspective it is not clear in which direction the states of Eastern Europe will develop in this respect (see as an example the article by Nadir Kinossian). The second step concerns the qualification of state/religion relations in Slovenia and Macedonia. In both cases, despite the assumption of secularization and hence religions/political separation, religion is well acknowledged in politics: in the case of Slovenia via the preferred treatment of traditional religions by some political actors; in Macedonia by the creation or forced ascent of politically active religions with connections to distinct ethnic parties of the political spectrum.

Sabine Riedel's chapter on *'The Role of State in Inter-Religious Relations—Lessons from East European History'* compares developments of the state/religion relationship in Eastern Europe by first categorizing Western European states in that respect. Here, historically, three forms emerged: The French case, where strong separation was implemented ('secular model' category); a cooperationist interplay between state and religion such as in Germany or the Netherlands ('cooperationist' category); and the 'state-church' category as in the examples of the United Kingdom and Denmark. In order to identify changes in the relationship within Eastern European societies, the chapter focuses on Bulgaria, Russia, and Bosnia-Herzegovina. The analysis demonstrates that all three—despite their secular constitutions—tend to the cooperationist and the state-church model, even if they are plural societies in the religious sense and share a socialist past. Hence, the ambiguity of social development in the region becomes obvious: modernization in the economic and technical sector, but diverse directions in the foundations of politics.

The second part of the book addresses the juridical outlook on state and religion. In his chapter on *'Law and Religion in Germany: The Case of Circumcision of Boys'*, Burkhard Breig analyzes the case of circumcision of boys by spiritual motivation in Germany. By discussing the latest issue of contention between religion and state in Germany from the legal perspective, he explains the tension between two basic individual rights in a modern state, namely between religious freedom (of the parents), and self-determination and physical integrity (of the child). In a bureaucratic masterstroke, the judges weighed the rights of the individuals involved and came to the Solomonic judgment that although the child has the right of physical integrity, the parents nevertheless cannot be punished for executing that particular religious norm that has been practiced for millennia.

Damir Gainutdinov's contribution on *'Russian Practice: Persecution for Criticism or Punishment for Blasphemy'* guides us back to Eastern Europe and summarizes various trials of artistic groups in the Russian Federation, especially in St. Petersburg and Moscow. He first emphasizes the fact that the juridical basis for the construction of a coherent identity of a people is also visible in the reshaping of criminal codes by the Russian Federation. As stated in one of the subsequent chapters by Inga Pylypchuk and Heike Winkel, state-defined 'religious feelings' have suddenly been introduced, and are conceived as primordial and unquestioned from the state perspective, thereby assuming a central position in new (but nevertheless ideally profane) juridical articles. Hence, in the Russian Federation today, the concept of a thick and coherently constructed culture encroaches from politics (indirectly activating religion via the tool of 'feelings') upon the sphere of law: The introduction of religious feelings into other fields of society by the state indicates the intention to develop a certain coherence of collective identity, especially when employing central aspects of a thick concept of culture.

The Russian Orthodox Church as an institution has been chosen by political elites to enhance the construction of a new coherent cultural in Russia. This has led to criticism in various segments of civil society. Recently, the Russian state has reacted harshly to protests against the Russian Orthodox Church. The Church itself carefully observes the cultural sphere and acts verbally and even physically if plurality exceeds the boundaries of its own acceptance, as Gainutdinov has experienced in his role defending artists in St. Petersburg's courts.

The third part of this volume is concerned with perspectives from political science, architecture, and literature studies towards the relationship between state and religion. While it might not at first appear logical to agglomerate these themes within one chapter, the reader will be able to connect them easily, not only by the geographical research field (the Russian Federation), but also by the keywords of coherence and thick culture introduced above: How are organized and so-called traditional religions utilized by political elites in Russia and Tatarstan? Have Russian Orthodoxy and Euro-Islam already become integral to politics in the resurgent Russian Federation?

In her chapter *'State-Identity Building in the New Russia'*, Julia Gerlach asks why Russian Orthodoxy became a key element of state identity building in the New Russia under the leadership of Vladimir Putin. She notes that in the process of transition, politics in the Russian Federation has been in need of legitimacy not only with regard to the foundations of the new state, but also in legitimizing the performance of everyday politics in improving the life of the people, which was and remains a challenging task for Russian politics.

In his contribution on *'Resurrection of the Temple: The Role of the State in Shaping the Regional Political Identity in Tatarstan'*, Nadir Kinossian deals with the relationship between politics and religion in Tatarstan. His case study focuses on two newly erected (or re-erected) religious buildings in the capital Kazan (a Sunni mosque and an Orthodox church), and investigates their spiritual and political functions as well as their historical embedment from a constructivist point of view. Financed and managed by the state and its regional representatives, the incentives and functions of the two religious buildings exemplify the close connection between religion and state today, and remind us that the course of separation between the two spheres we experience in Western Europe is not a one-way road. The links have become so close, and are maintained from the political side, such that religion itself has literally no space left for the movement and formulation of its own points of view on societal issues.

Inga Pylypchuk and Heike Winkel, in their chapter *'Strong Emotions, Weak Subjects: On the Role of Hurt Feelings in the Trial Against Pussy Riot'*, stress the new importance of emotions in the process of shaping ideal citizens that publicly represent the newly constructed collective identity in Russia. Here, the trial has symbolic functions and serves to design and publicly explain the coherence of identity in the individual, emotional sphere: "Navigating ones feelings according to the rules". State-standardized religious feelings and the definition of blasphemy and religious hate by politics are relatively new phenomena to Russian courtrooms. Nevertheless, this is not a mechanism intended to protect spiritual individuality; rather, it guides and channels feelings in order to construct a uniform and ideal type of citizen.

From a long-term perspective, the question for the overall organization of society is whether a top-down installation of norms and values aimed exclusively toward constructed coherence (an experience not exclusive to the Russian Federation) is able to reflect the real-world plurality of and within the differentiating spheres of societies that are engaged in modernization. Such forms of reflection are essential to maintain a certain degree of sharedness (meaning acceptance) among the affected people, since this consensus constitutes the basis for the sustainable development of a whole society (Smelser 1992:5).

In summary, it seems that politics in Eastern Europe is highly involved not only in the formation and canalization of attitudes towards everyday issues—which is their very task—but also in the construction of collective values and even identities, which is on the other hand inconsistent with a modern understanding of societal development. The editors are aware that the individual articles initially appear to address a wide range of topics. Nevertheless, by drawing on perspectives from law, political science, sociology, literature studies, and architecture, this volume presents a unique overview that can contribute to broadening the debate on a highly relevant issue.

References

Berliner Journal für Soziologie (1996) Das wissenschaftliche Kapital der Kultur. Neuere kultursoziologische Analysen. Berliner Journal für Soziologie Heft 1996(1):113–126

Mishler W, Pollack D (2003) On culture, thick and thin: Toward a neo-cultural synthesis. In: Pollack D, Jacobs J, Müller O, Pickel G (eds) Political culture in post-communist Europe: Attitudes in new democracies. Ashgate, Aldershot, p 237–256

Müller H-P (1994) Kultur und Gesellschaft. Auf dem Weg zu einer neuen Kultursoziologie? Berliner Journal für Soziologie 1994(2):135–156

Müller O (2013) Kirchlichkeit und Religiosität in Ostmittel- und Osteuropa. Entwicklungen – Muster – Bestimmungsgründe. Springer, Wiesbaden

Pickel G, Sammet K (2012) Transformations of religiosity in Central and Eastern Europe twenty years after the breakdown of communism. In: Pickel G, Sammet K (eds) Transformations of religiosity: Religion and religiosity in Eastern Europe 1989–2010. Wiley, Wiesbaden, p 7–20

Smelser N (1992) Culture: coherent or incoherent. In: Münch R, Smelser N (eds) Theory of culture. University of California Press, p 3–28

1.

Perspectives of Sociology

Concepts of Religion and the State: An Application to South-Eastern Europe

Jochen Töpfer

This chapter provides an overview of theoretical concepts between church and state, and examines the divergent cases of Slovenia and Macedonia. Slovenia and Macedonia, as relatively small countries of Eastern Europe, represent examples of constantly changing relationships between religious communities, the state, and the population since the initial post-socialist transition two decades ago. A common feature of social change is that religious communities are in search of their role within society and politics. Developments in Slovenia offer insights into the dynamics of the cleavage between traditional religions and new movements of indifference towards religious feelings. In Macedonia, the population is represented by two traditional religions (Christian Orthodoxy and Sunni Islam) that are interrelated with ethnic identity. Thus, following major political intervention, religion became a strong source of identity.

Introduction: Religion and State in South-Eastern Europe

Analyzing the relationships between religion, state, and society in Eastern Europe from the perspective of sociology means to enter areas of expertise of theology, cultural studies, history, anthropology, political science and even economics (see Segal 2006:vii). Researchers dealing with the topic should be aware of the academic context in order to facilitate and encourage open discussion among the scientific disciplines. Nevertheless, all share that most attention is focused on circumstances within the dominant societies of the region, such as the Russian Federation or Poland. In contrast, this chapter is concerned with the two cases of Slovenia and Macedonia. In these relatively small societies, religious communities reemerged as actors in the civic and political spheres after 1991. Therefore, they provide two useful cases for sociological analysis.

In Slovenia, a traditional religious community, the Roman Catholic Church (RKC[1]), is challenged in the public and political arenas by personal indifference to

1 RKC—Katoliška Cerkev v Sloveniji.

religion, and even atheist developments. Having no clear competitor in the religious sphere, the Catholic Church faces declining attention to its position in public, in politics, and on an individual level. The cleavage is manifest in attitudes among the population towards religion and religiousness, as well as in the political system, where parties can be localized near the two poles of the religious–atheist dimension. In Macedonia, several traditional religious communities inhabit a pluralist sphere and compete for attention in politics and society. Religion and ethnicity (and additionally social status) mostly coincide, which contributes to societal separation. The Macedonian Orthodox Church–Ohrid Archbishopric (MPC[2]) claims to represent the major ethnic community, the Slavic Macedonians. On the other side, a pluralist Islamic community represents mostly Albanians, Turks, and Muslim Macedonians. Ethno-religious alliances are translated into the political system, where the dominating political parties focus on members of one particular ethnic group as their voters.

A comparative analysis of recent processes in Slovenia and Macedonia promises to reveal interesting insights into two central cleavages of South-Eastern European societies: first between traditional religion and secular movements and, in the second case, between two historical religious communities actively seeking to influence identity. Which general processes and consequences can be revealed, which are important also to larger societies and other regions in Europe?

Historical Remarks

A short historical overview of general developments in Europe is necessary in order to classify the two cases with respect to the relationship between religion and state. The roots of sociology at the end of the 19th century are strongly connected to the first steps of distant scientific reflection of religion in society. Authors of the period were concerned with developments in Western Europe (France, United Kingdom, western lands of present-day Germany) and rearrangements of these relationships within this sub-region of the continent.

The religious–political sphere gradually separated here, within the context of modernization. The successive enforced retreat of traditional religion meant permanent subordination of the church to the state. The Catholic Church lost its function of legitimation of rule in formerly Catholic areas of Europe with the replacement of monarchic by democratic political systems. Today, the relations within these countries follow several models, ranging from official (and established) state churches via systems of cooperation to diverse patterns of separation of state

2 MPC—Makedonska Pravoslavna Crkva (Македонска Православна Црква—Охридска Архиепископија).

and church (Minkenberg 2003). Nevertheless, societies in Western Europe have in common that traditional as well as new religious communities share a relatively high degree of autonomy. The states mostly regulate the relationship to—but generally do not interfere in the internal affairs of—the organized religious associations. In Western European countries, the majority of the population has today developed a distinctly distant but overall tolerant attitude towards religion. It is assumed that this is connected to the finding that religion no longer plays a central role in the political sphere. Processes in societies beyond Western Europe differ from these developments.

Historically, the second major religious region of Europe is the Catholic South—a group of countries including Italy and Spain. Societies in this region are characterized by a close relationship between the church and the state—a long tradition of mutual collaboration and support, and a pattern surviving even monarchist rule by its application in modern dictatorships and later democracies in the 20th century.

The current consequence is that the formerly dominant traditional religious community lost its standing among significant groups of the population, especially among the young. Even if the majority of people ostensibly identify themselves as Catholic, young generations clearly distance themselves from respective major religious institutions. The Catholic Church faces a far-reaching loss of active members, and it remains uncertain whether the organization will ever again attract and influence significant groups within these societies.

The third part of Europe, described as Central Europe in this context, had a significant experience with the Protestant challenge to the Catholic Church. Examples here include large—mostly northern—parts of Germany, in addition to the Czech Republic and the Netherlands. Due to the tension between religious actors and modernization, a significant proportion of the population gradually developed an indifferent attitude towards religion and religious institutions. The pluralization of the religious sphere manifests as a pattern of distance but cooperation in the relationship of religion to present-day politics: The state variously subsidizes traditional religious communities, but otherwise does not significantly interfere in the religious sphere. Religious communities in the region have generally accepted their role as one player among several others within civil society. This position, to some extent preserved the reputation of mainstream religion within society, even if religiousness in its traditional form is declining on an individual level.

The fourth group of societies is located in Eastern Europe, with the core states of the Russian Federation, Poland, and Serbia. They share a long tradition of close relationship between political rule and a single dominant religion. As in the countries of Southern Europe, both spheres overlapped strongly. The important difference between the four groups is the period of socialist rule in Eastern Europe. Here, religion and its institutions were equated to symbols of the old, monarchist regime; Socialism, as the counter-reaction to the proximity of state and church, encouraged the prosecution, destruction, and expropriation of traditional religion and its organizations. Positioned in an oppositional role to the socialist regime, traditional religious communities were, among others, important actors at the beginning of the transition to democracy in the region; in many cases, they provided crucial parts of the infrastructure of oppositional movements (Pollack 2010:11). Nevertheless, the scale and rapidity of change surprised religious leaders in 1990 (as well as scientists and other groups involved in demanding democracy).

In contradiction to the transitional countries in Central Europe, such as the former East Germany and the Czech Republic, the respective Orthodox and Catholic Churches in Eastern Europe were able to develop permanent access to institutions of political power (Russian Federation) or at least to decisive parts of the established political parties and their elites (Poland). On the side of the population, the most recent data show—in contrast to other regions of the Continent—signs of increasing religiousness in Eastern Europe during the last twenty years (Pollack 2009:37). The process was also briefly observed in the transitional societies of Central Europe[3]. In Eastern Europe, further development is yet unclear, but the level of religiousness remains high.

When positioning Macedonia and Slovenia in this general, historical–religious classification of European societies, it is necessary to acknowledge that both cases are located in border regions. Slovenia has a strong Catholic background, similar to the second group of Southern European countries. It was a Crown land of the Habsburg Monarchy and located not far from its imperial capital, Vienna. Additionally to Austria, two other neighboring countries—Italy and Croatia—have long traditions of connecting their nationhood with Christian Catholicism. Nevertheless, two shifts in the history of Slovenia laid the basis for indifferent thinking towards religion and its traditional institutions, in this case the Catholic Church. The first shift was the local rise of the Protestant movement after 1550, which was fiercely suppressed by the Catholic Church. The leaders[4] of the movement were expelled from the Habsburg territories and exiled to ambitious Protestant duchies within the

3 See respective answer patterns in the World Values Survey for the Czech Republic and Eastern Germany, wave 1991/1992 and later. (http://www.worldvaluessurvey.org, 28/01/13; questions A006 “Religion important in life” and F025 “Religious denomination”).

4 Primož Trubar (1508–1586) and Jurij Dalmatin (1547–1589) are the most prominent bearers of the Protestant movement in Slovenia. They published several books in Slovene and translated the New Testament, which also represented the first steps in establishing Slovene not only as a spoken, but also written language.

Holy Roman Empire. Consequently, in the Duchy of Carniola (*Herzogthum Krain*) itself, parts of the Slovene population increasingly associated Catholicism with a foreign, intruding power.

The second shift resulted from the constellations during the Second World War. The wartime movements in Yugoslavia fighting for liberation from the fascist occupiers were very diverse in structure, background, and thus their goals. Apart from external influence of the Allies, leftist partisans grew to become the key player of the liberation movements, also because they were distinct from the other groups in one significant way: Their ideology was not based on exclusive forms of ethno-religious nationalism. All other relevant groups seriously seeking political power in Yugoslavia during the war—whether collaborating with the occupiers or not—based their ideology on a mono-ethnic nation connected to a single national religion. Consequently, a significant proportion of the population in Yugoslavia and in the small Slovenian lands, exhausted by ethnic conflict from monarchist Yugoslavia and the Second World War, sympathized with the partisans. After their success in Yugoslavia, the Catholic Church was blamed for its role during the war when it did not support the liberation movement. Thus, a distance between people and the Catholic Church was prescribed during the time of socialism by the state.

These historical roots indicate the positioning of Slovenia in a border region between the Catholic Southern- and a more secular Central Europe. Protestantism differentiated and qualified traditional religion (even though to a small extent); later political ideologies abused, oppressed, excluded, and replaced traditional religious organizations. Thus, the main cleavage in the society of Slovenia today is between the conservative position represented by the Catholic Church and a secular perspective of political and other public issues.

Macedonia, as the second case study, is located in the center of the Balkan Peninsula. Here, mainly two traditional religious denominations, Sunni Islam and Orthodox Christianity, have shaped cultural development and personal identity over centuries. Although significant proportions of the population converted to Islam during the long historical rule of the Ottoman Empire in the region, the majority of Slavic people maintained an association with Orthodox Christianity between 1400 and 1900. The Ottomans, following the Hanafi school of Sunni Islam, applied a form of rule based strictly on guidelines written in the Qur'an and the Sunnah. Formally a religious state, Ottoman rule consequently distinguished people mainly by their faith, regardless of ethnicity or other (previous) forms of identity. Christianity and Judaism are explicitly mentioned in the Qur'an as sharing some common sources with Islam, and therefore were not wiped out but officially acknowledged and granted relative autonomy by the Ottomans. Overall, religious denomination played a crucial role in identifying the Self and the Other, and there was no significant distinction between the arising ethnic peculiarities within the Empire until the mid-19th century (Karpat 1985:116).

The beginning of the 20th century was marked by the final withdrawal of the Ottoman Empire from the European continent. The consequences in the religious sphere were twofold: Firstly, many Muslims fled towards core Ottoman regions, thereby drastically changing the religious balance in favor of Orthodox Christianity. Secondly, there were frequent changes in the national denomination (e.g., Bulgarian, Serbian) of the institution representing Orthodox Christianity in the territory of today's Macedonia. Finally, the Macedonian appellation after the Second World War was independently organized in 1959 and granted autocephaly in 1967 by political will. Nonetheless, from a long-term historical perspective, it seems to be common that political power determined the name of the Orthodox Church and the faith of people within a territory. Of first interest in the context of this chapter is that Islam was represented as an intruding force by successive nation states of South-Eastern Europe, although it became an autochthonous religion within the Balkans during the preceding centuries. The binding force of Orthodox Christianity was the central contradiction to Islam in order to legitimate the expulsion of Ottoman rule and dominate the area. Secondly, succeeding powers (Serbia, Bulgaria, and Greece) quickly transformed religion into a nationalist instrument, declaring the Orthodox population within the territory of today's Macedonia as belonging to their respective ethnic group, national church, and therefore to their only nation (Ibid:50) in order to claim territory for their newly founded states.

The period from the end of the 19th century until the end of the Second World War was marked by permanent and violent ethnic rivalry, combined with religious elements; throughout the area of Macedonia, a repeated process of 'Serbization' and 'Bulgarization' took place. The effect on the attitude of the population in 1945 towards traditional religion and its relation to politics was similar to the situation in Slovenia—the vast majority of people were tired of ethno-religious conflict, and socialism was seen by many as a new chance to overcome rather than simply obscure the separation between societal groups. The following decades of a relatively high level of inter-ethnic cooperation in Yugoslavia demonstrated these intensions. After the collapse of socialism, Macedonia was constituted as an ethnically-defined nation of the Macedonian people[5]. This decision renewed tensions between social groups based on ethnic and religious sentiments, and revitalized the political focus on this issue. Hence, post-1991, people were focused on the question of ethno-religious

5 The Constitution of The Republic of Macedonia, adopted 17/11/1991, emphasizes in its preamble "[…] the historical fact that Macedonia is established as a national state of the Macedonian people […]". Other ethnic groups are mentioned as nationalities living in Macedonia, but not as constituting groups of the nation. Source: http://www.verfassungsvergleich.de/, 28/01/12.

belonging, and the proportion of the population with indifferent attitudes towards religion has subsequently declined to an insignificant level today.

The described historical path-dependencies also imply the positioning of Macedonia in a border region, yet between the Orthodox Eastern Europe and the former Ottoman-ruled region which is characterized by Islam today. Individual identity within this society is based predominantly on ethnic reference with constituting religious elements. Consequently, Macedonia shares main characteristics with the Orthodox Eastern countries regarding the development of religion after 1991: A revitalized role of religion in politics and the public spheres, as well as an increasing level of religiousness at the individual level.

Theoretical Approaches of Religion and the State

These historical path-dependencies frame the following reflection of theoretical approaches, which are concerned with the interplay of religion and politics. Established concepts of social science classifying the relationship between church and state mostly focus on developments in societies in Central- and especially in Western Europe. Here, a central problem of Christianity—the division between the Earthly and Heavenly kingdom, and thus the two powers ruling in the respective 'worlds'—shaped power struggles for centuries (Robertson 1987:153). Unique in comparison to other parts of Europe (and the world) was the successive separation, cumulating in their radical schism during the course of the French Revolution. The leap meant the final subordination of church to the state in the region until today. These developments constituted the framework for theorists who created the concepts of church and state described now. It is also necessary to acknowledge the Christian context, because religions and respective organized communities have various organizational structures and differing mental orientation. While the first dimension describes the organization of the hierarchic form of the institution representing a religion, the second distinguishes religions via their inner- or other-worldly orientation[6]. When focusing on Macedonia, where approximately 30% of the population follows Sunni Islam, it is important to emphasize that this religious confession has generally the same inner-worldly orientation as Christianity, but an

6 A typology of religions on the basis of the two dimensions `structure` (weak/developed) and `orientation` (inner-/otherworldly) was developed by Smith (1974) and replicated by Robertson (1987:157). While the structural dimension is self-explanatory, the mental dimension of orientation means the sphere with which the central religious-based activity of respective adherents is identified. Innerworldliness describes a group ethos that emphasizes reshaping the contemporary world according to traditional doctrines, whereas otherworldliness is the view that existing worldly circumstances are largely to be accepted.

entirely different structure—less hierarchical in the earthly organization, connecting the believer more directly to God compared to the Christian counterpart. The consequence is that religious dignitaries as the 'earthly' representatives cannot claim an absolute and final interpretation of the religion for today, as within the ecclesiastical Christian structures of Catholic, Orthodox, or Evangelical confession.

When reviewing classical concepts of religion and the state, one experiences that early sociologists like Max Weber followed what today would be described as an interdisciplinary approach. Weber combined sociologic, economic, cultural, and theological findings in his work at the beginning of the 20th century. Of primary importance regarding the issue of religion and the state is Weber's description of three general, ideal types (*'Idealtypen'*) of rule: the traditional, the charismatic, and the legal-rational form. Within each ideal type, institutionalized religion has a specific position towards the state, which makes the approach promising in the context of this paper.

The *traditional* ideal type of rule is generally characterized by a very close relationship between religion and the state. The spheres give mutual legitimation and mostly overlap. Here, Weber divides the category into two subunits: *hierocracy* or *theocracy*[7] on one side, in which earthly power is dominated by religion; and on the other *caesaropapism*, in which there is close subordination of church to political power (Weber 1922:200). This general category of traditional rule describes the traditional European monarchies that governed in Europe throughout the Middle Ages.

The second ideal type, *charismatic rule*, historically emerges directly after—and as the fierce counterpart to—the traditional form. Here, established religion and religious communities are excluded from political and civic life, and are replaced by doctrines of a movement with a charismatic leader, comprising an independent ideology[8]. Religion is tolerated by politics only during the first steps of establishing the charismatic rule if that serves the political goals of including wider parts of the population in the political movement, and to support and contribute to the legitimation of its leadership.

In terms of the relationship between religion and the state, the third ideal type, *legal-rational rule*, is positioned between the two forms described above. Here, politics and religion are not identical or mainly overlapping, but are separated, and religious communities enjoy relative autonomy. The state bases its legitimation not

7 Theocracy is subdivided into *incarnate*, direct rule of the founder of the religion; and *theocratic*, direct rule of priests of a small religious circle.

8 The political ideologies were constituted in contrast to religion with 'earthly-based' sources of legitimation. The historical background in this case was fascist Italy and the Socialist Soviet Union in the 1920s.

exclusively on religious or ideological foundations: the main characteristics of the ideal type are a constant confirmation of—and back-coupling to—the population as the source of legitimation of rule. Traditional religious communities may be acknowledged or slightly supported, although not necessarily. Subsumed within the category of legal-rational rule, the societies of Western Europe developed various forms of a general separation of church and state during the 19th and 20th centuries within the structures of democracy.

Weber set the three described ideal types into a chronological continuum, where the charismatic form overthrows the traditional and will be finally succeeded by legal-rational rule. These assumptions were accompanied by the observation that the relationship between religion and state in the societies of Europe became more diverse via the specific character of modernization. Following Weber's differentiation, monarchy was succeeded by charismatic rule; however, after 1945, the conflict line dividing the continent was between the democratic capitalist and the 'charismatic' socialist regimes. Consequently, charismatic and legal rule became a matter of more specific differentiation; social science now concentrated on the various political dominations of religion (Murvar 1967:71). In his description of forms of religious legitimation of the state, Roland Robertson advanced the concept of Weber and added *Eratianism* as a fourth ideal type (Robertson 1987:157), characterized by a separation of church and state and a low degree of autonomy on the part of religion.

A decade after Robertson, Juan J. Linz acknowledged the plural forms of treatment of religion by the two societal and political systems in Europe within one typology and generated five categories of church/state relations, organized according to an increasing distance of both spheres: theocracy/caesaropapism, politicized religion, friendly separation, hostile-laicist separation, and political religion as substitute (Linz 1996:134). Linz emphasized that the framework was not an ordinal dimension with end points; rather, it was arranged as a circle wherein the categories of political religion and caesaropapism are connectable because of the high level of integration between religion and state in both systems, regardless of the origin of the first element. Linz' typology is open for a wide range of forms of rule and therefore valuable to the context of this book, which is concerned with societies in transition. Linz' concept was applied to Eastern Europe in an analysis of church/state relations in Russia over a long-term historical perspective, and comprehensively advanced for this case (Riedel 2006:326).

Thus, the concept proposed by Linz proved useful for qualitative analysis of transitional societies in the region. In order to compare recent state/church relationships in Slovenia and Macedonia, additional quantitative assessment tools should be considered. Which concepts permit the evaluation of recent patterns?

The collapse of socialism left only democratic regimes in Europe, and therefore the concept of a general separation of politics and religion. The consequence for theoretical approaches to religion and state was the development of typologies focusing on the status of religion within democratic systems (see Fig. 1.1). Most prominent in this context is the categorization of Chaves and Cann, who provide a continuum between the three categories of: a) An established state-church; b) systems of cooperation between state and church; c) the complete separation of the two spheres (Chaves and Cann, 1992:280). They used six indicators that are similar to a Christian understanding of the interplay between the two spheres, of religion itself and of institutionalized religious communities[9].

Their concept was slightly modified by Detlef Pollack, who applied the approach to the classification of patterns in post-transition societies of Eastern Europe. He used the variable of the relations between state and church (plus the degree of religious plurality) in a society to explain the tremendous differences in religious vitality across Eastern Europe (Pollack 2002:18). Pollack retained the three general categories of Chaves and Cann, but focused the indicators more specifically on aspects of the involvement of traditional religious organizations in state institutions[10].

In 2003, Michael Minkenberg analyzed religion and politics in Western European democracies. While keeping the three general categories in state/church relations of Chaves and Cann as the basis for classification, Minkenberg widened the pool of indicators in regard to their concept and the one of Pollack, and thus expanded the scope (Minkenberg, 2003:128). The mentioned approaches represent approved concepts of social science, measuring the interdependence of religion and state within democracies (Kippenberg and Schuppert 2005:173). Nevertheless, the last decade was marked by developments in Eastern Europe in which the degree of democratic legitimation of the state significantly decreased or at least varied to a great extent (cf., Russian Federation, Ukraine, Moldova). Notwithstanding the multiple reasons, it is currently the case that traditional religion achieved unexpected but meaningful access to political power in several societies of Eastern Europe.

9 The six indicators are: a) the existence of a single official state-church, b) the official recognition of selected denominations, c) state interference in the appointment of religious dignitaries, d) the personnel of a religious community are paid (fully or partly) by the state, e) the existence of a church tax, and f) state investment in constructing/maintaining buildings of religious worship (see also Kippenberg and Schuppert, 2005:173). Each indicator is coded yes/no, so that the range of the variable is between zero (full separation) and six points (established state-church).

10 These are: a) existence of a state-church (two points), b) theological faculties at state universities, c) state-financed religious education at school, d) pastoral care in prisons and the military, and e) financial support (via taxes, etc.) of religious communities by the state (Pollack 2002:18). Coded as Chaves and Cann (1993), except indicator a), which is coded 0–2. Range 0 to 6.

In fragile transitional societies, religion re-entered the space of legitimation of the state. As mentioned in the section on historical path-dependencies, the majority of societies in Eastern Europe also have a long tradition of close ties between politics and religion. These processes leave the impression that theoretical concepts based exclusively on democratic forms of governance are not sufficiently broad to adequately encompass phenomena emerging recently across the region.

Weber (1922)	Robertson (1987)	Linz (1996)	Chaves/ Cann, Pollack, Minkenberg (1992–2003)[11]	Fox (2008)
Hierocracy	Theocracy			
(Theocracy),	Hierocracy	Theocracy /		Religious state
Caesaropapism	Caesaropapism	Caesaropapism		
Traditional rule				Active state religion
	Eratianism			State-controlled religion
		Politicized religion		
			Established state-church	Cultural state religion
Legal rule				Preferred treatment
			Cooperation	General support
		Friendly separation	Separation	Moderate separation
		Hostile-laicist separation		Nearly or full separation
Charismatic rule				Hostility
		Political religion		

Fig. 1.1: Concepts of State/Church Relations 1922–2008[11]

The latest theoretical concept, which addressed also this methodological gap, was the 'World Survey of Religion and the State' by Jonathan Fox (2008). Fox conceptualized an index of *Government Involvement in Religion* (GIR), which is a quantitative study on global level. Fox developed a differentiated pattern of nine categories for classifying state/church relations, including the group of Eastern European societies (Ibid:147). The categories range from a 'religious state', which can be equated to theocracy and caesaropapism in the previously mentioned concepts; five different forms of 'preferred treatment of specific religious communities'[12]; two forms of 'separation' (moderate and full) 'hostile' relationship (see Fig. 1.1). Contrary to the concept of Chaves and Cann (1992), the last category of 'hostility' is broader and additionally includes the system of an established political religion; here, Fox explicitly mentioned the former USSR (Fox 2008:48) and present-day countries of the Caucasus, which, during the last two decades, have shown strong indications of erecting new political religions with ideologies centered around a strong leader (Ibid:147, see Azerbaijan as an example).

Fox developed the variables for the classification in reviewing a broad set of other studies that measure the relationship between religion and the state (Ibid:39–45). He noted that previous concepts employ relatively few indicators and, consequently, measure single aspects (Ibid:46). The method proposed by Fox is, therefore, to collect numerous proven indicators from previous studies to create five variables measuring the relationship: a) the official role of religion in the state, b) state restriction and preferential treatment, c) restrictions on minority religions, d) regulation of the religious sector, and e) religious legislation. These five general variables, each normalized to a range 0–20, are combined, where their sum represents the 'General GIR' index (see Fig. 1.5).

An additional measurement, which also includes up-to-date data, is provided by The Religion and State Project (RAS)[13]. The project measures four independent indexes, a 'Government Regulation of Religion Index' (GRI), a 'Government Favoritism of Religion Index' (GFI), 'Social Regulation of Religion' and 'Religious Persecution'. Here, single aspects of the relationship are in focus. Slovenia and Macedonia are included in the study, and will be discussed later.

---

11 The concepts of Pollack (2002:18) and Minkenberg (2003:128) are based on Chaves and Cann (1993). Therefore, these are integrated into one column here. Chaves and Cann used six indicators, Pollack reduces the measurement to five factors, and Minkenberg expands it to eight characteristics. The differing number of indicators induces a different factor weighting in the evaluation (e.g., Minkenberg focuses on financial support).

12 The five categories are active state religion, state-controlled religion, cultural state religion, preferred treatment, and general support of one or more religions. See Fig. 1.1.

13 http://www.thearda.com/ras/, 28/01/13.

Figure 1.1 attempts to integrate the presented theoretical approaches for the categorization and analysis of the relationship between state and religion. The grid is not organized according to Weber's chronological dimension. Rather, it follows the concept of Fox, in presenting a continuum from a high/identical overlap of the spheres on the top (beginning with theocracy), to the greatest possible degree of separation—a situation of institutionalized hostility between religion and politics. Therefore, the ideal type of 'charismatic rule' (or category of 'political religion' in the concept of Linz) at the bottom of the figure is a specific case. The political system entirely replaces religion with a political ideology that is not a traditional but a newly created form of belief system[14]. Hence, this category does not exactly describe a relationship between two protagonists, since one—religion—is completely eliminated in its traditional sense. In established political ideologies[15], the center of orientation and behavior of the population is directed towards earthly issues by the doctrine (mostly in the form of nationalism towards a culturally and biologically coherent "nation of people"). It mostly omits issues of otherworldly transcendence or unsolved 'last' questions exceeding human capacity for recognition—all matters are to be resolved in this world. Thus, ideology attempts to substitute, but cannot equate to, traditional religion in this context. The category is not identical to that of caesaropapism; nevertheless, since religion and politics are merged into one unit, many common characteristics can be revealed and the categories are combinable by matching several characteristics[16].

Examining Fig. 1.1 in this sense, Weber's work can be interpreted from the perspective that charismatic rule succeeded traditional regimes as the polarized counterpart reacting to the former combination by eliminating and substituting religion. Later, consensus-oriented legal regimes balanced the relationship between state and church, and developed secular models of mutual understanding and consensus.

Religion, State, and Society in Slovenia

Slovenia is a small and ethnically homogenous country of two million (mil.) inhabitants. The religious sphere was dominated for centuries by one confession and the institution representing it, the Roman Catholic Church. A differentiation briefly emerged during the period of the Protestant Reformation, but the attitudes of the

14 The main difference between ideology and religion is the respective earthly and heavenly central orientation in the doctrine.

15 The term `political religion` (Linz 1996:134) is replaced here by `political ideology` as a description of the category.

16 See the arrow in the last row of Fig. 1.1.

population towards religion did not pluralize before the 20th century (see historical remarks). The traditional religious confession is Christian Catholicism. It is organized today at national level in the RKC, which claims to represent the majority of citizens in cultural and spiritual terms. However, today the sphere is appropriately described as heterogeneous.

Slovenia became independent in a gradual process that cumulated in its official secession from Yugoslavia in June 1991. At that time, it was the most economically and politically advanced society of the six republics constituting Yugoslavia. The political elite generally managed the change to democracy and a market economy by successfully applying gradual transition measures. Today, Slovenia is among the most developed countries in Europe and the most advanced transitional society of former socialist Eastern Europe. The Human Development Index (HDI) of the United Nations Development Programme ranked Slovenia 21st, between France and Finland for the year 2011 (UNDP 2011:127). In addition to economic development, international measures of democratic political and civil rights did not report limitations on the expression of political will or religious faith during the last twenty years. The regional environment of Slovenia is marked by democratic states with a long tradition of Catholic Christianity (Austria, Italy, and Croatia). Despite the fact that the highest organizational principal of the two largest religious communities, the Catholic Church and the Islamic Community in Slovenia, is located outside the country, there are no significant external influences having a definite negative impact on the religious sphere or on social integration.

The Population

Christian Catholicism is the largest faith group in Slovenia (recorded as 57.7% in the last official census of 2002[17]; see Fig. 1.2). However, in relation to these data, questions about church membership numbers[18] and the understanding of being a

17 Following data for Slovenia is based on the census 2002 (http://www.stat.si/popis2002/, 28/01/13).

18 The RKC itself declared the number of Catholics in Slovenia at 1,553,497 for 2011 (http://katoliska-cerkev.si/statisticni-podatki-o-cerkvi-na-slovenskem-za-leto-2011, 28/01/13). The number is challenged on the basis of results of surveys (see http://www.worldvaluessurvey.org) as well as the census of 2002, which reports 1,135,626 people declaring their religious denomination as Catholic. Since the gap is approximately 400,000 people, the difference concerns a share of 20 percent of the population in a small country like Slovenia. Here, there is an evident discrepancy in the conception of the religious institution and the people that are categorized, which has implications for the relations between religion and state.

follower of Catholicism[19] are current issues in Slovenia. Following the census of 2002, the second most widespread attitude towards spiritual belonging is those who did not wish to express an affiliation to a religious denomination (15.7%). An additional 10.1% explicitly declared themselves as atheist. In Slovenia, this is not a widespread phenomenon like the former East Germany or the Czech Republic, but is very high compared to neighboring states. Slovenia has also seen the emergence of an atheist association[20].

The fourth-largest category according to the 2002 census is the group for whom religious affiliation is not known (7.1%). Thus, it can be argued that, in total, one third (32.9%) of the population does not regard religion as a central point of individual orientation, or positions religion as not being a primary part of personal identity.

The second-largest religious denomination in Slovenia is Islam. In the 2002 census, 47,488 people described themselves as Muslim. Muslims mostly came from poorer regions of Yugoslavia, such as Bosnia-Herzegovina, and immigrated to Slovenia during socialism[21]. In a predominantly Slovene and Christian Catholic environment, Islam is strongly associated with ethnic belonging, and runs within families already born in the country. In general, quantitative data and interviews reveal no signs that the number of followers of Islam in Slovenia is growing by means of conversion. However, the number increased significantly compared with the 1991 census, which reported 29,361 adherents. It can be followed that this large difference between successive censuses is due to the belated naturalization/ legalization of citizenship among former Bosnian people in Slovenia during 1991 and 2002. Hence, Muslims have represented a stable 2.4% of the total population in recent decades. Internally, the Islamic sphere itself is dominated by one institution, the Islamic Community in Slovenia (ISRS)[22]. There are several other Muslim groups active within the territory, which are not included in this organization. Their memberships are relatively small, are based on family ties, and therefore predominantly concentrated in one location such as the capital Ljubljana or in industrial towns in the north. Muslim communities in Slovenia generally follow the Hanafi school of Sunni Islam.

19 There is a vital debate in sociology of religion within Slovenia about how to categorize people in this group between the cultural definition of belonging to Catholic faith (as a family tradition) and membership oriented understandings of belonging to the Catholic Church (as an institution).

20 ZAS — Združenje ateistov Slovenije (Association of Atheists in Slovenia).

21 Most of them were Muslims from Bosnia-Herzegovina or Albanians from Macedonia and Kosovo.

22 Islamska Skupnost v Republiki Sloveniji (ISRS) — Islamic Community in The Republic of Slovenia.

Population according to ethnic affiliation (as percentage of total population)							
Slovene	Croat		Serb	Bosn.[23]	other	n.a.[24]	unkn.
83.1	1.8		1.98	1.51	2.11	3.09	6.43
… native language							
Slovene	Croat	S.-C.[25]	Serb	Bosnian	other		unkn.
87.75	2.75	1.85	1.6	1.6	1.81		2.66
… religious affiliation							
Catholic	Atheist	Prot.	Ortho.	Muslim	other	n.a.	unkn.
57.8	10.1	0.9	2.3	2.4	3.6	15.7	7.1

Fig. 1.2 Religion and Ethnicity in Slovenia, 2002 Census[26]

The third religious denomination in Slovenia that is important in the context of this chapter is Orthodox Christianity, with approximately 46,000 adherents in the 2002 census. As with the Muslim community, Slovenian Orthodox Christians mostly originate from poorer regions of Yugoslavia and immigrated during the1960s and 1970s. Orthodox Christians are either Serbs from Bosnia-Herzegovina, Kosovo, or Southern Serbia; or are Macedonians. Almost 90% of Orthodox adherents are affiliated to the Serbian-Orthodox Church (SPC), the remaining to the Macedonian counterpart MPC.

The last religious confession in Slovenia—albeit very important, due to its historical role—is Christian Protestantism. The 2002 census reports 16,135 adherents; although a relatively small group, comprising less than 1% of the population, it is a traditionally rooted religious branch of Christianity in the area, which was suppressed in a conservative Catholic environment (see historical remarks). Today, the majority of adherents are organized in the Evangelical Church in Slovenia[27] (14,736 members); a further 1,399 people identified themselves as members of

23 Islamska Skupnost v Republiki Sloveniji (ISRS) — Islamic Community in The Republic of Slovenia.

24 No answer.

25 Serbo-Croatian.

26 State Statistical Office of The Republic of Slovenia, 2002 Census (http://www.stat.si/popis2002/, 28/01/13). Data as percentage of total population.

27 Evangeličanska cerkev AV v Republiki Sloveniji (ECRS)—Evangelical Church of the Augsburg Confession in The Republic of Slovenia. Subsequent total number of members as reported by ECRS and other groups.

other, mostly newly founded, Protestant groups.

Other religious communities present in Slovenia are predominantly new movements (mostly Evangelical Christian organizations from North America) or traditional religions that have no historical representation in Europe (e.g., Buddhism). The sphere of other religions in Slovenia is notably heterogeneous: respective organizations have in sum approximately 10,000 to 15,000 adherents, with no particular belief showing significant growth. Therefore, these groups do not have a noticeable influence on public or political debates.

Religious Organizations

The categorization of institutionalized religious groups in Slovenia follows that of the Office for Religious Communities in the Republic of Slovenia (ORC)[28] into: a) traditional, b) immigrated, and c) new religious communities. According to affiliates and infrastructure, the largest traditional religious community in Slovenia is the RKC. The two archdioceses that head its organizational structure, Ljubljana and Maribor, are subdivided into six bishoprics (additionally the bishoprics of Murska Sobota, Celje, Koper, and Novo Mesto). The heads of the six units constitute the Slovene Bishops Conference (SŠK[29]) as the highest organ of the Catholic Church in the country, which consists of eight members[30]. Its task is to regulate and organize relations between the community and the state. The six bishoprics host the 785 parishes of the Catholic Church in Slovenia[31], which constitute the lowest level of the church hierarchy. The bishoprics and parishes are legal persons under the Religious Freedom Act (2007, 2010).

In order to understand the attitudes of the population in Slovenia towards religion, and especially towards the Catholic Church, it is necessary to briefly highlight three current problems of the RKC concerning politics and society. The first issue is less concerned with spiritual than with economic matters. Since Slovenia's independence, the RKC has demanded comprehensive restitution of property nationalized in the former socialist Yugoslavia. If the claims would be fully accepted by political decision, it is argued that the largest religious institution would become also a key

28 Urad za verske skupnosti, http://www.mizks.gov.si/si/delovna_podrocja/urad_za_verske _skupnosti/, 28/01/13.

29 Slovenska Škofovska Konferenca — SŠK.

30 Currently, the body consists of the mentioned six bishops plus the Auxiliary Bishop of Ljubljana (Msgr. Dr. Jamnik) and a retired dignitary (Msgr. Pirih).

31 February 2012, ORC, http://www.mizks.gov.si/si/delovna_podrocja/urad_za _verske_skupnosti/, 28/01/13.

economic player (if not a monopolist) in various business areas in Slovenia. Due to the state's recent financial problems and mismanagement within parts of the Catholic Church, this issue remains one of intense public discussion. Secondly, the RKC remains passive in addressing its role during the Second World War. This issue marks a central source of value-normative separation between the Catholic Church and other significant groups of society. Thirdly, the RKC actively articulates its traditional and conservative position towards political and social issues. Thus, it intervenes in the political sphere by introducing its arguments to public debate. Due to these three dimensions, public trust in the institution remains low; only one third (34.8%) of the Slovenian population expressed general confidence in churches[32].

The second traditional and institutionalized religious community is the Evangelical Church of the Augsburg Confession in the Republic of Slovenia (ECRS). This relatively small church is concentrated in the northeastern part of the country, close to the borders with Austria and Hungary. It is organized in one bishopric (seat in Moravske Toplice), which compromises 14 parishes[33] in the region. Due to its progressive role in historically important events in the formation of a Slovene identity and nation (reformation, process of establishment of Slovene as a written language) and the liberal but inclusive position of its leaders in recent political debates, the church enjoys a widespread positive reputation, while only 0.75% of the population actually members of the church.

The RKC and the ECRS represent the traditional religious communities in Slovenia[34]. The second category provided by the ORC includes immigrated religions and religious groups. Here, most members are reported for the Islamic Community in Slovenia (ISRS), which claims to represent 98.5% of all Muslims in the country. The ISRS was registered in 1976 in Ljubljana with one imam, but could not be fully active until Slovenia became a sovereign state. Following independence of the state in 1991, the ISRS organized the structure and institutional integration of Muslims in Slovenia under the influence of the Islamic Community in Bosnia and Herzegovina[35]. Today, it is highly integrated into the structures of the Bosnian Islamic Community and holds 3 of 83 seats in the council of the Bosnian organization[36]. Internally, the ISRS is headed by the mufti (currently Dr. Nedžad Grabus), who is

32 World Values Survey, question E069 ("How much confidence do you have in the churches?"). Data available only for year 1999, see http://worldvaluessurvey.org (28/01/13).

33 Evangelical Church in the Republic of Slovenia, see http://www.evang-cerkev.si/, 28/01/13.

34 Judaism, which is registered as the third traditional religion by the ORC, comprises a very small community in Slovenia (total 99 people in the 2002 census).

35 ISRS, http://www.islamska-skupnost.si/, 28/01/13.

36 See official page of the Islamic Community in Bosnia-Herzegovina http://www.rijaset.ba/.

elected for a 5-year term by the council of the ISRS, which is required to a make two-thirds majority decision on this issue. The mufti must be approved by the authorities of the Bosnian Islamic Community in Sarajevo. The 15 local communities of the ISRS are located mostly in larger industrial towns. Each community sends members to the council of the ISRS in Ljubljana. In 2006, one imam and former mufti of the ISRS formed a separate group in Ljubljana, with approximately 200 followers. Other Muslim communities report fewer members, and therefore do not play a crucial role in the religious sphere.

The Serbian Orthodox Church (SPC) is the last important religious organization in Slovenia discussed in this paper. It was also registered in 1976 and faced similar restrictions to the Muslim organization during socialism. In the 2002 census, 43,285 people declared affiliation to Orthodox Christianity, most of which were within the SPC. The Serbian Orthodox Church in Slovenia is itself one of five parts of the district of the Metropolitan of Zagreb-Ljubljana[37] (a similar territorial unit to a Catholic bishopric). Internally, the church organizes eight local communities in Slovenia around its national center in Ljubljana. There are numerous other religious groups in the country, but their organizational status and infrastructure are limited by their low membership capacity. In total, there are presently 42 churches and other religious communities registered by ORC[38].

State Regulation and Political Involvement

Religion in general—and religious communities in particular—receive little attention in the Slovenian Constitution. Art. 7, para. 1 of the constitution notes that the state is separated from religious communities. The subsequent paragraph states that religious groups are equal and can pursue their activities in Slovenia in a free manner. Four additional articles[39] of the constitution are concerned with the issue, expressing freedom of religion in specific situations and merely on an individual level. No religious group is explicitly mentioned, and neither is the legitimation of the state based on historical or religious recourses.

The official state body responsible for religious affairs in the country, the Office for Religious Communities (ORC), registries religious groups, observes

37 See official page of the SPC http://www.mitropolija-zagrebacka.org/,

38 http://www.mizks.gov.si/si/delovna_podrocja/urad_za_verske_skupnosti/register_cerkva_in_dru gih_verskih_skupnosti/#c18716, accessed 28/01/13.

39 Additional articles are Art.14 (equality before the law), Art.16 (suspension and restriction of rights), Art.41 (freedom of conscience), and Art.63 (prohibition of incitement to hatred and discrimination).

religious communities, and supports the inter-religious dialogue in Slovenia. The administrative registration process is rather short and does not hinder groups from religious activities. To date, there is no instance of the ORC intervening in the internal affairs of any religious group, or rejecting an application for registration. The first registration of religious communities in Slovenia dates back to 1976. Since then, 44 religious communities enrolled in the register, of which two were recently deleted (2010 and 2012). In addition to the register, the state conducted special agreements on the legal status of six religious communities[40], most of them traditional and Christian. In these cases, the organizations have a certain size and structure that require further regulation for channeling relations with the state. Additionally, the Republic of Slovenia signed a special treaty with the Holy See on legal issues associated with the activities of the Catholic Church in the country[41].

Slovenia's political system is influenced by the religious sphere due to the specific historical path-dependencies that resulted in the cleavage of people with indifferent religious attitudes from those with traditional Catholic-oriented beliefs. Several Slovenian political parties position themselves in the tradition of the first Slovene parties, which appeared more than a century ago, and are therefore perceived as having a close relationship to the Catholic Church (Kerševan 1998:379). Links are not directed only from the political area, as parts of the RKC also expressed their preference for certain conservative parties in pre-election periods. On the other side of the political spectrum, parties explicitly canvass voters with a very distant attitude towards the Catholic Church. This major cleavage can also be observed in the party-specific handling of the key question of restitution of property confiscated from the Catholic Church after 1945. Some parties support the claims of the RKC, whereas others do not. The interests of political and religious players also coincide in the cultural and educational sector, particularly on the issue of interpretation of the role of the Catholic Church during the Second World War. Here, political actors express widely divergent views: Some adopt the position of the RKC; parties on the other side of the political spectrum accuse the church of collaboration with fascist occupiers (Ibid:381). Overall, the described basic cleavage in Slovenian society is also manifest in the political system.

The last twenty years have seen no major disputes between religious communities in Slovenia. Religious harmony is instead disrupted by political decisions

---

40 Ibid. Agreement on Legal Status with the Roman Catholic Church / Slovenian Bishops Conference (1999), the Evangelical Church (2000), the Pentecostal Church (2004), the Serbian Orthodox Church (2004), the Islamic Community (2007), and the Buddhist Congregation Dharmaling (2008).

41 Official Gazette of the Republic of Slovenia 04/2004.

or inactivity, as described above. This is also obvious in the case of the year-long unsuccessful application of the ISRS to build a new place of worship in Ljubljana. Compared to the wider regional situation, Slovenia experiences few societal conflicts, and religious involvement in such is limited and non-violent. Consequently, relations between religious communities and the state are characterized by a general separation, and by tolerance from the political side. The GIR index therefore evaluates Slovenia as having general support for some religions and a low level of restrictions on minorities (Fox 2008:147).

Religion, State, and Society in Macedonia

The second case study is that of the Republic of Macedonia, a country that was also a part of the former socialist Yugoslavia. Becoming independent in September 1991, the small state, inhabited by 2 million people, soon faced tremendous internal and external threats to its sovereignty and statehood.

Independence of the State and External Constraints

The external challenges to Macedonia were and are derived from the construction and interpretations of national identity within the neighboring nations, especially in Greece and Bulgaria. These circumstances affect crucial pillars of legitimation of the sovereign Macedonian state. The Federal Republic of Yugoslavia, bordering in the north shortly after its independence, was involved in the war in Croatia and Bosnia-Herzegovina and faced a UN Security Council trade embargo between 1992 and 1995. Macedonia was therefore unable to trade via these major economic channels, which had been established for decades within Yugoslavia. In 1999, many refugees fled the Kosovo war to Macedonia, which was then one of the poorest countries in Europe. Thus, Macedonia's early independence was accompanied by a constant potential for overspill of violence from the north. Political relations with Serbia on official level were generally non-hostile during the last two decades. Nevertheless, one unresolved issue continues to have far-reaching influences on the religious sphere in Macedonia: The Serbian Orthodox Church does not recognize the autocephaly of its Macedonian counterpart MPC and therefore does not accept the decisions taken during socialist rule to split the churches and establish an institution within each federal unit to represent the spiritual interests of the majority of the population within its borders (see historical remarks). From the official perspective of the SPC, the Orthodox Church in Macedonia remains part of their institution, and the area under their spiritual jurisdiction.

Bulgaria, to the west, has maintained good political relations with Macedonia since its independence. Bulgaria recognized the Macedonian state early, but yet denies a distinct ethnic and cultural Slavic identity in Macedonia (Riedel 2005:123). This point of view also influences the religious sphere in Macedonia: Part of the cultural negation from the Bulgarian side is the claim of a historical Bulgarian continuity of the Orthodox Church in Macedonia. The Bulgarian Orthodox Church (BPC) does not recognize the MPC. By glorifying a brief period of the Middle Ages, during which the territory was governed by Bulgarian rulers, the BPC continues to insist on its cultural supremacy over the MPC. Finally, the resulting situation for the Macedonian Orthodox Church is the same as the dispute with the SPC: external exclusion and denial of its existence. From the two sides, the MPC is in a constant state of probation to prove its legitimacy, and therefore the basis of its very existence.

Greece, in the south, immediately closed all border crossings following the declaration of the Republic of Macedonia in September 1991. It imposed various restrictions and demanded changes of official symbols of the newly founded state (including the constitution and the flag), with which Macedonia complied in most cases. The so-called 'name dispute' regarding the constitutional name of Macedonia, which was imposed by Greece at that time, continues to hinder the republic from full recognition in crucial European and global governmental organizations. The political dispute between the two countries is also present in the religious sphere. The Greek Orthodox Church does not recognize the MPC as an independent Orthodox church. There are no established interreligious consultations to resolve the status of the MPC—a situation similar to relations with the other two Orthodox churches of Serbia and Bulgaria.

Macedonia's western neighbor is Albania, the poorest country in Europe. Due to specific circumstances during socialism[42], there are only a few economic and cultural connections between the two states. On an official political level, relations are friendly but fragile, because of provocative elements within the Albanian minority in Macedonia declaring Albania as their center of national orientation. Since religion is not a primary source of identity and orientation for a majority of the Albanian population[43] and is handled very liberally there, its religious sphere provides no basis for potential negative influence on interreligious relations with Macedonia. The summary demonstrates that, with the exception of Albania, the surrounding

42 Relations between the leaders of Yugoslavia, Josip Broz Tito, and of Albania, Enver Hoxha, remained fraught since 1948, when Yugoslavia was expelled from the Cominform (Communist Information Bureau).

43 Compared to European societies, there are high rates of atheism and interreligious marriage among the population of Albania.

states have continually influenced the identity of the Macedonia (Slavic) population and therefore also influenced religious affairs.

When Macedonia declared independence, the country's economy and the political elite were not prepared for sovereignty to the same degree as in the Slovenian case. Macedonia was highly dependent on Yugoslavia in economic terms, since the state budget of the republic was financed mainly by federal financial aid from the developed republics Slovenia and Croatia via a fund in Belgrade. Alongside Kosovo and Bosnia-Herzegovina, Macedonia was among the poorest parts of the federation. Additionally, the markets for Macedonian products were exclusively within the borders of the collapsing Yugoslavia. The political elite, namely the first president of the republic, Kiro Gligorov, and the members of the first expert government, faced these challenges with sincere intentions but disagreed about the economic transition (e.g., measures of privatization). Partly due to the external constraints, successive governments failed to construct a functioning market economy and democratic political regime. Consequently, a vast majority of the population experienced lower living standards compared to socialist times. Economic emigration increased significantly at the beginning of 1990s. Today, Macedonia is among the least developed countries in Europe and is ranked 78th, between Mauritius and Jamaica, in the 2011 UNDP Human Development Index (UNDP 2011:128). Due to declining living standards and badly mismanaged privatization, economic wealth is now concentrated among a few. The Gini Index, which measures income equality within a country, increased dramatically during the transition period (today at 44.2)[44].

The Population

The 2002 census shows that 64.2% of the Macedonian population is affiliated to Christian Orthodoxy[45] (see Fig. 1.3).Since that census did not record membership in organizations such as the Serbian, Bulgarian, or Macedonian Orthodox Churches (Statistical Office 2002a:518), it is not possible to identify the exact distribution of followers.

Nevertheless, since religion and language are strongly linked to ethnic identity in Southeastern Europe, one can compare the numbers with the data on ethnic affiliation and native language in the census. In terms of ethnic distribution, 64.8% of the population identified themselves as Macedonian and 1.8% Serbian (Ibid. 2002b:62); percentages for native language are only slightly different to those for

44 Income Gini coefficient 2000–2011, see UNDP 2011:136.

45 The census of 2011 was not conducted regularly. Therefore, data from the 2002 census is presented here.

ethnicity (Ibid. 2002a:446). It can therefore be reasoned that the spiritual competence of the MPC is recognized by the majority of Christian Orthodox adherents in Macedonia[46].

Population according to ethnic affiliation (as percentage of total population)							
Mace.[47]	Serb	Alb.[48]	Turkish	Roma	other	n.a.	unkn.
64.2	1.8	25.2	3.9	2.7	2.2	-	-
… native language							
Mace.	Serbian	Alb.	Turkish	Roma	other	n.a.	unkn.
66.5	1.2	25.1	3.5	1.9	1.8	-	-
… declaration by religion							
Orth.[49]	o. Ch.[50]	Muslim			other	n.a.	unkn.
64.78	0.37	33.33			1.52	-	-

Fig. 1.3 Religion and ethnicity in Macedonia, 2002 Census[51]

The second-largest group according to religious affiliation is Muslims, who comprise 33.3% of the total population. The great majority follow Sunni Islam (Hanafi School), with a minority of Bektashi, a traditional Muslim dervish order. The Sunni group is ethnically highly heterogeneous, and consists of Albanians, Turks, Roma, Muslim Macedonians (Torbeshi, Pomaks), and Bosnians.

Ethnic Albanians represent 25.1% of the total population, and so dominate the Islamic sphere in Macedonia. The second-largest ethnic group of Muslim faith is the Turkish community, which, via the Ottoman Empire, has shaped Islamic religious traditions for centuries in what is present-day Macedonia. The share of 3.9% of the total population implies that the group accounts for at least 10% of Muslim believers in the country. Roma, as the third group, officially represent 2.7% of the

46 Additionally, tabular analysis in the World Values Survey for Macedonia 2001 reveals a strong overlap between of religious denomination (F025) and ethnic group (X051) variables (http://worldvaluessurvey.org, 28/01/13).

47 Macedonian.

48 Albanian.

49 Orthodox (in the census not differentiated between Macedonian and Serbian).

50 Adherents of other Christian branches.

51 State Statistical Office of the Republic of Macedonia, 2002 Census (see http://www.stat.gov.mk/, 28/01/13). Data as percentage of total population. Bulgarian is not declared separately, as ethnic affiliation or native language.

population, and therefore constitute approximately 8% of Muslims in Macedonia. Due to their marginal status in education, politics, and economy, they have little influence on major Islamic institutions within the country or on the character of their relations with the state. Thus, Roma are underrepresented in institutions of the religious sphere of society too. Recently, there have been complaints from local Muslim Roma groups that the Albanian dominated Islamic Religious Community of Macedonia (IRC) has attempted to expand its control over their communities[52].

Other religions active in Macedonia are predominantly new religious movements, such as American Evangelist Churches or Asian religions. In sum, they do not have a significant number of adherents and do not influence the political sphere. It is notable that the statistical analysis of the 2002 census omits those who did not provide an answer, identified themselves as atheist, or who chose not to declare a religious affiliation (Statistical Office 2002a:518). The census gives the overall impression that the majority of people belong to a religious denomination, and that there is no space for a predominantly indifferent attitude towards religion among the population[53].

Religious Organizations

The largest organized religious community in the Republic of Macedonia is the Macedonian Orthodox Church. Due to historical path-dependencies, its establishment was not accepted by the SPC or the BPC: Both tried to extend their spiritual jurisdiction over the territory of today's Macedonia following the collapse of the Ottoman Empire and the expansion of their respective kingdoms in the area, which started approximately 150 years go. After the Balkan Wars of 1912–13, the territory became part of Serbia and a 'cultural Serbization' took place. Together with the Bulgarian occupation during the two world wars, Orthodox Slavs in the area of today's Macedonia were frequently forced to change ethnic identity and description of their religious affiliation until 1945. By the end of the Second World War, a decision by the People's Liberation Front of Macedonia (ASNOM) introduced the foundation of the Macedonian Orthodox Church in order to end the dispute between the SPC and the BPC and to grant Macedonian Slavic people a source of their own national identity. Hence, the process of separation from the Serbian Orthodox Church was marked by political influence. Nevertheless, in 1959, under political pressure, the

52 http://www.setimes.com/cocoon/setimes/xhtml/en_GB/features/setimes/features/2012/11/29/feature-03, 28/01/13.

53 Despite the historical experience of socialism which indicates that these attitudes could be a relevant pattern among people living in Macedonia.

SPC officially accepted an independent church in Macedonia. Eight years later, in 1967, the MPC itself declared autocephaly as the final step in the establishment of an independent Orthodox Christian church. However, the declaration was never accepted by the SPC. Despite complaints from the latter, the Macedonian Orthodox Church began to build up its own structure; it slowly established its own parishes within the territory of the Socialist Republic of Macedonia, and benefited from the transfer of places of worship (especially after 1991) that were owned by the SPC before nationalization. Important for the current text is the fact that, today, the MPC is not headed by a superior institution outside the country, directly or indirectly influencing its decisions and activities.

The Macedonian Orthodox Church is internally structured into ten dioceses[54]. Seven are located within the country; three are established for the diaspora in America/Canada, Australia/New Zealand, and Europe, respectively. The dioceses are organized in the Holy Synod, the highest organ of the MPC. The synod is presided over by the Archbishop of Ohrid and Macedonia (currently Archbishop Stephen), the representative head of the church. The local institutions of the seven dioceses within Macedonia are the parishes, whereas the exact number of active ones is unclear. Estimations differ widely, and often include religious buildings without mentioning levels of spiritual activity performed by the MPC (Nikolovski-Katin 1999:92). With regard to the population of the country, the MPC claims to be a central source of identity of the Slavic Macedonian people, as recently reiterated by Archbishop Stephen[55]. It is necessary to note that the church currently supervises religious places and symbols that are of central importance for the whole of Christian Orthodoxy in Eastern Europe (see the cultural heritage surrounding Lake Ohrid).

The second-largest religious organization in the country is the Islamic Religious Community in Macedonia (IRC[56]). Similarly to the MPC, it is constituted independently and does not have a superior institution outside the country setting guidelines for its activities. The IRC is dominated by the ethnic Albanian group in multi-ethnic Macedonia but claims to represent all Muslims in the country, irrespective of their ethnicity. Nonetheless, especially for religious Turks and Bosnians, the Islamic institutions of their respective countries are central points of orientation. It is reported that Roma—who are also mostly Muslim—have the least religious conscience and institutionalization. This ethnic group organizes religious life at the

54 See http://www.mpc.org.mk/, 28/01/13.

55 Christmas address of Archbishop Stephen, 6 January 2013 (http://evesti.mk/2013/01/05/g-g-stefan-bozik-e-praznik-na-mirot-prazink-na-slgata-i-edinstvoto/, 28/01/13).

56 Albanian BFI—Bashkësia Fetare Islame në Republikën e Maqedonisë, http://www.bim.org.mk/, 28/01/13.

local level, and here quite independently. As mentioned earlier in the text, local Muslim communities of Roma complained about the expanding efforts of the IRC. There are no coherent data available about the number of local communities included in the IRC. The community has its own educational institutions, the Madrassa Isa Beg (a secondary school) and the Faculty of Islamic Sciences, both located in Skopje. Macedonia has another small but prominent Muslim organization: the traditional Bektashi Religious Group of Macedonia (BRG). Similarly to the majority of Muslims in Macedonia, the members of the Bektashi order are concentrated in the northwest of the country; however, in contrast to the larger Muslim communities, they follow a form of Islam which cannot be subsumed under the two main Sunni and Shia branches of the religion. Instead, Bektashi is characterized by syncretic elements of various branches of Islam. After independence in 1991, a dispute occurred between the BRG and the state, regarding restitution of places of worship that were confiscated from the Bektashi under socialist nationalization. This also included the question of ownership of an old and historically significant mosque compound (*tekke*) near Tetovo. In 2002, a radical Muslim group staged a violent occupation of the compound, in response to which the state did not intervene. More recently, the compound was partly transferred by the state to the ownership of the IRC, which clearly discriminates against the Bektashi group.

In total, there are 30 religious communities registered at the Commission for the Relations with Religious Communities and Groups[57]. Since other religious communities combined represent less than two percent of the population, they are not crucial players in the Macedonian religious sphere. Generally, religious leaders in Macedonia express interreligious understanding and cooperation. Instead, the main potential for religious disputes in Macedonia is between institutions of one religious denomination rather than between the two major organizations MPC and IRC, which claim to represent the vast majority of citizens. The conflict line within the religious denominations is located between small organizations and the dominant one, which is indirectly supported by crucial political actors. In the two cases of MPC and IRC, it is possible to identify highly significant political factors in the religious sphere of Macedonia (see 'state regulation', described below). Since independence, groups of armed rebels have sporadically proclaimed areas 'independent', often located in the northwest of the country. Such groups attempt to use religion as a divisive factor between Albanians and Macedonians, but major religious institutions distance themselves from these groups, whose activities are mostly motivated by criminal goals. In general, it is doubtful whether the activities of armed rebel groups have any form of religious motivation.

57 http://www.kovz.gov.mk/?ItemID=BFF253DF95C8884785FFD6B65A39654E, 28/01/13.

State Regulation and Political Involvement

The reformed 2001 constitution of Macedonia emphasizes in its preamble seven ethnic groups living in the country. It mentions issues concerning religion in six articles[58]. In five of the six, the individual right of freedom of religion is regulated. Article 19 additionally highlights the separation of religion from the state and the establishment of religious educational facilities, and therefore concentrates on collective rights of religious communities. Here, the MPC, the Islamic Religious Community, the Catholic Church, the Evangelical Methodist Church, and the Jewish Community are explicitly referenced.

The state requires religious communities to be registered via the Commission for Relations with Religious Communities and Groups, which is an independent government body[59]. The commission categorizes registered religious organizations into churches, religious communities and religious groups[60], yet on an unexplained basis. The first category of *churches* compromises 15 Christian religious groups, the most prominent being the MPC, the Catholic Church, and the Evangelical Church in Macedonia. The others are all very small Christian churches, both traditional and newly founded. The second category, *religious communities*, includes seven institutions: the Islamic Community (IRC), the Jewish community, as well as five others[61], yet all are of different nature. The last category is termed *religious groups*, and compromises eight associations—six Christian and two Muslim. The Bektashi order is also registered in this category, which is an indicator of an applied ranking of preference by the state, and hence of unequal treatment in comparison to the IRC. An additional indicator is the duration of registration which differed in these two cases.

Furthermore, the Serbian Orthodox Church is not mentioned in the register. Statements from representatives of the SPC in Macedonia point out that numerous unsuccessful applications for registration were launched during the last twenty years. The state also uses violent means to prevent the establishment of the SPC in Macedonia, in terms of administering places of worship. Bishop Jovan, official representative of the SPC on Macedonian soil[62], was repeatedly arrested by the police, who also damaged the place of worship and his property. He was also prevented

58 Articles number 9, 19, 20, 48, 54, and 110 of the Macedonian constitution.

59 http://www.vlada.mk, 28/01/13.

60 http://www.kovz.gov.mk/?ItemID=BFF253DF95C8884785FFD6B65A39654E, 28/01/13.

61 Jehovah's Witnesses, Islamic Community of the Holy See and the Crown, Sathya Sai Centre, Vaishnavska Religious Community Iskon, Community "Universal Life".

62 http://spc.rs/, 28/01/13.

from entering the country in religious clothing.

The next issue between religion and politics in Macedonia concerns the construction of religious buildings. In 2009, the conservative government announced the construction of an Orthodox church in the city of Skopje, which would be run by the MPC. This provoked other communities, first of all the IRC, and resulted in their claim for state funding for their places of worship. There is also criticism from smaller religious associations, who claimed that they have been repeatedly denied government permission to erect places of worship, even from their own financial budgets[63]. Here, a qualitative discrepancy in the treatment of religious communities is manifest. The issue forms part of a broader context which includes, for example, the re-shaping of the capital city of Skopje[64], where the government of Macedonia has spent 200–250 million euros[65] on new museums, monuments, and sculptures. These projects are part of the attempt of certain political actors to construct a new national Macedonian consciousness among the ethnic Macedonian citizens. Besides the antique and often odd symbols of the new architectural projects, the MPC became part of the construction of Macedonian identity. Consequently, an overlap of goals of ethno-political parties and religion can be detected. In addition to the bizarre combination of the historical background of the region and current national identity, other societal groups not targeted by these symbols are obviously excluded from the process of cultural and national construction.

The repeated discrimination and sometimes persecution of other religious groups—especially other Orthodox Churches—as well as the documented favoritism of one (MPC) and gradually a second religious organization (the IRC) indicates the establishment of 'state favored religious communities' in the case of Macedonia. The MPC is seen by decisive political parties, as well as from its own perspective, as a pillar of modern Slavic Macedonian identity. Therefore, politics is involved in defining ethno-religious identity. The reaction from the other main ethnic part of the political spectrum is favoritism of one Islamic association, the IRC. It can be followed that a system with two cultural state religions is emerging in Macedonia, because there is political support for the deep involvement of the two dominant religious organizations in the formation of identity on a national level. The structures and dynamics of the relationship of religion and politics in Macedonia are not comprehensively described here, but provide good examples of why Jonathan Fox allocated a rating of 27.17 on the scale between full separation

63 See http://www.forum18.org/, 28/01/13.

64 The project was labeled 'Skopje 2014'.

65 http://www.balkaninsight.com/en/article/macedonia-s-skopje-2%C3%A5aa4-eats-quarter-billion-euros, 28/01/13.

of religion and state (0 points) and a religious state (100 points) (Fox 2008:141). Hence, relations in Macedonia are characterized by preferred treatment for some religions, and by a high level of restrictions on minorities. Since the data series used by Fox ends in 2005 (Ibid:47), developments during the last eight years are not included in his study. Nevertheless, processes during the last decade show that the country is tending towards the category of cultural state religion (see Fig. 1.1): Other indicators, such as the Government Regulation Index (GRI) and Government Favoritism Index (GFI) of the State and Religion Project[66] evaluate the situation as having an even closer relationship between religion and state (values 3.1 and 4.1 respectively[67], see Fig. 1.5).

Before summarizing the relations between religion and state within Macedonia, external constraints must be acknowledged. Since crucial neighboring states dispute the very existence of a Macedonian nation, and particularly the legitimation of the MPC as a basic pillar of the nation, the state and the main religious organization in Macedonia are in a constant state of probation. This translates into internal developments, wherein domestic politics becomes an issue of identity construction and search for legitimation. Here, political forces declare religion—and employ the two favored religious organizations for that goal—as one main source of personal identity. Other religious groups or minorities are comminuted between the two ethno-political powers of Macedonians and Albanians. This conflict already reached high levels of intensity compared to Slovenia, because violence and the threat of violence are used for political blackmail on a daily basis. According to Fox (2004), the religion variable is most likely to intensify external and internal conflicts, as can be observed in the case of Macedonia.

Conclusions

The religious spheres of the small societies of Slovenia and Macedonia share a pluralistic character. In both countries, the population can be divided into two dominant groups: In Slovenia, between Catholic Christianity and indifferent attitudes towards religion; in Macedonia, between adherents of Orthodox Christianity and followers of Sunni Islam. In each society, on the organizational level, at least 30 religious communities are registered, comprising both traditional groups and new, mostly minor Christian, movements. Additionally, religious communities of all sizes have shown no significant growth in either country. The qualitative differences between Slovenia and Macedonia lay in the relationship between religion and state

66 http://www.thearda.com/ras/, 28/01/13.

67 The range of both values is between 0 (full separation) and 10 (religious state).

following the collapse of socialism. Developments in Slovenia over the past decade reveal consistently declining trust in the main traditional religious community, the Catholic Church. Thus, political influence by the church is not supported by the population. In Macedonia, the Macedonian Orthodox Church, representing the majority religion, became a pillar of legitimation of the state by political will; the church actively fulfills this function, also to legitimate its own existence. However, in spiritual terms, it is not representative of at least one third of the population and cannot function as a basis for national identity. The legitimation of the involvement of religion in politics remains limited in Macedonia and Slovenia, as demonstrated by the attitudes of citizens, shown in Figure 1.4.

	Politicians who do not believe in God are unfit to hold public office		Religious leaders should not influence how people vote		Religious leaders should not influence government	
	MK 01[68]	SLO 05[69]	MK 01	SLO 05	MK 01	SLO 05
Agree	32.4	10	75.1	69.3	67.9	65.8
Neither	16.8	15.1	8.7	10.7	12.9	12.3
Disagree	44.1	69.4	9.6	14.2	11.5	16

Fig. 1.4 Attitudes towards the involvement of religion in politics[70]

Figure 1.4 clearly indicates that the populations of both countries generally oppose the influence of religious leaders in politics (and elections). Nevertheless, 32.4% of the Macedonian population agrees that politicians should believe in God in order to hold public office (68.8% of Muslim and 25% of Orthodox respondents). Compared to Slovenia, both response rates are very high, even though agreement was predominantly expressed by Muslim respondents. Nevertheless, the involvement of religions in Macedonian politics is not legitimized with regard to the attitudes of the population.

The relationships between religion and state in Slovenia and Macedonia are summarized in Fig. 1.5. Slovenia belongs to the category of countries which institutionalized a generally civil separation of the spheres (with moderate political support for religion). In contrast, Macedonia is among the countries demonstrating

68 Macedonia 2001.

69 Slovenia 2005.

70 http://worldvaluessurvey.org/, 28/01/13.

preferential treatment of specific religious communities.

Since the data series does not include the most recent developments, it is assumed that the situation for Slovenia did not change significantly, whereas in Macedonia specific religious institutions are brought into the political arena by specific but crucial actors. Hence, the influence of religion in politics increases and significant characteristics of a cultural state religion legitimating the nation and state can be observed. Nevertheless, since the population largely opposes this influence, mentioned political actions lack legitimacy.

	GIR[71]	GRI[72]	GFI	SRI	RP
	0–100	0–10	0–10	0–10	0–10
MK	27.17	3.1	4.1	5.8	1
SLO	11.96	0.9	4.5	5.9	0

Fig. 1.5 Summary of indices of religion/state relations

The findings on religion and state reveal further important implications for the three central theoretical paradigms of sociology of religion (secularization, individualization, or 'market of religions'). Reviewing them in the context of developments in Macedonia and Slovenia, it is noted that a 'market of religions' presumes that historical path-dependencies are weak and that state regulation of religion is low. In both cases, this assumption neglects important variables that are crucial to explain general processes in the religious sphere. Slovenia displays a consistently high level public indifference as well as a steady decline in the number of adherents of traditional religious organizations. Secularization is manifest at the public, political, and even personal levels, where indifference towards religion is widespread today. The conflict line is thus between institutionalized traditional Catholic and secular organizations, which leaves little space for other religious communities to exert public or political influence. A good example is the situation of the Evangelical Church in Slovenia, which expresses very liberal positions to societal questions but gains no new members or adherents besides reputational benefits among the population. In Macedonia, the inclusion of two religious organizations into the political arena by ethno-political parties channels the attention of the population towards the issue: religion has regained a presence in the public sphere with political intentions.

71 Fox 2008:141.

72 See http://www.thearda.com/, 28/01/13. "The GRI, GFI, and SRI values reported on the National Profiles are averages from the 2003, 2005, and 2008 International Religious Freedom reports, while the Religious Persecution (RP) measure is an average from the 2005 and 2008 reports".

References

Chaves M, Cann D (1992) Regulation, pluralism, and religious market structure. Rationality and Society 4(3):272–290

Forum18. Religious Freedom. http://www.forum18.org/

Fox J (2004) Religion, civilization, and civil war. Lexington Books, Oxford

Fox J (2008) A world survey of religion and the state. Cambridge University Press, Cambridge

Karpat K (1985) Ottoman population 1830–1914. Demographic and social characteristics. University of Wisconsin Press, London

Kerševan M (1998) Religion und Kirche in der slowenischen Zivilgesellschaft nach 1990. In: Pollack D et al. Religiöser Wandel in den postkommunistischen Ländern Ost- und Mitteleuropas. Ergon, Würzburg, p 371–394

Kippenberg H, Schuppert G (eds) (2005) Die verrechtlichte Religion. Der Öffentlichkeitsstatus von Religionsgemeinschaften. Mohr, Tübingen

Linz J (1996) Der religiöse Gebrauch der Politik und/oder der politische Gebrauch der Religion. Ersatzideologie gegen Ersatzreligion. In: Maier H (ed) Totalitarismus und politische religion. Konzepte des Diktaturvergleichs, München, p 129–154

Macedonian Orthodox Church . http://www.mpc.org.mk/

Minkenberg M (2003) Staat und Kirche in westlichen Demokratien. In: Minkenberg M, Willems U (eds) Politik und Religion. VS Verlag, Wiesbaden, p 115–138

Murvar V (1967) Max Weber's concept of hierocracy: A study in the typology of church–state relationships. Sociological Analysis 28(3):69–84

Nikolovski-Katin S (1999) Small religious communities and groups in the republic of Macedonia. Philosophy and Sociology 2(6):91–99

Office for Religious Communities, Slovenia. http://www.mizks.gov.si/si/delovna_podrocja/urad_za_verske_skupnosti/

Office for the Relations to Religious Communities and Groups, Macedonia. http://www.kovz.gov.mk/

Pollack D (2002) Religion und Politik in Mittel- und Osteuropa. Aus Politik und Zeitgeschichte (42):15–22

Pollack D (2009) Renaissance des Religiösen? Erkenntnisse der Sozialforschung. Osteuropa 06 (2009):29–45

Pollack D, Wielgohs J (eds) (2010) Akteure oder Profiteure? Die demokratische Opposition in den ostmitteleuropäischen Regimeumbrüchen 1989. VS Verlag, Wiesbaden

The Religion and State Project. http://www.thearda.com/ras/
Riedel S (2005) Die Erfindung der Balkanvölker. Identitätspolitik zwischen Konflikt und Integration. VS Verlag, Wiesbaden
Riedel S (2006) Kirche und Staat in Russland. Transitionen und Kontinuitäten. In: Bunčić D, Trunte N (eds) Iter philologicum, München, p 319–331
Robertson R (1987) Church–state relations in comparative perspective. In: Robbins T, Robertson R (eds) Church–state relations: Tensions and transitions. Transaction Books, Oxford, p 153–160
Roman Catholic Church, Slovenia. http://katoliska-cerkev.si/
Segal R (ed) (2006) The Blackwell companion to the study of religion. Wiley–Blackwell, Oxford
Statistical Office of the Republic of Macedonia (2002a) Census of population, households and dwellings in the Republic of Macedonia. Book IX, Skopje
Statistical Office of the Republic of Macedonia (2002b) Census of population, households and dwellings in the Republic of Macedonia. Book X, Skopje
Statistical Office of the Republic of Macedonia. http://www.stat.gov.mk/
State Statistical Office of Slovenia. http://www.stat.si/
UNDP (2011) Human development report 2011. United Nations Development Programme, New York
UNDP. Database: Human development indicators. http://hdrstats.undp.org/en/indicators/
Weber M (1922) Wirtschaft und Gesellschaft. Mohr, Tübingen
World Values Survey. http://worldvaluessurvey.org

The Role of Democratic State in Inter-Religious Relations: Theoretical and Historical Considerations in Respect of Countries in Transition

Sabine Riedel

Since the end of the Cold War and the fall of the Berlin Wall in 1989, all the countries of Eastern Europe began a deep transition process characterized by the opening of their economies and changes in their political systems towards democracy. The new political framework directly affected the status and working conditions of churches and religious communities in many respects: First, the collapse of the socialist systems was mainly caused by the loss of political legitimacy of the ruling communist parties. New democratic values pushed back their socialist ideology together with its anti-clerical and anti-religious views. Secondly, the disappearance of an official state doctrine initiated a search for a new national identity in cultural and religious terms. Thirdly, people were no longer afraid to openly express their religious consciousness or affiliations, so that societies gradually developed forms of cultural and religious pluralism. Finally, all Eastern European countries adopted the European Convention on Human Rights (1950) and joined the European Council of Europe, ensuring freedom of religion as well as self-determination for religious groups and their institutions. In short, *identity*, *legitimacy*, *autonomy*, *cultural rights*, and *religious values* became key issues in transition countries describing and rewriting the relationship between state and churches and inter-religious relations. The first section of this chapter will give a short theoretical introduction to this topic.

This paper analyzes the new church/state and inter-religious relations in three transition countries characterized by their cultural, ethnic, and religious diversity: the Russian Federation, and two Balkan countries: Bulgaria, and Bosnia and Herzegovina (section 3). To this day, all these countries suffer from democratic deficits, which raises the question of whether the lack of democratic structures is responsible for the existing interethnic and inter-religious tensions; or, to pose the question another way: To what extent have state institutions and public bodies already developed concepts or strategies for managing and resolving social conflicts between groups with different religious consciousness, values, and identities? In order to understand the essential task of democratic states as a neutral authority in interfaith disputes, the second section of this article covers Europe's experience with monarchies and authoritarian regimes, where ruling elites justified their power and privileged position through specific cultural or religious values. A further section examines the advanced democracies of Western Europe, which needed to adopt methods to integrate large numbers of immigrants of different faiths. This comparison may serve to illustrate that countries in transition—similarly to other modern societies—face choices between various approaches to mediating inter-religious tensions. Finally, we have to discuss not only the necessities but also the boundaries of governmental regulation, which are determined by norms of democracy and human rights.

The Meta-theoretical Framework in Shape of an Archimedean Spiral

In analyzing church/state and inter-religious relations, we can use well-known theories of social sciences dealing with the mentioned topics of: identity, legitimacy, autonomy, cultural rights, and religious values. An especially useful approach derives from the scientific work of Émile Durkheim (1858–1917), the founder of sociology as an academic subject in French universities and a representative of the Modernization Theory. Durkheim described the development of society as a process of differentiation initiated by the social division of labor (Degele and Dries 2005:52). In pre-modern societies, by and large, people perform similar activities and share the same values and religious beliefs. In accordance with their simple way of life, they have the sense of belonging to a group of individuals characterized by specific peculiarities such as language, religion, or profession, which Durkheim defined as 'mechanical solidarity'. However, the modern industrial society is highly complex and functionally differentiated by vocational specialization, whereby traditional costumes and beliefs have changed radically or even disappear. Religion as an important source of solidarity loses its function for social integration, thereby necessitating the creation of new forms of solidarity in order to ensure continuing social cohesion. Durkheim was convinced that only people's awareness of their mutual dependence leads to a so-called 'organic solidarity' that newly defines traditional religious beliefs and values in terms of trans-religious and secular norms.

Apart from this and individual awareness, he also assumed the existence of a collective consciousness representing the totality of opinions, beliefs, feelings, and customs among members of a society. With the further process of modernization, this collective consciousness weakens such that social cohesion and integration increasingly depend on individuals' consciousness and their personal willingness (Kruse 2012:79). Based on Durkheim's assumption of the social division of labor, we can state that individuals within modern societies experience a changing sense of social belonging. They create new identities concerning state institutions and authorities that are responsible for the setting of social norms and ensuring compliance with these standards. Therefore, modernization processes involve the birth of national identities within the framework of a particular nation-state. Modern national identity may still be connected with the cultural and religious traditions of certain communities; or may be oriented towards the whole society, whose socioeconomic organizations and political institutions are replacing the roles of culture and religion in ensuring social inclusion.

The modernization of European societies at the end of the 19th century presented enormous social challenges such as migration to the cities and urbanization, unemployment, urban poverty, and the lack of housing and healthcare. All these factors undermined social cohesion and the creation of the necessary 'organic solidarity'. In particular, questions were raised regarding social reforms as well as political representation and the participation of underprivileged people. Increasingly, social movements and political parties throughout Europe demanded the democratization of their political systems and constitutions. Until the beginning of the 20th century, most European empires had a ruling elite comprising the monarch followed by the military and the aristocratic nobility. As a result of the general decline of religious doctrines and institutions due to modernization, the new political forces had serious doubts about the legitimacy of kingdoms, which derived their legitimacy from the supposed divine right of their sovereigns. It was proposed that the monarchal structure should be replaced by democratic legitimacy, guaranteeing the free expression of the will of the people through a free and undisclosed vote.

Although such demands for democracy appeared especially impressive between the two World Wars, social sciences focused their primary research interest on the theory of democracy until after the end of the Second World War. The reign of the Nazi terror required a deeper analysis of the social and political origins of authoritarian and totalitarian rule in searching for democratic alternatives. In this historical context, important scientific contributions included the 'The origins of totalitarianism' (1951) by the German sociologist Hannah Arendt (1951/1986) and 'A Preface to Democratic Theory' (1956) by the US political scientist Robert Dahl, which even today remains one of the most important works in this field. Dahl defines democracy as the self-government of citizens (demos), and regards it as a normative model which is yet to be realized anywhere. For that reason, his actual subject is the democratization process and the question of the extent to which democratically governed states, which Dahl regards as "polyarchies", tend to approximate this model.

The necessary conditions for such a 'polyarchal' democracy are "popular sovereignty" and "political equality" (Dahl 1956/2006:75), from which follows the legitimacy of a democratic government. Dahl considers that political legitimacy has nothing to do with a religious belief in the "divine right" of monarchs, nor does it have an ethical background. Instead, it has a psychological meaning, in the sense of "a belief in the rightness of the decision or the process of decision-making" (Ibid:46). In other words: the legitimacy of modern democratic governance depends on the attitudes and opinions of the people of one country. In addition, the citizen is the focus of the following five criteria, according to which we can describe and evaluate the democratization process and the level of development: 1. Effective participation, 2. Voting equality, 3. Enlightened understanding, 4. Control of the agenda, and 5. Inclusion (Schaal 2006:248–274, 260). This means that a highly developed democracy must guarantee all citizens equal opportunities not only for expressing their preferences but also for validation their choices.

Of special interest for our considerations is the fifth point that "the demos must include all adult members of the association" (Ibid:261). Currently, the question being discussed in intercultural and inter-religious conflicts is: Who belongs to the 'association' of a certain country? Obviously, in his fifth criteria of inclusion, Dahl refers to people of an identical citizenship having the same entitlements and duties towards a certain country. Whereas the Democratic Theory deals with 'demos' as an abstract term in the sense of a political community, Systems Theory pays attention to the complexity and diversity of society. The American sociologist Talcott Parsons is regarded as the founder of this approach in social sciences, which first appeared in the 1950s and dominated until the end of the Cold War (1989). Of prime importance is the internal diversification of modern society into further sub-systems such as social classes and professionals, as well as different milieus, lifestyles, and ethical values. Talcott assumes that all these social sub-systems are—to a certain level—self-controlled or "self-sufficient" and affected by each other (Parsons 1963:232–262).

For optimal development of the politically-, socially-, or culturally-oriented sub-systems, it would appear necessary to guarantee the inclusion of all these communities into a comprehensive civil society with its system of common values termed the 'demos' by Robert Dahl. This implies, however, common political institutions as 'regulating systems' and 'communication media', which permit the free transfer of political power to representatives regardless of their race, ethnic origin, mother tongue, religion, age, or sexual orientation (Münch 1995:625–635, 628). But there is another reason why social integration is an important commitment by a state with respect to peaceful and friendly relationships between different cultural and religious communities: During their internal diversification, modern societies are becoming more complex—a trend that tends to overburden the capacity of the public sector. Therefore, greater decision-making power is transferred from the central administration to stakeholder communities. This creates not only new political power but simultaneously delegates it to various social sub-systems that lack political legitimacy.

This legitimacy deficit has been taken up and broadly developed by the theory of Multiculturalism. According to this relatively new approach, which appeared after the end of the East–West conflict, Dahl's criteria for evaluation of democratic systems are insufficient. As the Canadian political philosopher Charles Taylor argues, the condition of equal opportunities for participation led to an 'equalization' that affected only civil and voting rights but which has not been expanded into either the socioeconomic or the cultural spheres. For this reason, Taylor (1994:25–74, 38) calls for a "politics of difference", recognizing not only the identity of individuals but also of groups and their right to "distinctness from everyone else". Whereas the classical ideas of Liberalism that were recently presented by the American philosopher John Rawls have generally ignored cultural differences, the multicultural concept attempts to re-establish the importance and social function of communities as social sub-systems.

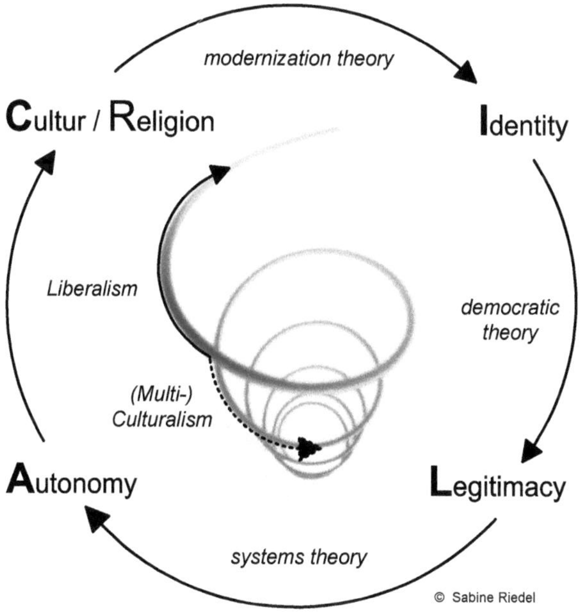

Figure 2.1: Meta-theoretical framework represented as an Archimedean spiral for the analysis of inter-religious relations in modern societies

Another prominent exponent of the Multicultural Theory also mentioned as Communitarianism is the Canadian academic Will Kymlicka. According to Kymlicka (1995), the recognition of cultural differences is not only a philosophical question or a moral obligation but, foremost, a political imperative of democratically constituted states. The fundamental point is the implementation of additional collective rights for such cultural communities that are in a minority position. He confirms that only the legal guarantee of positive accommodation of group differences would ensure the equal treatment and equal opportunity for political participation promised to citizens of disadvantaged and marginalized groups. From the perspective of the Systems Theory, Kymlicka attempts to solve the lack of legitimacy caused by the internal diversification of modern society and the transfer of political power to differentiated sub-systems. New group-differentiated rights for cultural, ethnic, or religious minorities ought to ensure the needed political legitimacy in favor of the newly created authorities.

If we take the above theories together—Modernization Theory, Democratic Theory, Systems Theory, Multiculturalism, as well as Liberalism, we are able to examine the question of how to combine them coherently in order to analyze inter-religious relations in modern societies. Figure 2.1 shows one possible combination in the form of a circle: The starting point is the pre-modern society as it existed in Europe during the 19th century. The Modernization Theory explains that the social division of labor created new national identities. At that point, the decline of traditional religious values already represented a significant threat to political institutions if they failed to ensure social inclusion in the absence of new social norms that were multi-faith, trans-religious, or religiously neutral. Whereas the democratic theory discusses the importance of equal political participation and voting in generating the necessary social cohesion in modern societies, the Systems Theory demonstrates the necessity for central political institutions elected by all citizens in supporting an optimum differentiation of social sub-systems and protecting their autonomy. Finally, the controversy between Multiculturalism and Liberalism about adequate legal structures to endure equal political participation leads us to a crossroad and the key question: Do group-differentiated political rights really support the integration of religious minorities, or do they risk new inter-religious conflicts? Our hypothesis here is that such collective rights tend to strengthen not only religious differences and contrasts but also their politicization, which could result in political and social stagnation and regression as well as in violent conflicts. In front of this consideration the circle of interconnected theories appears as an Archimedean spiral indicating different directions of social development.

Historical Background of Church/State Relations in Transition Countries

The transformation processes that started in Eastern Europe in 1989 and the political changes in North Africa since the beginning of the Arab spring in 2011 can be described as a global trend towards modernization and democratization. Many political and social forces calling for greater participation consider Western or European countries as exemplars of democratic values such as the rule of law, human rights; and fundamental freedoms, including the freedom of association, expression, culture, and religion. However, not for the first time in history, neighboring countries wish to orient themselves by Europe. As a consequence of colonialism, European empires became centers of socio-economic progress and scientific innovation, with the result that they are considered to epitomize modernization. This perception also concerned the political sphere, within which imperialist rule has established an absolutist reign of state power. Therefore, economically disadvantaged countries regarded the doctrine of absolutism as key for development, prosperity, and empowerment. We can conclude that there was a first attempt towards modernization in the form of 'Europeanization' during the period of imperialism.

What did this exemplary role mean with regard to church/state relations? The answer is that those monarchies with non-European territories began to orientate themselves according to the doctrine of absolutism. This legitimized the monarch's political power as deriving from the will of God, thereby creating the so-called divine right of sovereigns as one of the central components of their absolutist rule. The symbiosis between church- and state institutions, a typical element of pre-modern forms of society, was no longer an attractive model. Instead, the symbiotic relationship should become that of dominant state power subordinating the spiritual sphere, insofar as the monarch simultaneously became the leading authority of the official state-church or state religion. One of the best-known representatives of absolutist rule was King Louis XIV of France, who not only created a centralized state but also proclaimed a Catholic Church of France. According to the Gallican Articles (1682), the papal primacy was limited and the clergy nominated no longer by the Vatican, but by the monarch himself. This model of absolutism is well known as 'caesaropapism' in accordance with the Roman Empire, where the 'Caesar' was the secular emperor and at the same time the supreme head or the religious leader of the church (papa) (Linz 1996:129–170).

The French 'Sun King' was not the first absolutist to depose the powerful influence of the Roman Pontiff, nominating his own clergy and church doctrines completely independent of Rome. More than one century earlier, King Henry VIII founded the Church of England, declaring the English crown as its supreme head. Since his Supremacy Act (1534), the British monarch still bears the title 'Fidei

Defensor' (Defender of the Faith) and designates the government of the ecclesiastical hierarchy, comprising the bishops with the Archbishop of Canterbury as their spiritual leader. This historical period also saw the Protestant Reformation and the establishment of the national Lutheran churches in German-speaking and Scandinavian countries: In 1526, the Swedish King Gustav I officially broke with Roman Catholicism; eleven years later, the Evangelical Lutheran Church of Denmark and Norway was founded by Christian III of Denmark (1537). In the first decade of the 21st century the Swedish and Norwegian parliaments voted in favor of a separation between church and state, whereas in Denmark both institutions remain closely intertwined although the church is subordinate to the Danish Parliament.

As the Russian Tsar Peter the Great aimed to transform his country into a modern European power, he started profound administrative reforms—adopting the new model of church/state relations of his mighty European competitors, especially from the Swedish empire. Thus ended the 200-year period in which both institutions cooperated closely in a symbiotic relationship. The Tsars and the Russian Orthodox Church (ROC: Русская Православная Церковь) pursued their common goal of accepting the inheritance of the Byzantine Empire conquered by the Ottomans. For this purpose, they had adopted insignia and regalia of power such as the double eagle, which symbolized the dual rule of state and church. In 1700, the death of Adrian, the Holy Patriarch of Moscow and all Russia, gave Peter I the opportunity to keep the position vacant, replacing it two decades later by a Holy Synod whose 12 members were nominated by state authorities. State control of church-related institutions by the absolutist ruler also extended to the education and salary of the clergy (Кондаков (Kondakov) 2003:278). Monks and priests were required to support the religious as well as the cultural conquest of newly occupied territories.

About a hundred years later, Tsar Nikolas I appointed himself the official head of the ROC (1833) whereby state domination over the Orthodox Church not only continued but was transformed into one of the three ideological pillars of the tsarist empire, namely Orthodoxy, Autocracy and Nationality (православие, самодержавие, народность). Their autocratic character became apparent in internal as well as in external policies: On the one hand, the connection of Orthodox religion and Russian nationality initiated a pre-modern nation-building process that created a so-called 'confessional nation' in the sense that Russian nationals ought to be a member of the Orthodox Church. This kind of Russification posed an existential threat to other religious communities. According to the first census of 1897 only two-thirds of the whole population belonged to the ROK, with 11 percent belonging to an Islamic faith, 9 percent to the Roman Catholic Church, 4 percent Judaism, and 3 percent Protestants (Demoscope 2013). On the other hand, this nation concept was designed to lay claim to the role of a protective power vis-à-vis the population outside Russia belonging to Orthodox Christianity. This applied mainly to the Greek Orthodox Church, which was subordinate to the Ottoman Empire and included a large part of the Slavic- and Romansh-speaking populations.

At the turn of the 19th century, the Ottoman sultans followed a similar path to modernization. However, in contrast to the Russian tsars and their absolutist way of rule, the Ottomans adopted the model of enlightened absolutism. Even then, this model was represented by the Habsburg monarchy under its ruler King Joseph II, who declared the Patent of Toleration (Toleranzpatent, 1781) and recognized religious freedom. Nevertheless, Joseph II supported the Catholic Church in fulfilling its role as an official state-church by its transformation into a national institution controlled by the state. This model was a better fit than Russian autocracy for the diverse Ottoman Empire because of its millet-system, which recognized the autonomy of other religious communities. The Tanzimât reforms (1839–1876) initiated by Abdülmecit I aimed to adopt the millet system but, additionally to religious jurisdiction, an over-denominational legal system should be created in compliance with the principle of equal treatment. One result was the reform of the territorial administration (1864/67), which included political participation of all religious communities and the introduction of a citizenship beyond religious, ethnic, or linguistic boundaries with the elaboration of a new Civil Code (1869).

In order to implement these reform projects, even Abdülmecit I felt the need to take control of Muslim institutions such as their superior authority (the şeyhülislam) in order to break the resistance of conservative powers among Islamic theologians (ʿulamā') and lawyers (fuqahā'). This also reflects the role of enlightened absolutism and the Ottoman's orientation towards Western and Central Europe. However, because this path of Europeanization would mean a substantial loss of privileges for Muslims, their critics enjoyed a wide measure of support within Muslim communities, which accounted for around two-thirds of the whole population. In this historic context, Islamist concepts of society appeared for the first time or became stronger, such as Wahhabism on the Arabian Peninsula and Salafism in Egypt. These presented new interpretations of Islamic culture and history, according to which Islamic law given by God would be incompatible with secular law. These narratives were not only a response to the Tanzimât reforms and therefore a part of the modernization process itself, but also contradicted historical reality: The Ottomans already created their new Civil Code on the basis of sharia law and the (secular) Sultans' Law (Plagemann 2009:102).

The European empires supported the Tanzimât reforms insofar as the rights of the Christian minorities were concerned. However, they were not interested in the consolidation of the Ottoman Empire through a modern nation-building process, and regarded the millet system as a welcome opportunity to interfere in the internal affairs of the Ottoman state as protective powers for the Christian minorities. In order to avoid losing their influence, they now aimed to convert the Christian millets into national states whose Orthodox population would form the nucleus of a new confessional nation according to the Russian model. In addition to Greece and Serbia, further examples include Bulgaria, which was first transformed as Danube Vilayet (Tuna vilâyeti) into an autonomous and tax-paying principality (1878). Its nation-building was based on religion, ethnicity, and language, and therefore disrupted the creation of the Ottoman nation as a political alternative. When Bulgaria declared its independence as a Christian kingdom (1908) with the Bulgarian Orthodox Church (BOK—Българска православна църква) as its established church (Bulgarian Constitution 1879), the Muslim minority founded its own denomination (главно мюфтийство) and elected their own spiritual leader (Главен мюфтия). Subsequently, the Ottoman şeyhülislam only retained the right of veto in Bulgarian affairs for a matter of decades (The Muslim Denomination in the Republic of Bulgaria undated). Since that time, the clergy of the BOK as well as the Muslim community have been paid by the Bulgarian Government.

In the same year, 1908, Austria-Hungary as successor of the Habsburg Monarchy announced the annexation of Bosnia and Herzegovina, which at that time was still part of the Ottoman Empire but had been occupied by Vienna since 1878. In contrast to Bulgaria, where the BOK became an established church, the Orthodox and Muslim populations occupied minority positions, whereas Catholics were privileged but controlled by the Austrian government. This had caused tensions not only with the Ottoman Sultan, who officially served as head of state until 1908, but also with the Muslim population, whose spiritual leader was nominated by the Ottoman şeyhülislam. Lastly, Serbia claimed the right to represent the interests of Orthodox Serbs in Bosnia and Herzegovina, although they belonged to the Patriarchate of Karlovci (Vojvodina). Shortly after Austria's annexation, the First World War broke out, which ultimately ended with the dissolution of Austria-Hungary. From 1918, the newly established Kingdom of Yugoslavia pursued for the first time a neutral policy and equal treatment of the various religious communities. Under these conditions both Serbian Patriarchates could be united by relinquishing the position as the established church of the former Serbian Kingdom. The Muslim community also created a self-governing administration with the rais-ul-ulama as the spiritual leader for all Muslims in the former Yugoslavia (The Islamic Community in Bosnia and Herzegovina undated a).

We can summarize the historical review as follows: The first attempts at 'Europeanization' by the Ottoman and Russian Empires during the period of imperialism followed the model of absolutism, which was regarded as the key not only to economic growth but also for political stability. The adoption of absolutist rule included the subordination of churches and religions under state control so that most of the religious groups lost their autonomy. Since the beginning of the 19th century the Russian tsar as well as the Ottoman sultan proclaimed themselves head of their state-churches. The nomination and payment of the clergy—including their spiritual leaders—as public officials enforced state influence on faith communities. This form of modernization during the period of imperialism was similar to the so-called 'development dictatorships' during the 20th century. Beside these similarities there were significant differences: Russia initiated a nation-building process by creating a Russian confessional nation and excluding one-third of their population which belonged to other faith communities; in contrast, the Ottoman Empire followed the model of enlightened absolutism, giving their religious minorities the same rights and Ottoman citizenship.

The Role of State in Inter-religious Relations of Transition Countries

Before we start our comparative analysis of inter-faith relations in Bosnia-Herzegovina, Bulgaria, and Russia, we have to mention the period of totalitarian and authoritarian rule during the 20th century. While the majority of the European monarchies were transformed into constitutional monarchies or democracies, in Central and Eastern Europe, democratization processes were halted after the Second World War by the imposition of one-party communist systems. Despite major structural changes, these new political systems ensured continuity of state control over faith communities (Riedel 2006:S 319–331). In contrast to the Russian tsars, who utilized the Orthodox Church to legitimate their absolutist rule, the Bolsheviks used state dominance to enforce their anti-religious ideology: First, they accepted the restoration of the self-government of the Orthodox patriarchate, but very soon after the October Revolution (1917) they started anti-religious campaigns and persecutions in which thousands of priests were victims. When the new Patriarch Tikhon died in 1925, the Bolsheviks barred a successor, as had Tsar Peter I. In order to ensure its survival, the ROK issued an official declaration of its absolute loyalty to the Soviet government. Nevertheless, the new Act on Religious Affairs (1929) limited the autonomy of all religious communities, leaving them to the arbitrary decisions of state authorities until the 1980s (Gassenschmidt and Tuchtenhagen 2000:156). From 1944, religious communities were placed under the direct state supervision of two government councils, which were unified into the Council for Religious Affairs (Совет по делам религий undated) in 1965.

Establishing a socialist system, Bulgaria fell under the sphere of influence of the communist Soviet Union following the Second World War. This also resulted in a change of church/state relations towards the Soviet model of state interference:

Initially, the new communist regime created the Directorate for Religious Communities (Дирекция на вероизповеданията) as a supervisory body of the Ministry of the Interior. This gave the opportunity to persecute priests and monks charged with crimes against the state. The subsequent death of the Soviet dictator Josef Stalin (1953) also brought substantial changes for Bulgaria: In the same year, the Bulgarian communists suddenly permitted the Orthodox Church to restore its Patriarchate, which had been dissolved following the Ottoman conquest (1393). Therefore, the BOK could now realize its vision since 1870, of achieving full autonomy and independence from the (Greek) Patriarchate of Constantinople, which had eluded the previous tsarist government. Obviously, this was a political stratagem of the communist party, strengthening its dominance over religions and restructuring the Directorate into the 'Committee for Religious Affairs of the BOK and Religious Cults' (2012), which was subject to the authority of the Council of Ministers.

The Kingdom of Yugoslavia, founded in 1918, differed from other monarchies with regard to its secular system: There was neither a state religion nor state control over various religious communities. This rapidly changed following the creation of the Socialist Federal Republic of Yugoslavia (1943), which included Bosnia and Herzegovina as one of five republics. Although the new constitution guaranteed religious freedom, the Yugoslavian communists, like their brother parties in Eastern Europe, first started anti-religious campaigns and soon changed their priorities towards political instrumentalization of religions. In contrast to Bulgaria, Tito's administration in Yugoslavia founded not only the Republic's commission for religious affairs at the federal level, but additionally ministries of religious affairs in every republic as well as offices at the local level (Perica 2002:134). Since the 1960s, the various ethnic national movements started to utilize these structures for their own benefit. In this historical context, Bosnian communists demanded national status, which indeed led to the recognition of Muslims not as a religious group but as a sixth nation within the former Yugoslavia. This can be described as the return of the confessional nation model of the 19th century, which in addition to the ethnic nation concepts of Slovenians, Croats, Serbs, Montenegrins, and Macedonians, weakened the process of Yugoslav nation-building.

Inter-ethnic tensions were able to build up over more than two decades and finally broke out after the end of the Cold War. The main venue of these violent conflicts in the early 1990s was Bosnia and Herzegovina, which still suffers from the rivalry between the three main ethnic groups: the Serbs, Croats, and Bosniaks. Whereas this ethnic nation concept previously only had legal status within the former Yugoslav Federation, the international Dayton Peace Agreement (1995) officially recognized them as "constituent peoples" instead of fostering the citizenship of Bosnia and Herzegovina (Sarajlić 2013). Ten years later, the Progress Report of the

European Commission (2005) noted that this legal framework has proven to be an obstacle *"towards a State based on citizenship rather than on ethnic representation"*. However, there is another critical point: As a consequence of the national status as 'Muslim' within the former Yugoslavia, the ethnicity of 'Bosniak' refers today more to religious consciousness than to linguistic differences, so that the Bosniak community of about two million citizens is polarized: Secularist politicians defend the Bosnian Law on Freedom of Religions (Official Gazette of Bosnia and Herzegovina 2004) and its principle of separation between state and faith communities, which is the only way to conserve state unity. In contrast, the Islamic community (Islamska Zajednica—IZ) and its grand mufti (Rais-ul-ulama) expect to play a leading role in Bosnian society as well as in the European Muslim community.

Mustafa Cerić, the former grand mufti of Bosnia, and his successor, Husein Kavazović, represent a Bosnian Islam that follows a policy of exclusion and expansion similar to that of Croatian and Serbian nationalists: First, their association structure is similar to state institutions, consisting of a 'Council' as their representative and legislative body, which elects the Riyasat, the highest Islamic religious and administrative organ; as well as the 'constitutional court' based on their Islamic 'constitution' (The Islamic Community of Bosnia and Herzegovina undated b). Furthermore, about twenty percent of the 83 elected members of the Council come from abroad: 13 members are representatives of former Yugoslav territory (Sandžak/Serbia and Montenegro, Croatia, and Slovenia), and five additional members are from Germany, Norway, Australia, and the USA. The Bosnian Islamic Community therefore has a transnational orientation and missionary activity, although it *"regards itself a part of the universal Islamic community of Muslims around the world, a part of the Umaah"* (The Islamic Community of Bosnia and Herzegovina undated c). Vice versa, Islamic groups of Salafists or Wahhabists are present in Bosnia and Herzegovina, who immigrated during or shortly after the Bosnian war. Their religious activities are financed by the ministries of religious affairs or by foundations based in the Gulf States like Saudi Arabia and Qatar, which export conservative and fundamentalist interpretations of Islamic doctrines and culture (International Crisis Group 2013).

In addition to Bosnia and Herzegovina, Bulgaria—with its Muslim population of about 13 percent or about one million citizens—is within the sphere of influence of such oil states governed by absolutist monarchs. Similarly to European empires until the 19th century, they legitimate their political power through God, and with the support of a fundamentalist clergy under the leadership of the Saudi Arabian Wahhab dynasty. By the beginning of the 1990s, these groups had begun financing fundamentalist groups in order to penetrate the Bulgarian Muslim community—an aim in which they have achieved some success. On the occasion of charges against

13 muftis from Pazardzhik in South Bulgaria accused of fundamentalism (2012), Grand Mufti (The Muslim Denomination in the Republic of Bulgaria undated) Mustafa Hadzhi rejected any Islamist influence on his community (TV7 2012). However, he has come under pressure about his close ties with the religious ministries of Qatar, Saudi Arabia, Turkey, and Kazakhstan. Bulgarian public opinion and the state authorities have expressed concern about direct subsidiaries of foreign ministries. The result would not be a reconstruction of Bulgarian Islamic traditions but the importation of new Islamic doctrines embedded in political ideologies. To resolve this dilemma, the newly elected President, Rosen Plevneliev, recommends the accreditation of the High Islamic Institute as a research and educational center, a claim which was dismissed for a long time (Vissi Islamic Institute undated). Bulgarian Muslims have to go abroad in order to study Islamic theology and respective Islamic law.

The work of the Bulgarian Directorate for Religious Communities (the former Committee for Religious Affairs during the socialist period) is problematical, as Article 13 (3) of the Bulgarian Constitution (1991) mentions the Bulgarian Orthodox Church as the traditional faith community. However, this privilege and the state support benefits have their dark sides—namely the direct influence of the state, as occurred at the beginning of the post-socialist transition period. The first elected democratic government uncovered the entanglements of Patriarch Maxim in state security during the socialist regime and accepted Metropolitan Pimen as the new head of the BOC—who was elected in 1996 as rival patriarch by an alternative synod (Pravoslavieto 2013). This schism within the Church is a heavy burden and was not resolved either by mediation attempts on the part of Patriarch Bartholomew I of Constantinople and Patriarch Alexy II of Moscow, or by the death of Pimen himself (1999). First, a complaint by the canonical synod led to a judgment by the European Court of Human Rights (2009), which found the Bulgarian government had violated the neutrality of religious affairs. Furthermore, in 2012 it emerged that Pimen was also closely involved with state security during the socialist period. These backgrounds explain the current problems within the Church community under its new Patriarch Neophyte, who was installed in 2013 (Bulgarian Orthodox Church Undated): The organizational structures are weak, ineffective, opaque, and susceptible to corruption (Arndt 2013).

The democratization progress within the Russian Federation had already begun with Gorbachev's policies of glasnost and perestroika in the mid-1980s and specifically affected church/state relations. When the Russian Orthodox Church celebrated its thousand-year anniversary in 1988, the Soviet state officially participated in a number of festive events (Behrens 2002). This laid the cornerstone for new Acts on Religious Affairs at both federal and regional levels (1990) giving faith communities the freedom to practice religion, as a result of which the Council for Religious Affairs was dissolved. Shortly afterwards, the Russian Federation as the successor of the former USSR established a new Council for Cooperation with Religious Associations (2013) administratively attached to the Russian President. Although the new legislation has not led to an established church, there is preferential treatment of the ROC; the personnel composition of this advisory body also reinforces this hierarchy of faith communities (traditional and non-traditional). This plays to the interests of the Orthodox clergy under the new patriarch Kirill I of Moscow (installed 2009), who seeks to play a greater role in Russian society as lawyer and defender of ethical and moral values. In this context, there is also talk of *"crafting 'symphony' with state"* (Interfax 2011), which reminds more of the Middle Ages than of modern pluralistic societies (Mitrokhin (Митрохин) 2004).

One of the few state representatives on this Council is Alexander Ignatengo, the president of the 'Institute of Religion and Policy' (undated) and an expert on political Islam. His personality reflects the external dimension of inter-religious relations, namely the threat of Islamist ideology and extremism, mainly in Tatarstan and Bashkortostan. As a result of their oil and gas deposits, these republics are amongst the richest areas in Russia and enjoy substantial autonomy. Moreover, the majorities of their populations are Muslim (about four million) and are represented in the Russia Muftis Council under its Chairman Grand Mufti Rawil Gaynetdin (RMC—Совет Муфтиев России undated). In contrast to Bulgaria, Tatar Muslims have their own centers offering academic training for imams and theologians, for example the Central Spiritual Administration of Muslims of Russia (Центральное духовное управление мусульман России). Its chief, Talgat Safa Tajuddin, bears the title of Grand Mufti and Shaykh al-Islam from the Soviet era (Biography of Grand Mufti, Shaykh al-Islam 2003), which provokes tensions. Further potential for conflict arises from Salafists or Wahhabists abroad, which puts the Tatar Muslims under pressure and divides their community (Поляков (Poles) 2003). Nevertheless, one cannot ignore the fact that the political systems of these republics represent a new form of authoritarianism appearing in democratic garb (Hunter 2004), which reinforces the political abuse of Islam (Interfax 2013).

In conclusion, after the dissolution of the former Soviet Union and Yugoslav Federation, the representative bodies of their churches and religious communities suddenly found themselves in a new transnational phase, and in the dangerous position of potentially being misused in order to advance national interests or separatist objectives. The result was a substantially closer connection between state authorities and their privileged churches respectively, between political actors and their preferred faith groups. As the case of Bulgaria shows, such preferences cause increasing polarization between different religious communities. This tendency is reflected by the conversion of the former councils or ministries of religious affairs into an advisory body with the task of moderating inter-faith relations rather than controlling them. This kind of transition did not lead to separation between church/religion and state but, on the contrary, to increasing interdependence of both spheres. Against this background, state institutions really cannot play a neutral role—for instance by preserving the religious pluralism of their societies and guaranteeing inter-religious freedom. Instead, due to their partisanship and preference for a specific religious community, they lose authority and legitimacy with respect to the whole society, thereby promoting social and national disintegration rather than fostering a democratic process of nation-building.

European Democracies as Models for Church/State and Inter-religious Relations?

In this final section, we examine different models of church/state relations among Western European democracies to determine whether or not a democratic model developed during the 20th century. At this juncture, it should be pointed out that there is nowhere a genuine democracy in the ideal sense used by Robert Dahl, but only attempts to approach this model. Within this process, the democratically governed countries of Western Europe represent three main models of church/state relations due to their historical developments: The first model is characterized by the existence of an established national church as in the United Kingdom, Denmark, or Greece. The second model has no official state-church but grants religious communities the status of a public body or corporation. As Germany and the Netherlands illustrate, this cooperationist model has given churches or faith communities the possibility to conserve their own social services in the health and educational systems. The third secular model rejects such state subsidies, regarding religion as a private matter so that church and state institutions are totally separated. Examples are France, which adopted its secular model in 1905 via the Law on the Separation of the State and the Church; and Sweden and Norway, which only recently abolished their state-churches (in 2000 and 2012 respectively).

In the 1960s and 1970s, Muslims emigrated as guest workers from the Balkans, Turkey, North Africa, and the Middle East to Western Europe. Large numbers eventually decided not to return to their countries of origin but to stay in their new host countries. The benevolent receptiveness of the state towards family reunification and the payment of social welfare benefits led to the further arrival of young people and women affiliated to Islamic communities. Today, the national statistical institutes of the member states of the European Union estimate the total number of Muslims to be over 16 million or four percent of the population. This is slightly less than the proportion of Muslims among the Russian population (about 20 million), but more than that in the Balkans (about 9 million). Within the EU, Muslim communities have been established in member states that have completely different church/state relations: Germany and France each have approximately 4 million residents with a Muslim background, compared with approximately 2.5 million in the UK and 1 million in the Netherlands. Due to legislative differences, these countries developed very different approaches to integration of immigrant populations. The interesting question is whether these measures are successful, and how far they have an effect on church/state as well as on inter-religious relations.

In the 1990s, the United Kingdom tried out a new multicultural approach based on the theories of Canadian academics Charles Taylor and Will Kymlicka, although *"The British model of integration has never been clearly defined"* (Saggar and Sommerville 2012). The idea was to encourage representatives of the various Muslim communities to become more engaged in social integration; they should assume greater responsibility for improving education, employment, and social welfare within their communities. The British Government began to recognize and institutionalize Muslim organizations without establishing whether they were definitively faith communities, or instead represented cultural associations or political interest groups. This approach failed to meet those challenges of integration because although most Muslim representatives accepted this strategy, they tended to simultaneously oppose the social integration of 'their community' into the common British society. It became apparent that the multicultural approach mainly refers to the binding power of culture or religion but is not able to generate social cohesion beyond cultural or religious communities. A convincing argument in favor of the British integration policy is its commitment to awakening sensitivity and tolerance to cultural, ethnic, and religious diversity. However, it became clear that such cultural rights as freedom of religion or freedom of association can only be achieved if state institutions are created that transcend religious or cultural boundaries. In this respect, the 'established church' model has proved to be a hindrance.

In contrast to the UK, France has developed special integration measures on the basis of an etatist approach. On the one hand, this corresponds to the principle that state institutions have a duty to defend their neutrality concerning religious affairs as laid down in the 'Law on the Separation between State and Church' (1905)[1]. In this context, France has initiated an anti-discrimination policy within the European Union, following the example of the European Convention on Human Rights

1 See: "La République ne reconnaît, ne salarie ni ne subventionne aucun culte", in: Loi du 9 décembre 1905 concernant la séparation des Eglises et de l'Etat. Version consolidée au 01 janvier 2006. http://www.assemblee-nationale.fr/histoire/eglise-etat/sommaire.asp#loi [5.7.2013].

(1950). This policy of equal treatment is the most convincing aspect of the etatist approach, because it rejects any limitation of human rights and fundamental freedoms. However, on the other hand, the etatist approach contradicted the principle of state neutrality because the French government institutionalized the French Council of the Muslim Faith (Conseil Français du Culte Musulman—CFCM) under the then Minster of the Interior and future president, Nicolas Sarkozy (2005). The government's promised financial support has its price: The French president appointed the first chairman of this new council, thereby exerting influence over the CFCM as during colonial times. This approach also failed to deliver positive results: on the contrary, it strengthened the authority of Islamist organizations among French Muslims, marginalizing imams who were born and educated in France (Riedel 2010).

The current German approach to integrating Muslims could be described as a socio-cultural one; it differs from culturalism—with its linkage between ethnicity or religiosity and nationality; as well as from multicultural concepts, which are based on the same principle but adopt an egalitarian approach. One reason for Germany's own specific concept is the coexistence of two major Churches—Catholic and Protestant—which necessitated achieving a balance of power within state institutions founded at the end of the 19th century. The other reason is Germany's experiences of totalitarianism and authoritarianism during the 20th century: The self-determination of churches is one of the key benefits of democracy after the Nazi period and the socialist regime of the former East Germany. Facing the new challenges of integrating immigrants from Muslim countries, the German Federal Ministry of the Interior created the German Islam Conference (Deutsche Islamkonferenz—DIK). Since 2006, state authorities and Muslim representatives regularly discuss key items of social integration. However, Muslim umbrella organizations demand recognition as public bodies in order to acquire state subsidies. The state has rejected such demands on the grounds that many Muslim organizations operate more as cultural associations or interests groups than faith communities.

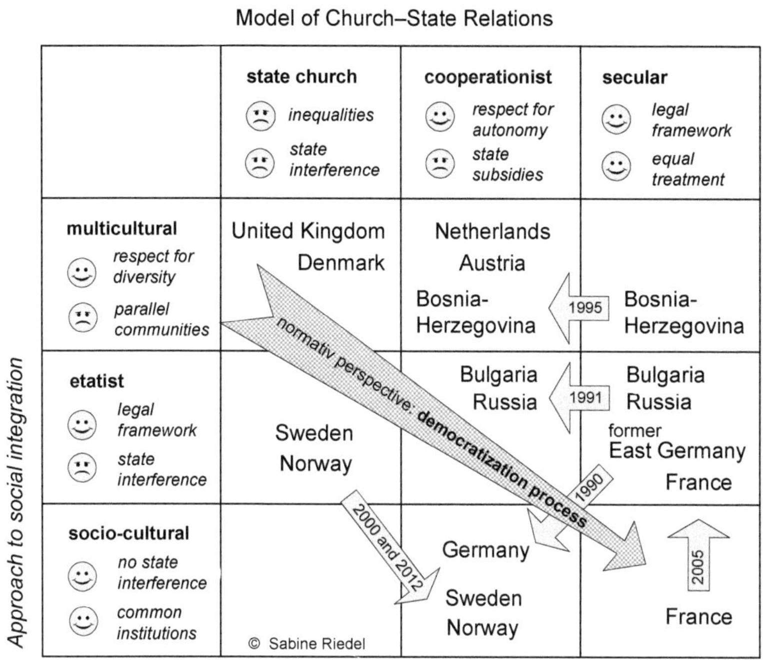

Figure 2.2: Democratization processes in Western and Eastern Europe in terms of social integration and church/state relations

Another way to guarantee the equal treatment of faith communities in Germany could be to replace the current cooperationist model of church/state relations with a secular model. The Christian churches would then have to relinquish subventions worth approximately 19 billion euros per year, in addition to the church tax (DRadio Wissen 2011). Such reform of the constitutional law on church/state relations is difficult but possible—as demonstrated by the examples of Sweden and Norway, which both recently revised their established church models to cooperationist models (Figure 2.2). Furthermore, since German reunification in 1990, Catholic and Protestant churches located in the eastern part of Germany receive state subsidies as well as church taxes collected by the state. At that time there was no public debate about alternatives, although only 26 percent of the population of eastern Germany today belongs to one of the two established churches (Catholic and Protestant) compared with 59.4 percent for Germany overall (Statistisches Bundesamt 2011).

There is a further argument in favor of the secular model: Even the recognition of Muslim organizations as public bodies within the framework of the cooperationist model does not promise any solution to their unequal treatment. An interesting example is provided by Austria, which also follows the cooperationist model and a multicultural approach to integration. In 1912, during monarchist rule, the Islamic Community of Austria (Islamische Glaubensgemeinschaft in Österreich—IGGiÖ 1912) was officially created and recognized as a public body via the Law on Islam (Islamgesetz). Today, it is responsible for training teachers of Islamic religious education at public schools. However, the largest Muslim organizations reject this form of cooperation, instead demanding recognition as a faith group and public body of their own. In the Netherlands, a further example of the cooperationist mode, there is no need for such a legal recognition by state authorities: In accordance with their multicultural approach to integration, every cultural community has to be publicly funded. One result is that it is very difficult to prevent the abuse of cultural and religious rights by associations with an Islamist political agenda.

How should we view the examined countries in transition and their models of church/state relations and social integration? The earlier discussion illustrates that these countries have recently given up their special secular model under which state institutions have been involved in inter-ethnic and inter-religious disputes. Since the 1990s, Bosnia and Herzegovina, Bulgaria, and the Russian Federation have introduced cooperationist models but with quite different results. If we consider the various approaches to social integration of their multi-religious populations, Bosnia and Herzegovina is in a situation similar to Austria or the Netherlands. Its multicultural approach, which goes back to the socialist period of the Yugoslav Federation as well as to the Habsburg Monarchy, has led to the formation of parallel communities along ethnic and religious lines. However, it must be concluded that the criteria of tolerance and respect for diversity inherent in the multicultural approach are yet to be fulfilled in this Balkan state. Inter-religious tensions persist in Bulgaria and the Russian Federation, where the Orthodox Churches are in the position of the traditional Catholic and Protestant Churches in Western Europe. Their new cooperationist model enables these churches to demand a dominant role within their societies and serves as a pretext for perpetuating state influence on religious affairs and their associations.

Conclusion: Boundaries and Necessities of Government Regulations

State control over religious communities provided an instrument for authoritarian systems to control civil society and prevent the emergence of oppositional forces. The simple transformation of the relevant controlling authorities into advisory bodies with the cooperation of faith communities will not be enough to meet the challenges of democratization. With a view to Bulgaria and the Russian Federation, we can draw the conclusion that indirect state influence on faith communities could indeed prevent further escalations of interreligious tensions. Without a neutral state authority and functioning state institutions as in Bosnia and Herzegovina, faith communities will still be misused for political purposes. However, even moderate state influence does not provide a sustainable solution to inter-religious conflicts, because in the long term the state can only retain its authority while it heeds the principle of autonomy and self-governance of religions. Furthermore, the new co-operationist model of church/state relations gives the illusion that state interference has almost disappeared, whereas in reality it continues indirectly through public subsidies. These financial handouts strengthen and intensify the competition among faith communities by demonstrating their unequal treatment.

Apart from these abuses of state influence, there is a need for government regulation in order to guarantee the neutrality of public institutions involved in religious affairs. A legal framework is necessary simply because some method is required to define church/state and inter-religious relations. In democratic states, this legislation dealing with various religions and cultures must first respect the European Convention for the Protection of Human Rights and Fundamental Freedoms as well as internationally accepted standards of human rights. Furthermore, it must guarantee high priority to the secular law in the sense that religious traditions and religious rights must be permitted their place within their respective communities but must accept secular legislation as a superordinate and final authority. Otherwise, the domination of a religious legislation would lead not only to situations of conflict with other faith communities but also to social disintegration. This is the most important point of criticism related to the multicultural approach that connects cultural or religious belonging with specific collective rights. The respect shown towards religious differences alone is worth nothing if faith communities do not treat other groups with the same respect, whether other churches, religious groups, or humanist communities.

References

Arendt H (2012) The origins of totalitarianism, New York 1951, German Translation: Elemente und Ursprünge totaler Herrschaft, Piper Verlag, München 1986.

Arndt M (2013) Nach den Stasi-Enthüllungen. Die Bulgarisch-orthodoxe Kirche in Staat und Gesellschaft, Konrad-Adenauer-Stiftung, Länderbericht Bulgarien, 29.3.2013. http://www.kas.de/bulgarien/de/publications/30619/. Accessed 2 July 2013

Behrens K (2002) Die Russische Orthodoxe Kirche: Segen für die „Neuen Zaren"? Religion und Politik im postsowjetischen Rußland (1991–2000). Schöningh, Paderborn, p 77

Biography of the Chief of the Central Spiritual Administration of Muslims of Russia, Grand Mufti, Shaykh al-Islam Talgat Safa Tajuddin. http://cdum.ru/en/mufti/index.php [3.7.2013]; Николай Константинов, Страсти по поводу юбилея. Что думают мусульманские лидеры России о праздновании 1400-летия прихода религии Мухаммеда на территорию нашей страны? Независимая Газета 10 (118), 18 июня 2003 г.

Bosnia and Herzegovina (2004) Official Gazette: Freedom of religion and legal status of churches and religious organizations in Bosnia and Herzegovina, Law 28 gennaio 2004, n°5. In: Cardia C, Università degli Studi ROMA TRE, Centro Europeo di Documentazione sulle Istituzioni Religiose. http://host.uniroma3.it/progetti/cedir/cedir/Lex-doc/Bos_l-2004a.pdf. Accessed 1 July 2013.

Bulgarian Constitution (1879) Verfassung des Königreichs Bulgarien, unterzeichnet in Tarnowo am 16./28. Chapter IX, Article 37. April 1879. http://www.verfassungen.eu/bg/verf79-i.htm; Bulgarian version: http://parliament.bg/bg/17. Accessed 25 Jume 2013

Bulgarian Orthodox Church (Undated) Българска православна църква. http://www.bg-patriarshia.bg/. Accessed 2 July 2013

Committee on the Bulgarian Orthodox Church and Religious Cults. Bulg. комитет по въпроси на българската православна църква и религиозните култове—КВБПЦРК. I: Пенка Ненова Цонева, Просветна политика и дейност на църквата в етапа на умерената дестабилизация 1953–1962, In: Пенка Цонева (ed.), Теоретичен семинар „Актуални проблеми на историята и управлението на българското образование"г., Sofia, 2012, pp 9–29, p 14. Accessed 7 May 2012

Council for Cooperation with Religious Associations (2013) Президент России, Совет по взаимодействию с религиозными объединениями, Состав Совета. http://state.kremlin.ru/council/17/staff. Accessed 3 July 2013

Council on Religious Affairs under the USSR Council of Ministers. (Undated) Совет по делам религий при совете министров СССР. 1943–1991. http://www.prlib.ru/Documents/contentproccessing/7_guide.pdf

Dahl R A (2006) A Preface to Democratic Theory, University of Chicago, Expanded Edition 2006, p 75.

Degele N, Dries C (2005) Modernisierungstheorie. Eine Einführung, Wilhelm Fink Verlag, Paderborn, p 52. Original French title: Émile Durkheim, De la division du travail social: Étude sur l'organisation des sociétés supérieures. Félix Alcan, Paris 1893.

Demoscope (2013) Первая всеобщая перепись населения Российской Империи 1897 г. Распределение населения по вероисповеданиям и регионамПервая Всеобщая перепись населения Российской Империи 1897 г. Под ред. Н.А.Тройницкого. т.I. Общий свод по Империи результатов разработки данных Первой Всеобщей переписи населения, произведенной 28 января 1897 года. С.-Петербург, 1905. Таблица XII. Распределение населения по вероисповеданиям, in: Национального института демографических исследований (INED) (ed.), Демоскоп Weekly, № 559–560. http://demoscope.ru/weekly/ssp/rus_rel_97.php?reg=0. Accessed 10 June 2013.

Deutsche Islamkonferenz, What is the DIK. http://www.deutsche-islam-konferenz.de/DIK/EN/DIK/UeberDIK/WasIstDIK/wasistdik-node.html. Accessed 6 July 2013

DRadio Wissen (2011) Verflechtung zwischen Staat und Kirche, 23.9.2011, http://wissen.dradio.de/finanzen-verflechtung-zwischen-staat-und-kirche.33.de.html?dram:article_id=12523. Accessed 7 July 2013

European Commission (2005) Bosnia and Herzegovina: 2005 Progress Report, Brussels, 9 November 2005, SEC 1422 p 24. http://ec.europa.eu/enlargement/archives/pdf/key_documents/2005/package/sec_1422_final_progress_report_ba_en.pdf

European Court of Human Rights (2009) Case of Holy Synod of the Bulgarian Orthodox Church (Metropolitan Inokentiy) and Others v. Bulgaria, Applications nos. 412/03 and 35677/04, Strasbourg, 22.1.2009, Final 02/06/2009

IGGiÖ (1912) Islamische Glaubensgemeinschaft in Österreich, Islamgesetz, Österreich, Wien, 9.8.1912. http://www.derislam.at/?c=content&cssid=Englisch&navid=886&par=10&navid2=906&par2=886. Accessed 7 July 2013

Institute of Religion and Policy. http://www.i-r-p.ru/. Accessed 3 July 2013

Interfax (2011) Russian Orthodox Church will continue crafting "symphony" with state - priest (updated). Interfax, 7.11.2011. http://www.interfax-religion.com/?act=news&div=8860. Accessed 3 July 2013

Interfax (2013) Russia's Council of Muftis wants to form alternative Muslim board in Tatarstan—expert. Interfax, 29.8.2013. http://www.interfax-religion.com/?act=news&div=980. Accessed 3 July 2013

International Crisis Group (2013) Bosnia's dangerous tango: Islam and nationalism. Policy briefing, Europe briefing N°70, 26 Feb 2013. http://www.crisisgroup.org/~/media/Files/europe/balkans/bosnia-herzegovina/b070-bosnias-dangerous-tango-islam-and-nationalism.pdf. Accessed 1 July 2013.

The Islamic Community in Bosnia and Herzegovina (Undated a) History. http://www.rijaset.ba/english/index.php/modules-menu/history. Accessed 25 June 2013

The Islamic Community of Bosnia and Herzegovina. The structural organisation of the Islamic community.

http://www.rijaset.ba/english/index.php/modules-menu/the-structural-organisation-of-the-islamic-community. Accessed 1 July 2013
The Islamic Community of Bosnia and Herzegovina. The Islamic community—sentinel and principles. http://www.rijaset.ba/english/index.php/modules-menu/the-islamic-community-sentinel-and-principles. Accessed 1 July 2013
Gassenschmidt C, Tuchtenhagen R (Hg.) Politik und Religion in der Sowjetunion: 1917–1941. Harrassowitz, Wiesbaden 2000, p 156
Hunter ST (2004) Islam in Russia: The politics of identity and security. New York, S. 270
Kondakov YE (2003) State and the Orthodox Church in Russia: the evolution of relations in the first half of the XIX century. St. Petersburg, p 278; Кондаков Ю Е (2003) Государство и православная церковь в России: эволюция отношений в первой половине XIX века. Санкт-Петербург, p 278.
Kruse K (2012) Geschichte der Soziologie. UVK Verlag, 2, Auflage, Konstanz, 2012, p 79
Kymlicka W (ed) (1995) Multicultural citizenship: a liberal theory of minority rights. Oxford University Press, Oxford, 1995.
Linz JL (1996) Der religiöse Gebrauch der Politk und/oder der politische Gebrauch der Religion. Ersatz-Ideologie gegen Ersatz-Religion. In: Maier H (Hg.) Totalitarismus' und, Politische Religionen'. Konzepte des Diktaturvergleichs (Politik-und Kommunikationswissenschaftliche Veröffentlichungen der Görres-Gesellschaft, Band 16). München, pp 129–170
Mitrokhin N (2004). The Russian Orthodox Church: Present State and Challenges. Moscow; Митрохин Н (2004) Русская православная церковь: современное состояние и актуальные проблемы. Москва
The Muslim Denomination in the Republic of Bulgaria (Главно мюфтийство на мюсюлманското изпошедание в рпублика България). http://www.grandmufti.bg/en/about-us/institutions-history.html. Accessed 2 July 2013
Münch R (1995) Systemtheorie und Politik. In: Nohlen D, Olaf-Schultze R (eds) Lexikon der Politik, Band 1 Politische Theorien. Beck, München, pp 625–635, p 628
Parsons T (1963) On the concept of political power. Proceedings of the American Philosophical Society 107(3):232–262. http://www.jstor.org/stable/985582, see also: http://de.scribd.com/doc/125232136/On-the-Concept-of-Political-Power
Perica V (2002) Balkan idols: Religion and nationalism in Yugoslav states. Oxford University Press, New York, p 134
Plagemann G (2009) Von Allahs Gesetz zur Modernisierung per Gesetz. Gesetz und Gesetzgebung im Osmanischen Reich und in der Republik Türkei. Lit Verlag, Münster p 102

Poles KI (2003) The Arab East and Russia: the problem of Islamic fundamentalism. Moscow; Поляков КИ (2003) Арабский Восток и Россия: проблема исламского фундаментализма. Москва

Pravoslavieto (updated 2013) Хронология на разкола в Българската Православна Църква (БПЦ). http://www.pravoslavieto.com/docs/razkol_chronology.htm. Acessed 2 July 2013

Riedel S (2006) Kirche und Staat in Russland. Transitionen und Kontinuitäten. In: Trunte N, Bunčić D (Hg.) Festschrift für Helmut Keipert zum 65. Geburtstag, Iter philologicum, Die Welt der Slaven, Sammelbände/Sborniki. Band 28, München S. 319–331

Riedel S (2010) Der vielstimmig Islam in Europa, Muslimische Beiträge zu Integrationsdebatten, SWP-Study, S17, June 2010, p 24. http://www.swp-berlin.org/fileadmin/contents/products/studien/2010_S17_rds_ks.pd. Accessed 5 July 2013

RMC—Совет Муфтиев России. http://www.muslim.ru/. Accessed 3 July 2013

Saggar S, Somerville W (2012) Building a British model of integration in an era of immigration: Policy lessons for government. University of Sussex, and the Migration Policy Institute, Washington. http://www.migrationpolicy.org/pubs/uk-countrystudy.pdf. Accessed 5 July 2013

Sarajlić E (2013) Country report: Bosnia and Herzegovina. In: EUDO Citizenship observatory. Revised and updated January 2013. European University Institute, Florence, RSCAS/EUDO-CIT-CR 2013/07. http://eudo-citizenship.eu/docs/CountryReports/Bosnia%20and%20Herzegovina.pdf. Accessed 1 July 2013

Schaal GA (2006) Die politische Theorie der liberal-prozeduralistischen Demokratie: Robert A. Dahl. In: Brodocz A, Schaal GS (eds) Politische theorien der Gegenwart I, Eine Einführung, 2., erweiterte und aktualisierte Auflage. Verlag Barbara Budrich, Opladen, pp 248–274, p 260

Statistisches Bundesamt, Datenreport (2011) Der Sozialbericht für Deutschland, Kapitel 13 Freizeit und gesellschaftliche Partizipation. Wiesbaden, 29.11.2011, p 355. https://www.destatis.de/DE/Publikationen/Datenreport/Downloads/Datenreport2011Kap13.html. Accessed 7 July 2013

Taylor C (1994) The politics of recognition. In: Godmann A (ed) Multiculturalism. Expanded paperback edition. Princton University Press, pp 25–74, p 38

TV7 (2012) Актуален гост. Има ли радикален ислям в България? интервю с Мустафа Алиш Хаджи, in: TV7.bg, 30.09.2012. http://tv7.bg/vinagi-v-nedelia/VideoDetails&id=9464062. Accessed 2 July 2013

Vissi Islamic Institute (Undated) Висш ислямски институт, За нас. http://www.islamicinstitute-bg.org/main.php?sec=2&page=10. Accessed 2 July 2013

2.

Law and Religion

Law and Religion in Germany: The Case of Circumcision of Boys

Burkhard Breig

Introduction

The Basic Law for the Federal Republic of Germany (*Grundgesetz für die Bundesrepublik Deutschland*, hereinafter: "**Basic Law**") (Tomuschat and Currie 2010), which functions as the German constitution, states that there is no state church; freedom to form religious communities shall be guaranteed; religious societies shall enjoy independence from state interference (Art. 140 of the Basic Law in connection with Art. 137 of the German Constitution of 11 August 1919); and the freedom of religion of individuals is guaranteed (Art. 4 of the Basic Law). This implies openness of the state to religious plurality, and the corresponding duty of the state to neutrality, equal treatment, and tolerance (Bergmann 2013).

While these guarantees aim to provide protection for both the state and religious societies, neither exists within separate spheres: people live in a state but have also personal religious convictions; people's behavior is the subject not only of state law but also of religious norms. State legislators and courts can, therefore, very well be in a situation where their decisions might impinge upon religious norms and convictions. Such collision between legal and religious norms was the subject of a recent court decision in Germany that led to a broad public discussion (see II, III below). While the legislator reacted quickly and enacted a statutory amendment (see IV below), the discussion is on-going. Even the constitutionality of the new law has been questioned by some commentators within the legal literature. The case can be seen within the context of the decline of external foundations for the legal system, and the development of legal systems towards universal norms that are accepted regardless of religion. If, thus, the last measure and source of law is to be found in commonly accepted principles such as human dignity (Art. 1, para. 1, first sentence of the Basic Law), and religious tradition is no more seen as a direct foundation of law, the consequence may be that the law is incompatible with religious tradition.

The Decision of the District Court of Cologne

Recently, German courts were required for the first time to deal with the question of whether circumcision of a child, if it is not medically indicated, constitutes the crime of causing bodily harm (Section 223 of the German Criminal Code).

The facts of the case that gave rise to the prosecutor's indictment and subsequently to a famous decision by the district court of Cologne (*Landgericht Köln*): The parents of a four-year-old boy asked a physician in Cologne to circumcise the child. The parents belonged to the Muslim faith and wanted to comply with tradition. There was no medical indication for circumcision. The physician circumcised the boy in his surgery under local anesthetic. Two days later, in order to medicate secondary bleeding, the mother took the boy to the accident and emergency department of the University Hospital of Cologne. The Office of Public Prosecutor in Cologne subsequently brought a charge against the physician who performed the circumcision.

The local court of Cologne (*Amtsgericht Köln*) acquitted the physician on the grounds that, even if the elements of the crime were fulfilled, the circumcision was justified by the parents' legal consent (Section 1626 para. 1 of the German Civil Code) (Langenscheidt Translation Service). The consent was valid, as it was exercised in the best interests of the child (Section 1627 of the German Civil Code). The boy's right to physical integrity had to be weighed against the parents' right to bring up their children and to practice their religion. According to the court, as a traditional ritual act, circumcision is an expression of cultural and religious identity as a member of the Muslim faith, and prevents social stigmatization of the boy within that community (Amtsgericht Köln 2011). The Office of the Public Prosecutor challenged this decision.

In June 2012 the district court of Cologne as the appellate court decided that circumcision of a child constitutes a crime under Section 223 paragraph 1 of the German Criminal Code. According to the court, the action is not justified by the parents' consent. The parents of a boy that is not able to assess the consequences of circumcision cannot effectively overrule the child's consent. The parents are obliged to wait until the boy is capable of assessing for himself whether or not to undergo circumcision.

Nevertheless, the court acquitted the accused, as he had acted without guilt. As the court pointed out, the accused was not aware that circumcision constitutes a crime under German law, and this mistake was unavoidable because the legal situation was very unclear (cf. Section 17, sentence 1 of the German Criminal Code) (Landgericht Köln 2012).

While in that specific case the actors were not convicted, all groups who practice infant circumcision in Germany (mainly the Jewish and Muslim communities) were concerned about whether the practice would still be legal. The German Bundestag responded rapidly to these concerns, and in July 2012 adopted a resolution asking the Federal Government of Germany to present in autumn 2012 a draft law ensuring that circumcision of boys is legally permissible when performed in accordance with professional medical standards and in such a way that it does not cause avoidable pain. The Bundestag adopted the resolution by a vast majority in the last legislative session before the 2012 summer recess (for the law implementing this resolution, see IV below).

Elements of a Legal Analysis of the Case

The Cologne decision could refer to a rather active discussion among legal scholars that was initiated by a book contribution in 2008[1]. Following the decision, the discussion in the literature has quickly evolved to explore different aspects of the case from the perspectives of social, criminal, constitutional and civil law (Rox 2012a; Goerlich and Zabel 2012; Rox 2012b; Walter 2012; Roxin 2012; Wiater 2012; Jarouschek 2012; Ring 2012; Isensee 2013; Steinbach 2013).

Before analyzing the criminal liability of the parents or the person performing the circumcision, it will be useful to give a brief analysis of the fundamental constitutional rights of the participating persons, as granted by the Basic Law.

Fundamental Rights

Multilateral Constellation

The fundamental rights of several persons are involved: If the parents are prohibited by the Criminal Code from having their minor son circumcised, this may constitute a limitation on the right to exercise one's faith and the parents' right to

1 *After Putzke* (2008). Subsequently, there were a number of further contributions, e.g., *Günter Jerouschek*: Beschneidung und das deutsche Recht. Historische, medizinische, psychologische und juristische Aspekte, NStZ 2008, 313–319 (318); *K.-A. Schwarz*: Verfassungsrechtliche Aspekte der religiösen Beschneidung, JZ 2008, 1125 ff.; *Rolf-Dietrich Herzberg*: Rechtliche Probleme der rituellen Beschneidung, JZ 2009, 332–339; *Kai Zähle*: Religionsfreiheit und fremdschädigende Praktiken. Zu den Grenzen des forum externum, AöR 2009, 434–454; *Rolf Dietrich Herzberg*: Wann ist die Körperverletzung durch Zirkumzision gerechtfertigt?, ZIS 2010, 471–475; *Fateh-Maghadam*, RW 2010, 115 ff.; *Thomas Exner*: Sozialadäquanz im Strafrecht. Zur Knabenbeschneidung, Berlin 2011 (PhD thesis); Arbeitsgemeinschaft Rechtsanwälte im Medizinrecht e.V. (Hrsg.): Die Zirkumzision im Spannungsfeld zwischen Glaubenstradition und Strafrecht, 2011.

bring up their children (see b below). Similarly, prohibition of circumcision can constitute a limitation of the rights of the person who carries out the circumcision (see c). Both the parents and the person carrying out the circumcision can refer to their fundamental rights in their function of protecting individuals *from the state.*

On the other hand, circumcision, as a serious physical intervention, affects the right of the child to physical integrity (see d). However, in this case, as the circumcision is carried out by the parents or a person mandated by them, the physical integrity of the child is not limited by state action, but by the action of private persons. The fundamental rights granted by the Basic Law are in the first instance subjective rights of citizens vis-à-vis the state; they do not have direct effect in relations between private persons, i.e., they do not directly create obligations of private persons. This means, in the situation at hand, that they do not give the boy a direct claim versus his parents to refrain from circumcision.

Nevertheless, this does not mean that the legal relationship between private individuals is entirely unaffected by obligations to fundamental rights. According to the Federal Constitutional Court of Germany, the fundamental rights form the normative basis of the whole legal system constituted by the Basic Law; the state is obliged to protect the fundamental rights of individuals from infringements. Furthermore, the fundamental rights have to be taken into account for the interpretation of all non-constitutional law. Where the fundamental rights of one person compete with other legal positions, e.g., with the fundamental laws of others or with other interests protected by the constitution, it is necessary to search for ways to co-ordinate these positions in order to avoid contradictory legal orders. Hereby, it is necessary to minimize, as far as possible, any limitations to the fundamental rights affected (principle of harmonizing interpretation, in German also: *praktische Konkordanz*) (For this concept, see Hesse 1995).

The Parents' Rights: Freedom of Religion; Right to Free Upbringing of Children

Prohibiting the circumcision of children arranged by their parents may be seen as a limitation of the parents' freedom of faith (Art. 4 of the Basic Law) and the care and upbringing of children as "the natural right of parents and a duty primarily incumbent upon them" (Art. 6, para. 2, of the Basic Law).

Article 4 (para. 1 and 2) of the Basic Law states:

> "(1) Freedom of faith and of conscience, and freedom to profess a religious or philosophical creed, shall be inviolable.
>
> (2) The undisturbed practice of religion shall be guaranteed."

This provision protects the freedom of faith, including the undisturbed practice of religion and the freedom to profess one's religious creed. Along with the undisturbed practice of faith and religion in the private sphere (*forum internum*), it also grants the freedom to live and act in accordance with religious convictions (*forum externum*) (Bergmann 2012).

Unlike many other fundamental rights of the Basic Law, the rights under Article 4 are granted unconditionally, without reference to limitations by the laws. These rights can therefore be limited only based upon other fundamental rights and other goods protected by the Basic Law (Antoni 2012).

According to a widely used formula, freedom of faith does not convey a right to interfere with the rights of others2. Some authors therefore hold that Article 4 of the Basic Law cannot be used as an argument in favor of the parents' right to circumcise their son (Isensee 2013).

Others are of the opinion that Article 4 covers all forms of exercising one's faith and religion, including such forms that interfere with the rights of third persons. They argue that the freedom of religion presumes the freedom to define what religion is, and refer to cases in which the German Federal Constitutional Court ruled that courts must take into account the understanding of the relevant religious community3.

In any case, freedom of religion has to be weighed against other fundamental rights.

Article 6 (para. 2) of the Basic Law states:

> "(2) The care and upbringing of children is the natural right of parents and a duty primarily incumbent upon them. The state shall watch over them in the performance of this duty."

The provision grants parents priority and independence in determining and performing the care and upbringing of their children. Parents have a subjective right vis-à-vis the state to non-interference. At the same time, the state has the duty to watch over the parents. The central criterion is the child's best interest. The parents' right under this provision (in connection with Article 4 of the Basic Law) includes the parents' right to determine the religious (or non-religious) foundation of education. It is disputed whether the provision also grants parents the right to interfere with the fundamental rights of their children.

Person Carrying Out the Circumcision

The circumcizor may claim that a prohibition of circumcision constitutes a limitation

2 Cf., e.g., Bergmann (2012) Rn. 10.

3 Bergmann (2012); *Kyrill-A. Schwarz*: Verfassungsrechtliche Aspekte der religiösen Beschneidung, JZ 2008, pp. 1125–1130 (1128).

of his/her occupational freedom (Art. 12 of the Basic Law). However, Article 12 does not protect the circumcizor's interest in performing a circumcision against the will or interest of the boy without valid consent.

Child

The child has the right to life and physical integrity (Art. 2, para. 2, sentence 1 of the Basic Law). Circumcision is a serious physical intervention which in any case constitutes a limitation of physical integrity. This is also true for circumcision motivated by religious convictions. The social or religious meaning must be taken into account where the fundamental rights of different persons are weighed against each other, but it does not affect the fact that a physical intervention constitutes a limitation of the fundamental right of Article 2, paragraph 2 of the Basic Law (Isensee 2013:320).

Article 2, paragraph 2, sentence 3 stipulates limitations to this fundamental right: according to that provision, the rights granted by Article 2 may be interfered with only pursuant to a law. Such limitation—and the law on which it is based—must comply with the principle of proportionality, i.e., they must serve fundamental rights of others or other constitutional goods, must be limited to those which are necessary, and must be proportional to the benefit pursued.

In a specific case of circumcision, therefore, the boy's right to physical integrity must be weighed against the parents' right to determine the religious and cultural upbringing of their children.

Application for Criminal Law Analysis

Elements of the Crime of Causing Bodily Harm (Sec. 223 of the German Criminal Code)

Under Section 223, sentence 1 of the German Criminal Code, "whosoever physically assaults or damages the health of another person, shall be liable to imprisonment not exceeding five years or a fine"4. The removal of the foreskin fulfills the elements of this provision.

Some authors in the legal literature argue that religious circumcision, if it is performed in a medically correct manner, is exempt from criminal law as "socially adequate action" (*sozialadäquates Handeln*) (Exner 2011). According to German doctrine, a person cannot be held liable if they act within the limits of common

4 German translation by *Michael Bohlander*: http://www.gesetze-im-internet.de/englisch_stgb/.

social practice (i.e., if the action is "socially adequate"), even if the action results in damages for others. However, according to the majority of scholars, the category of social adequacy as a limitation of material criminal law can only be applied to exclude criminal persecution of actions that do not create a significant risk or a risk that is expressly allowed by a legal provision5. This is not the case for circumcision, which not only involves risk but results in physical harm. On the one hand, it has to be accepted that there is a broad range of educational measures that are covered by common practice and which are also accepted. Parents are allowed to choose the educational methods they deem appropriate. On the other hand, in recent decades it has become common opinion that no physical violence is permitted in education; an expression of this tendency is the ban on physical punishment introduced in 2000, in Section 1631, paragraph 2, sentence 2 of the German Civil Code. The educational environment provides no less intense protection of children's rights. Therefore, each physical intervention has to be assessed using the common legal criteria, including criminal law.

As a result, according to German law, circumcision contravenes Section 223, paragraph 1 of the German Criminal Code.

Justification

Circumcision is justified when medically indicated, as in cases of phimosis. In Germany, the sanitary and medical situation is such that there is no reason for preventive circumcision without acute symptoms (Herzberg 2009:332, 334).

An act that fulfills the elements of a crime can, nevertheless, be lawful if it is justified by the victim's consent. Valid consent requires that a person has the capacity to assess the significance of the action to which they are consenting. This ability is not equivalent to the capacity of contracting or religious maturity. There is no doubt that a four-year-old boy is unable to give valid consent to circumcision.

He must therefore be represented by his parents.

The relevant provisions of the German Civil Code are as follows: According to Section 1626 paragraph 1, parents have the duty and right to care for their minor children (parental custody—*elterliche Sorge*). Parental custody includes, in particular, the care for the person of the child (*Personensorge*). As long and insofar as the child is not able to take responsibility for its own actions, the parents are obliged and entitled to represent the child. In doing so, they must act for the best

5 Cf., e.g., *Thomas Fischer*: Strafgesetzbuch, 60. Auflage 2013, § 223, Rn. 11; *Barbara Rox*: Annotation to the decision of *Landgericht Köln* of 7 May 2012, JZ 2012, p. 606 f.; *Günter Jerouschek*: Beschneidung und das deutsche Recht. Historische, medizinische, psychologische und juristische Aspekte, NStZ 2008, pp. 313–319 (318).

interests of the child (*zum Wohl des Kindes*; Section 1627, first sentence, of the German Civil Code).

In assessing whether circumcision of a minor boy can be in his best interest, it is necessary to balance the disadvantages and risks of circumcision against the advantages. The assessment has to take into account constitutional law and, in particular, the fundamental rights of the persons involved (for the fundamental rights involved, see 3 above). The key question is therefore whether the parents' rights under Articles 4 and 6 of the Basic Law may result in circumcision being in the child's best interest. In contrast to female circumcision—which according to general opinion is forbidden in Germany and cannot be justified by parental consent—there is no common opinion among legal scholars as to whether male circumcision can be justified.

In favor of circumcision it is often claimed that male circumcision is a religious duty according to Jewish faith and has been practiced for thousands of years all over the world by Jews and Muslims. As such, it helps the boys to integrate within their religious community (see Schwarz (note 13), in Bergmann 2012:1128–1129).

Others hold that under the Basic Law no religious commandment is able to justify such a serious intervention (Cf. Eschelbach 2012a, with many references to other authors); and that if the practice of circumcision was not questioned in previous decades, this was only due to social taboos (Eschelbach 2012b).

Amendment of the German Civil Code

While the legal discussion on elective circumcision of minor boys in Germany began in 2008, it became a political issue only after the court decision of June 2012. That decision made it clear that the current legal situation does not grant the Jewish and Muslim communities the certainty that circumcision of boys is permissible.

The legislator therefore acted quickly, and on 28 December 2012 a law came into effect that aimed to clarify the conditions under which parents are able to give valid consent to elective circumcision of their minor child.

The law introduced a new Section 1631d into the German Civil Code:

> Section 1931d. Circumcision of a male child. (1) The care for the person of the child [Personensorge] comprises the right to give consent to the circumcision of a child who is unable to assess the situation themself even if there is no medical indication for circumcision, provided that such circumcision is to be exercised according to the rules of medical art. This does not apply if, even taking into account the aim pursued by the circumcision, there is a risk that it is contrary to the best interest of the child.

> (2) During the first six months after the child's birth, circumcision according to paragraph 1 above may also be performed by a person appointed by a religious community if such person—while not being a physician—has completed special training and is equally able to perform a circumcision as a physician.

The amendment was met with relief by representatives of the Jewish and Muslim communities in Germany. However, the new act did not end the legal discussion around religious circumcision. Critical voices within the literature hold that the new law is unable to resolve the collision of interests—and eventually also of religious and secular norms—regarding circumcision (Herzberg 2014). In addition, certain authors argue that Section 1631d of the German Civil Code is a violation of the principle of non-discrimination between women and men, as circumcision of boys is an intervention that can be as equally serious as light forms of female circumcision (Putzke 2013).

While some scholars hold that circumcision of boys for purely religious reasons cannot be justified at all under the German Basic Law6, others argue that the legislator is generally entitled to propose a general solution that balances the interests and rights of the parents, the religious communities, and the boys7. The legislator did not spell out in detail the criteria for legally binding consent by parents. The law does not limit elective circumcision to cases of religious motivation. In the first court decision8 dealing with Section 1631d of the German Civil Code, the judges argued, however, that the motivation of the parents is a material consideration in assessing whether circumcision was in the best interest of the child. Other circumstances that may be relevant to the child's interest include the child's own wishes, medical peculiarities, and others. It is self-evident that, in addition, the person performing the circumcision must give the parents full information on the risks associated with circumcision (see Putzke 2013).

As can be seen from this short overview, the new law was not able to put an end to legal uncertainties, and the first case that came to court showed a possible development: In the absence of detailed legal regulations, courts can clarify the requirements to information of the parents and—where appropriate—the child; and also to the circumstances under which a religious motivation for circumcision can be respected. This would help to gradually establish greater legal clarity for

6 Not completely clear: See Putzke (2013).

7 Cf. a recent court decision: OLG Hamm, Beschluss vom 30. August 2013 – 3 UF 133/13, NJW 2013, 3662 (with annotation: *Peschel-Gutzeit*: Die neue Regelung zur Beschneidung des männlichen Kindes. Kritischer Überblick und erste Reaktionen der Rechtsprechung, NJW 2013, 3617–3620).

8 *Ibid.*

all concerned.

Unless the new Section 1631d of the German Civil Code is declared unconstitutional, persons performing circumcisions may be able to rely on this norm: even an author who considers Section 1631d invalid holds that, at present, physicians can claim that they acted without guilt.

Conclusion

The discussion around religious circumcision of boys came as a surprise for most of the German public and even for the majority of the legal academic community. Prior to the decision of the Cologne *Landgericht* and the precedent article by Putzke there was virtually no legal debate on the topic of religious circumcision. It was manifest that boys' circumcision is a part of the culture of fairly large parts of the German population, predominantly the Jewish and Muslim communities, and their right to do so was not disputed.

The case exemplifies the process of re-constitution and re-formulation of the whole legal system under the influence of human rights, which gained emphasis after the adoption of the Basic Law for Germany in 1949. Another example of this process is the principle of non-discrimination between men and women. While the seemingly simple and obvious principle is expressly stated in Article 3, paragraph 2 of the Basic Law, it took the legislator more than forty years, via a long series of decisions by the German Constitutional Court and the European Court of Human Rights, to eliminate even cases of direct sexual discrimination between women and men, and the process is still ongoing.

One of the reasons why male circumcision was not discussed earlier is certainly also German history—there was likely anxiety that prohibition of boys' circumcision according to Jewish tradition would be regarded by the Jewish community as a limitation on Jewish life in Germany. Rather than providing a definitive resolution, the amendment to the German Civil Code is an attempt to achieve a compromise between the different positions; at present there is no consensus for a feasible solution.

References

Antoni M (2012) In: Dieter Hömig (Hrsg.): Grundgesetz für die Bundesrepublik Deutschland, 10. Auflage 2012, vor Art. 1, Rn. 15.

Amtsgericht Köln, Urteil vom 21. September 2011 – 528 Ds 30/11. http://www.justiz.nrw.de/nrwe/ag_koeln/j2011/528_Ds_30_11_Urteil_20110921.html. Accessed 22 August 2013.

Bergmann R (2012) In: Hömig D (Hrsg.): Grundgesetz für die Bundesrepublik Deutschland, 10. Auflage 2012, Art. 4 Rn. 2.
Bergmann R (2013) In: Hömig D (Hrsg.): Grundgesetz für die Bundesrepublik Deutschland, 10. Auflage 2013 Art. 4 Rn. 1.
Eschelbach (2012a) In: von Heintschel-Heinegg B (Hrsg.): Beck'scher Online-Kommentar StGB, 21st edition, § 223, Rn. 9.1-9.12.
Eschelbach (2012b) In: von Heintschel-Heinegg B (Hrsg.): Beck'scher Online-Kommentar StGB, 22nd edition, § 223, Rn. 9.
Exner T (2011) Sozialadäquanz im Strafrecht. Zur Knabenbeschneidung, Berlin; Tröndle/Fischer: Strafge-setzbuch, 55. Auflage, § 223, Rn. 6b.
Goerlich H, Zabel B (2012) Säkularer Staat und religiöses Recht, JZ 2012, 1058–1061.
Josef Isensee, Grundrechtliche Konsequenz wider geheiligte Tradition, JZ 2013, 317–327 (319).
Herzberg RD (2014) Der Abwägungsgedanke und der „evidenzbasierte Blick" in der Beschneidungsdebatte, ZIS 2014, S. 56 65.
Hesse K: Grundzüge des Verfassungsrechts der Bundesrepublik Deutschland, 20. Auflage, Heidelberg 1995, Rn. 72.
Isensee J (2013) Grundrechtliche Konsequenz wider geheiligte Tradition, JZ 2013, 317–327 (p. 319).
Jarouschek G Beschneidung – Heileingriff, religiöses Gebot oder strafbare Körperverletzung, in: Wilhelm Degener / Michael Heghmanns (Hrsg.): Festschrift für Friedrich Dencker zum 70. Geburtstag, Tübingen 2012, S. 171 181.
Landgericht Köln, Urteil vom 7. Mai 2012 – 151 Ns 169/11, NJW 2012, 2128. http://www.justiz.nrw.de/nrwe/lgs/koeln/lg_koeln/j2012/151_Ns_169_11_Urteil_20120507.html. Accessed 9 March 2013.
Langenscheidt Translation Service. Regularly updated by Neil Mussett: http://www.gesetze-im-internet.de/englisch_bgb/englisch_bgb.html.
Putzke H (2008) Die strafrechtliche Relevanz der Beschneidung von Knaben. Zugleich ein Beitrag über die Grenzen der Einwilligung in Fällen der Personensorge. In: Hardtung B u.a. (Hrsg.): Festschrift für Rolf Dietrich Herzberg, Tübingen 2008, S. 669–709.
Putzke H (2013) Das Beschneidungsgesetz (§ 1631d BGB). Fauler Kompromiss und fatales Signal. In: Monatsschrift für Kinderheilkunde 2013, 950–951.
Ring G. Die medizinisch nicht indizierte Beschneidung von Jungen im deutschen Recht – zur Rechtslage seit dem 28.12.2012, NJ 2013, 148 ff.
Rox B: Anmerkung zum Urteil des LG Köln vom 7.5.2012 – 151 Ns 169/11, JZ 2012, 806–808.
Rox B (2012) Schlusswort, JZ 2012, 1061–1063.

Roxin C (2012) Der Streit um die einverständliche Fremdgefährdung, GA 2012, 655 ff.

Steinbach A (2013) Die gesetzliche Regelung zur Beschneidung von Jungen, NVwZ-Extra 2013, 1 10. http://rsw.beck.de/rsw/upload/NVwZ/NVwZ-Extra_2013_09.pdf. Accessed 30 August 2013.

Tomuschat C, Currie DP (2010) Basic Law for the Federal Republic of Germany. https://www.btg-bestellservice.de/pdf/80201000.pdf.

Wiater P (2012) Rechtspluralismus und Grundrechtsschutz: Das Kölner Beschneidungsurteil, NVwZ 2012, 1379 1382.

Walter T (2012) Der Gesetzentwurf zur Beschneidung – Kritik und strafrechtliche Alternative, JZ 2012, 1110 ff.

Russian Practice: Persecution for Criticism or Punishment for Blasphemy

Damir Gainutdinov

Art critics Yuri Samodurov, Andrei Yerofeyev, and Lyudmila Vasilovskaya; artists Alexander Savko and Artem Loskutov; members of Pussy Riot; human rights defender Maxim Yefimov; and many other activists might have been sentenced to between three and five years in prison if a proposed Russian law on blasphemy had been adopted earlier.

On 9 April 2013, draft Bill #142303 on blasphemy passed its first reading in the Russian State Duma (Russian Federation 2013). Very soon, it will be signed by the president and come into power. The bill establishes responsibility for insulting the beliefs and feelings of adherents of the religions "which are an integral part of the historical heritage of the peoples of Russia". The maximum punishment under the bill is five years imprisonment.

Mikhail Saltykov-Shchedrin was credited with the idea that the severity of Russian laws is mitigated by the fact that obeying them is optional. This situation can be seen to persist into the 21st century; however, in recent years, another distinctive feature of Russian legislation has emerged: ultimately ambiguous wording, which allows arbitrary interpretation and implementation according to the requirements of the political situation. This typifies most of the significant legal acts released from "the rabid printer": The Meetings Act, the Blacklist Law, the Law on Foreign Agents, etc.

Finally, Russia's legislative deputies have given their attention to the feelings of religious believers. The draft bill is entirely opaque in defining which religions are regarded as an integral part of Russian heritage, and what kinds of feelings are to be protected. No further details are provided in the draft or the accompanying explanatory note. However, there is no doubt that the law will be applied against critics of the Russian Orthodox Church, and against artists whose works employ symbols associated with Orthodox Christianity. For many years, there has been discussion on introducing criminal responsibility for blasphemy, but only now was the command issued to the deputies. We can therefore presume that the bill is a kind of reaction to the latest high-profile story concerning the Russian Orthodox Church—the Pussy Riot case.

Presently, the laws on liability for words and actions concerning religious feelings are rather broad, and are strongly criticized by experts, practical lawyers, and human rights defenders. Existing anti-extremism laws proscribe illegal incitement of religious hatred and determine several criteria to prohibit the spread of materials identified as extremist. Articles 280 and 282 of the Criminal Code establish liability for public appeals to extremist activity; incitement of national, racial, or religious enmity; and abasement of human dignity by reason of their attitude to religious, national, or racial affiliation. A huge number of existing rules within the Criminal Code acknowledge motives of religious enmity and hatred as an aggravating circumstance, including: encroachment on life and health, hooliganism, and vandalism. Article 5.26 (2) of the Code of the Russian Federation on Administrative Offenses establishes liability for insulting the religious feelings of citizens or the desecration of articles, marks and emblems symbolizing religion. However, officials regard the sanctions provided by existing legislation as being too weak. The new Blasphemy Law is set to become the cherry on top of the cake representing the coalescence of state and church.

In point of fact, if we look through the most recent well-known cases on blasphemy and insulting religious feelings, we can easily establish that all of them deal with public activities and criticism of the political authorities or the Russian Orthodox Church. Taking into consideration Russia's extensive experience in the persecution of adherents of 'non-conventional' creeds, the enthusiastic ignorance of prosecutors and police, and the total dependence of the courts, then the forthcoming implementation of the law is obvious.

'Caution, Religion!' and 'Forbidden Art'

In early 2003 a contemporary art exhibition titled 'Caution, Religion!' opened at the Sakharov Center (Moscow). More than forty artists from Moscow, Armenia, Georgia, Bulgaria, the Czech Republic, Japan, Cuba, and other countries participated in the project. The title of the exposition was intended to underline issues concerning the perception of religion in contemporary society; and the mutual relations and contradictions between art and religion, the state and the church. The exhibition was smashed and routed by Orthodox fundamentalists, who destroyed some of the showpieces. Nevertheless, none of the attackers were brought to justice; on the contrary, a criminal prosecution was initiated against the organizers of the exhibition: Yuri Samodurov and Lyudmila Vasilovskaya were fined 100-thousand rubles according to Article 282 (1) of the Criminal Code. The main evidence of their guilt consisted of a few expert reports, stating that the exhibits were sacrilegious and expressed intolerance to Orthodoxy as a basis of Russian culture. In the opinion of the experts, the aim of the exhibition was to deface Orthodoxy and the Russian Orthodox Church.

In 2007 a new exhibition titled 'Prohibited Art' opened at the Sakharov Center, presenting works of art that were declined by Moscow museums during 2006. Some of the showpieces used religious symbols or topics, including an Alexander Savko painting from the series entitled 'Mickey Mouse's Travels Though Art History'; a collage with the cross and the Order of Lenin by Vagrich Bakhchanyan; and 'Icon-Caviar' by Alexander Kosolapov. The organizers, Samodurov and Yerofeyev, as expected, were sentenced to fines of 150-thousand and 200-thousand rubles respectively under Article 282 (1) (New York Times 2010). The criminal prosecution was initiated by the ultra-right 'People's Union' party, whose leader Sergey Baburin declared that, "most of the exhibit items are of anti-religious, anti-state, and extremist character, and denigrate Russia's armed forces and the Russian Orthodox Church" (Sakharov Center 2007).

The spirit of free-thinking and opposition soared over the exhibition. This was apparent from the choice of the Andrei Sakharov Museum and Public Center as the location of the exhibition, from the content, and from the reactions of officials: for instance, Patriarch Kirill publicly expressed support for the criminal sentencing of the organizers (Lenta 2010).

The 'Mickey Mouse Case'

Among many works of art exhibited at the Sakharov Center during 'Prohibited Art' was an Alexander Savko painting based on the engraving 'Sermon on the Mount' by the 19th century German artist Julius Schnorr von Carolsfeld. In the center of the painting, instead of Christ surrounded by followers there appears Mickey Mouse, symbolizing mass culture as an object of worship.

After the organizers of the exhibition were sentenced, the Prosecutor's Office applied to the District Court of Tarusa to have the Savko painting classified as extremist material; the demand was fulfilled by the court. This means that any dissemination of the work is prohibited under the threat of criminal or administrative prosecution. Despite the provisions of the anti-extremist law, the court decision was based on an expert's conclusion that the painting is offensive to religious believers.

Pussy Riot

Probably the best-known case of recent years is the criminal prosecution of members of Pussy Riot, a feminist punk band. They loudly declared that the Russian Orthodox Church is no more than a service organization for the state. The authorities could not confess that the action was of a feminist and anti-government nature. On the other hand, the criminal prosecution in this case seemed to pursue personal vengeance on behalf of the 'former-next' president. This resulted in the pre-trial arrest, torture, and demonstrative cruelty of the verdict (two years imprisonment). A remarkable contrast is that Yuri Piotrovsky, who spilled black dye on the icons in the same Cathedral of Christ the Savior, was sentenced only to one year of probation, and was released in the courtroom (Interfax 2013). The difference was that Piotrovsky did not declare any political slogans, nor criticize Putin or Kirill.

Artem kissmybabushka.com Loskutov

Artem Loskutov, an artist from Novosibirsk who held an action in support of the arrested members of Pussy Riot, was fined for offending believers (under new legislation, he could get up to five years in jail, but at that date the only sanction was administrative, and Loskutov escaped with a fine of 1000 rubles). The core idea of the action was that activists placed stylized icon banners in support of Pussy Riot in three advertising lightboxes. The owner of the lightboxes later declared that he had not suffered any damage via that action.

To the Nuthouse for Criticism of the Bishop: The Case of Maxim Yefimov

Petrozavodsk activist Maxim Yefimov used an online newspaper, 'The Zero Hour' to publish several articles critical of funding for the Karelian eparchy of the Russian Orthodox Church. He was then subject to criminal prosecution for inciting hatred against Orthodox believers, and also the real prospect of being confined to a psychiatric hospital: the investigator twice ordered Yefimov to undergo forensic psychiatric examinations. As a result, Yefimov fled Russia and sought asylum in Estonia, where the authorities considered his prosecution in Russia to be politically motivated.

Film Prohibition: Innocence of Muslims

In autumn 2012, riots occurred in several countries following the publication of excerpts from the film 'Innocence of Muslims'. Radicals attacked US, UK, and German embassies, burned flags, and clashed with local police; the rioting even claimed lives. As usual, Russian authorities considered extremists to be the authors of the film rather than those who killed people and smashed-up embassies. This highlights another problem—that of censorship and the extrajudicial blocking and filtering of websites. Under the pretext of defending the feelings of believers, Russian officials once again tested mechanisms for the efficient blocking of undesirable information. Pre-empting any court decision categorizing the film as extremist material (inasmuch as such a decision can provide a legal basis for blockage), the Prosecutor's Office and regional branches of the Federal Service for Supervision in the Sphere of Telecommunications, Information Technologies and Mass Communications instructed internet service-providers to block access to the film. Almost all of the providers reluctantly complied.

Analyzing Russian law enforcement practices, we can summarize the following:

1. Only adherents of the Russian Orthodox Church can count on the protection of their 'religious feelings', as can, to a lesser extent, Muslims of state-oriented groups. Followers of all other religions, including Christians, are dubbed sectarians at best; and at worst are persecuted, as in the case of Jehovah's Witnesses.
2. The most severe official reactions are triggered not only by criticism of church orders, but by expressions connected to criticism of the authorities and which have a social and political dimension: both Pussy Riot and Maxim Yefimov primarily criticized the government.
3. On the whole, prosecution is not relevant to defending the feelings of believers. Instead, the blasphemy laws are used as a tool to formalize the claims connected to public activity. The authorities deliberately provoke and deepen religious contradictions within society. This is typified by official attempts to portray those awaiting trail following the Bolotnaya Square demonstration[1] as being opponents of Russian Orthodoxy and its supporters. As a result, while judging such cases, the courts do not seek the appropriate balance between freedom of expression and the defense of religious feelings; do not apply the 'three-part' test[2]; and do not query the justification for such serious restrictions on the freedom of speech within a democratic society. None of these things are required, simply because the aim of the campaign is completely different.
4. The draft bill that passed through the Duma is a spontaneous counter-reaction by some officials to the growing public discontent with the persistent violation of

1 The Bolotnaya Square demonstration was a mass protest in Moscow on 6 May 2012 against the inauguration of Vladimir Putin as the president of the Russian Federation the following day. It encompassed a wide range of opposition movements and individual demonstrators who together demanded transparency in the election process and called for a democratic change in Russia. The demonstration started as the so-called 'March of Millions' through the center of Moscow and ended at Bolotnaya Square in a violent clash between protesters and the police; hundreds of participants, including famous opposition leaders, were arrested during and in the aftermath of the event.

2 The three-part test or Miller-test is applied by the Supreme Court of the United States of America since the late 1970s in order to evaluate whether a public expression of opinion is obscene, and therefore a matter of criminal prosecution. The test sets high limitations for state restrictions on the freedom of expression.

the principles of the secular state and the budgetary funding of the pastimes and caprices of the church elite. It is unlikely that the authors of the bill conducted a rigorous scientific evaluation of its consequences. Illiterate wordings speak for themselves: An extremely low level of professionalism, and a yearning to please the boss who shows obvious religiosity, produce laws that are used to persecute individuals for their opinions and their dissent.

References

Interfax. Defiler of icons in the Cathedral of Christ the Savior was sentenced to restriction of freedom. 2013. http://www.interfax-religion.ru/?act=news&div=50478 [In Russian].

New York Times. Art trial reveals clash of Russian cultures. The New York Times. 8 July 2010. https://www.nytimes.com/2010/07/09/world/europe/09iht-russia.html?_r=2&ref=global-home& [In Russian].

Russian Federation (2013) Draft Bill #142303: Amendments to the Criminal Code of the Russian Federation and certain legislative acts of the Russian Federation in order to counter the insult of religious beliefs and feelings of citizens, desecration of objects and objects of religious worship (pilgrimage), places of worship, and ceremonies". http://asozd2.duma.gov.ru/main.nsf/%28SpravkaNew%29?OpenAgent&RN=142303-6&02

Sakharov Center. Baburin: No to obscurantism at the center of Moscow. 2007. http://old.sakharov-center.ru/museum/exhibitionhall/forbidden-art/whois/baburin-english/

Lenta. Patriarch condemned Samodurov and Yerofeyev for the lack of love. 2010. http://lenta.ru/news/2010/07/22/condemn/

3.

The Political Interpretation of Religion

Religion and State Identity-Building in the New Russia

Julia Gerlach

Introduction

The Russian Federation (New Russia) is known for diversity in almost every aspect. Managing diversities has been both a crucial political project and a major challenge, particularly accompanying the dissolution of the Soviet Union. Along with the breakdown of the Soviet Union, existing Soviet narratives and identities that had served as the glue for decades were lost. Counter narratives and identities of the 1980s and early 1990s almost exclusively focused on ethnic and religious diversity and became the ideology of the independence movements that promoted the building of titular nation states. For some ethnic groups who have not felt represented in the emerging 15 independent republics, including the New Russia, those events paved the way for separatist movements that led, overall, to political trauma of gradual territorial disintegration and instability, and in some cases escalated into terror attacks, counter-terror measures, and even bloody civil wars.

Ever since, managing diversity has *nolens volens* become a priority for Russian policy. Current formal institutions are not sufficient to manage diversity in Russia. The state's federalist organization at least reflects ethnic diversity in some respect by granting 21 territories the status of *national republics* and a few smaller entities the status of *autonomous territories* (either *oblast* or *okrug*), which provides political and fiscal autonomy of different scale and to a certain degree. Nevertheless, there seems to be demand for informal institutions that unite or glue, and thus stabilize the vast territory. This refers to identity building by the state, subsequently called state identity-building, which is understood as the making or construction of collective political identities promoted through narratives by political elites. In this respect, it is an ongoing and dynamic top-down policymaking process

New Russia's state identity-building has been shaped primarily by the leadership of Vladimir Putin, who became acting president in December 1999 and has since been the key political actor, both as president and prime minister[1]. His vision of

1 Vladimir Putin became acting president of the Russian Federation when Boris Yeltsin resigned

state identity seeks to overcome diversity—which is perceived as destabilizing—by constructing a common spiritual core that is closely linked to Russian Orthodoxy and to Russia's Orthodox history. This "religious turn" gradually became visible after Putin took office. With his first inauguration in 2000, Putin established a new type of inauguration ceremony comprising both political and sacral components. Following the political ceremony in the Moscow Kremlin, Putin received blessings from the Patriarch of the Russian Orthodox Church (ROC) during a service at a prominent Orthodox cathedral. The double ceremony reflects an explicit turn (especially considering the violent exclusion of religion from public life during the Soviet period) and symbolically unites state and church as servants of the same master—the New Russia.

In his first inauguration speech, Putin emphasized the relevance of state identity-building for his upcoming term as president: "I consider it my sacred duty to unite the people of Russia and to gather citizens around the clearly defined tasks and aims, and to remember, every minute of every day, that we are one nation and we are one people. We have one common destiny" (Putin 2000a). By defining state identity-building as his "sacred duty", Putin adopts it as a policy priority and at the same time anticipates the spiritual core of his state identity-building project.

Vladimir Putin has adhered to the intentions stated in his first inauguration. State identity-building has been and remains a focal area of his domestic policy (Putin 2013a). There is also no doubt that Orthodox religion and the ROC play a crucial role for what is promoted as the state's identity. In public addresses, Putin consistently underlines the special role of Orthodoxy for Russia's historical and present-day state identity: "The Russian Orthodox Church plays a major role in bringing people together around common spiritual values. Today (…) it is doing much to strengthen civil accord and moral principles (…) and to educate young people in the spirit of patriotism and respect" (Putin 2013b). In addition, links between state and church have become increasingly intimate and more obvious, culminating in the 2011/2012 presidential campaign. The zenith was reached when Patriarch Kirill (Vladimir Gundaev) regained the historical Patriarch's residence in the Moscow Kremlin in December 2011, and in February 2012 called the years of Vladimir Putin's rule, compared to Boris Yeltsin's term, a "miracle of God" (Gundaev 2012a).

The newly emerging relationship between religion and politics in state identity, and between state and ROC in policy, has not only attracted academic attention,

in December 1999. He was later elected president and served two presidential terms in arrow from May 2000 until May 2008. For one term from May 2008 until May 2012, he was appointed prime minister. His third inauguration as president took place in May 2012.

but has also led to criticism and even protest within the New Russia and abroad. Particularly, the guaranteed secularity of the state and the explicit rejection of the establishment of a state church stipulated in the *Constitution of the Russian Federation* (1993) seem to be contradicted by current political reality. As exemplified by the case of *Pussy Riot*, society in the New Russia is obviously divided about the role that Russian Orthodoxy should play in state identity—and that of ROC for the state. Historically, state identities towards religion have been a matter of change. Russia's imperial traditions stand for the inclusion of religion and the ROC under the roof of the state in an arrangement of unified and symbiotic terrestrial and ecclesiastic powers that has been referred to as *symphonia*. In contrast, Soviet traditions draw on the exclusion of both religion and churches from the public and thus the political sphere, as an atheist utopia. The constitutional tradition from 1993 both enshrines freedom of religion and declares the Russian Federation a secular state. It is contested by the *Law on Freedom of Conscience and Religious Associations* (1997) that explicitly grants the ROC a special role out of all the "traditional faiths"[2] (Law on Freedom of Conscience and Religious Associations 1997).

A large body of literature along with mainstream media tells what can be referred to as the two myths about the role of religion in state identity-building in the New Russia. The first myth portrays the "religious turn" as some natural—even deterministic—development in Russian policy. This is a misleading simplification of a very complex political process, as will be shown in this chapter. The second myth concerns the love-match between religion and politics / state and church. In practice, the relationship is much more ambiguous and complicated than it may appear in the first instance. Instead of sentiment, power politics are at work, and the situation can be best captured as mutual instrumentalization or *do ut des*.

The key question of why Putin decided to strengthen the religious factor with respect to Orthodoxy as a part of his state identity-building 'mission'—despite the diversity of and violent conflicts in the name of religions in Russia; conflicting traditions of how to deal with religion politically; and growing criticism on the relationship between politics and Orthodoxy—has not yet been systematically and sufficiently answered. This chapter hopes to contribute to closing that gap in our understanding. Following the 'rational actors' paradigm and controlling for the variable of potential personal preferences, the construction of New Russia's state identity around a religious core is assumed to form part of a rational political process.

Taking into account Putin's first inauguration speech, state identity-building—or, in his words, "to unite the people of Russia"—has been a crucial part of the actual

2 The 1997 law defines in its preamble "Christianity, Judaism, Islam, and Buddhism" as "traditional faiths".

mission to realize the political vision of integrating and stabilizing the country. It is evident that Putin needed to gain popularity among the citizens of the New Russia in order to convince them to identify with his narratives on state identity. As a matter of course, the narratives themselves had to be convincing. In order to gain popular or mass support and to sustain power, Everhard Holtmann and Werner J. Patzelt suggest that political actors must meet three requirements: (1) Responsiveness, (2) legitimacy, and (3) performance (Holtmann 2008:8; similarly, Sarcinelli 2011:89). The first requirement of *responsiveness* tells political actors to respond to the demands and needs of citizens or voters. This means that the masses (or at least the majority of the population) need to be served by the range of the political program. As for state identity-building, it is easier to reach, convince, and integrate people when the narratives address fields that touch the target audience. Spirituality and religion only work when there is some need or demand for them. I argue that the top-down "religious turn" coincidently correlated with the bottom-up development in the society of the New Russia that has been referred to as the "religious revival" or "religious vitality". The second requirement of *legitimacy* suggests that political acting needs a basis that is perceived to be legitimate. It has a formal or legal, and an informal or political dimension. Political acting must be perceived as harmonious with both the legislation and with the political system, including political culture and political traditions. There are many ways of constructing legitimacy politically. In any case, religion—as well as its historization and culturalization—can be employed to enhance legitimacy. I argue that the "legitimating effect" of religion, combined with an invented history and culture that has been referred to as the "(re)invention of tradition", is to strengthen legitimacy. The third requirement of *performance* refers to the perception of politics, and requires political actors to produce positive policy outcomes. Progress and optimization regarding both public demands and policy objectives are expected. Well-perceived performances also stimulate legitimacy and may even broaden what is considered politically legitimate. I argue that Vladimir Putin believes that state identity-building around an Orthodox core will strengthen his overall domestic and international political performance, particularly regarding the creation of unity as the base. Overall, for the political elites in the New Russia, the "religious turn" makes rational sense in order to demonstrate responsiveness, strengthen legitimacy, and enhance performance

This study employs a process-tracing methodology as well as data and narrative analysis to answer the research question of why a political decision was made to base state identity-building around a core of Russian Orthodoxy. The focus of the research is on the state and key political actors. In this sense, the results can help explain why the decision can be regarded as rational for key political actors and the state. The chapter will not investigate the perspectives of religious actors, the church, or bottom-up identity-building processes[3]. This localization is not to imply a one-sided use or instrumentalization of religion by the state. Conversely, it is assumed that religious actors and the ROC, as well as grassroots movements and regional actors, follow similar rational patterns, which should be explored in further research.

The structure of the article follows the vein of this research question in eight sections. Subsequent to this introduction, a literature review discusses the present understanding of the politics/religion nexus and the relationship between the Russian state and the ROC (section 2). Then, theoretical approaches on state identity-building and the role of religion are discussed (section 3). Process tracing is used to contextualize the historical role of religion in state identity-building in Russia (section 4). The subsequent section then analyzes the dependent variable, which is the inclusion of religion in state identity-building in the New Russia (section 5). The next three sections deal with three independent variables. They are borrowed from theoretical approaches to rational political decision-making and political communication, and will be applied to the case of the New Russia: state's strategy of responsiveness and the vitality of religion (section 6); the state's strategy of legitimacy and the legitimizing effect of religion (section 7); and the state's strategy of performance and the creation of unity (section 8). The final section summarizes the findings and presents conclusions (section 9)

The research is based on primary sources and the relevant literature on religion and politics. The data analyzed include various surveys on religion in Russia conducted by the Russian research institutes *Sreda*, the *Yuri Levada Analytical Center* (subsequently referred to as *Levada*), *Romir* affiliated to *Gallup International*, and the *Russian Academy of Science* in cooperation with the *Academy of Finland*. In addition, public addresses of the presidents of the New Russia, published on official government websites, are analyzed. To avoid changes of meaning through translation, the study is based on the English translations provided on the official website. The research period covers the leadership of Vladimir Putin from 2000 to 2013

Literature Review

International research contributing to the understanding of the role of religion, particularly Russian Orthodoxy, in state identity-building in Russia derives from three different areas: humanities, regional studies, and social sciences. The body of literature can be divided into two meta-approaches. The first approach focuses on the

3 Two recently published studies focus on the side of religious actors and the ROC: Richters (2013) and Knox (2009).

nature of religion(s) in Russia, including their (historical) proliferation, social status, rites, and the lives of believers (subsequently referred to as the *nature-approach*). The second approach aims to explore the relationship between church(es) and the state, and the overall nexus between politics and religion (subsequently referred to as the *nexus-approach*). For both approaches, the number of contributions has recently increased significantly, reflecting the growing attention and relevance of the topic. Major public attention was generated by the discourse on the case of *Pussy Riot*[4], which highlighted the relationship between ROC and state in the New Russia.

For this study, the nexus approach contains the most relevant body of literature. Only a few international monographs have been dedicated to this field so far. The first studies from 2005 and 2006 approach the role of the ROC from the church's perspective and examine its relevance for Russian civil society. In *Russian Orthodox Society and the Orthodox Church* (2005), the Australian scholar Zoe Knox focuses on the ROC's social role and influence on society. She identifies factions within the ROC: One faction would promote democratic development and the establishment of civil society, while the other, led by the politically influential Moscow Patriarchate, tended to oppose (Knox 2005b). In several articles and book chapters, Knox elaborates on the relationship between politics and religion, particularly on the nexus of nationalism and Orthodoxy (Knox 2005a) and the development of freedom of religion under the leadership of Vladimir Putin (Knox 2008). In 2006, the American Historian Wallace L. Daniel, in *The Orthodox Church and Civil Society in Russia*, examines the process of post-Soviet identity-building in Russia from the inner perspective of the ROC. He analyzes how the church makes its way and tries to increase its social influence through the promotion of values (Daniel 2006).

Later monographs particularly focus on the relationship between politics and religion / church and state. In her book *Believing in Russia*, the French journalist

4 The group of young women had performed a music piece called *Punk Prayer* in the Moscow *Christ the Savior Cathedral* without permission. In the context of the ongoing presidential election campaign in February 2012, they criticized the close relationship between ROC and state. After the performance was interrupted and stopped by staff and security in the cathedral, *Pussy Riot* uploaded the video they had taken to the Internet platform *YouTube*. Three members were arrested, charged with hooliganism motivated by religious hatred, and sentenced to two years imprisonment in a penal camp. One of the sentences was later suspended on probation (Willems 2013:5). The discourse about the case made the relationship between religion and politics in Russia the focus of public attention, both within the Russian Federation and abroad. While the evaluation of the case seems to divide society in the New Russia between critics of the state and critics of *Pussy Riot*, public opinion in Western countries almost unanimously supports the activists. The Russian Federation was harshly criticized for the status of human rights, legal procedures, and a strong state (EU Statement on Freedom of Expression in the Russian Federation 2012).

Geraldine Fagan elaborates on the development of religious policy in Russia after 1991. She finds the state has gradually promoted Orthodoxy and the ROC during the last two decades, both legally and politically. Nevertheless, she concludes (contrary to what the mainstream media suggests) that there is no consensus on the preferred role of the ROC in society and state (Fagan 2012). The German scholar Katja Richters analyzes the relationship between ROC and state from the church's perspective. She finds extensive convergence of ideas, especially on the Russian nation, but doubts the often-claimed one-sided influence of the state on the church. Her findings in *The Post-Soviet Russian Orthodox Church* instead emphasize a rather mutual relationship between two actors with two sometimes conflicting agendas (Richters 2013)

Most contributions assigned to the nexus approach make sense of the relationship between ROC and state through the lens of nationalism. In this respect, Orthodoxy is understood as an ideological tool used by political actors to strengthen "the national Russian idea". The main argument is most commonly borrowed from history (Panov 2010), only rarely from current surveys on identification (Kääriäinen 2009). It suggests that Orthodoxy substitutes as a mono-ethnic identity within the country.

With a few exceptions, research on the role of religion and the ROC in the New Russia tends to go in circles, repeatedly applying the same concepts (nationalism, instrumentalization of religion by the state) and arguments (path-dependencies, historic determinism) and reaching similar conclusions. One reason is the lack of valid data on religion in Russia, especially for the period before 1991. After 1991, many scholars refer to their research colleagues rather than collecting or evaluating primary data. This produces a very one-sided picture of the relationship and the role of the ROC. The present study therefore approaches the field from a different perspective, by applying the meta-theory of rational choice in political decision-making and setting responsiveness, legitimacy, and performance as independent variables. The analysis also relies predominantly on primary data (surveys and speeches), not on the literature.

Theoretical Approaches to the Role of Religion in State Identity-Building

Making sense of the role of religion in state identity-building will follow the line of conceptualizing identity, elaborating on the process of identity building by the state through narratives, and exploring the role of religious factors in state identity-building. To begin with, the state in this chapter refers to the nation state. In modern times, states are almost exclusively organized as nation states. This is why most of the literature understands state identity-building as part of nation building.

This classification is appropriate. However, the concepts of nation building and nationalism as the underlying ideology have been excessively applied to explain almost every aspect of the transformation in Central and Eastern Europe. I argue that applying them as the key concepts to address the aims of this study would not only be redundant in repeatedly following the same patterns, but would further result in limited research outcomes. Hence, the main focus will be on the construction of identity in a broader sense, not one restricted to national identity

The term "identity" is used in two contexts: debating identity policy, and discussing an analytical category (Brubaker/Cooper 2000:2). For this chapter, the branch of identity policy is more relevant, yet the analysis requires making sense of identity conceptually. Identities matter—this has been the consensus for decades. In social sciences, research focusing on identities started in the 1960s and 1970s. Crucial for studying identities were the social movements and uprisings that addressed civil rights, decolonization, and emancipation and thus challenged existing identities. This context indicates that identities became relevant for social sciences when they were in transition and/or caused social and sometimes violent conflict. The awareness of identity seems to increase when it is in crisis (Erikson 1968). Political science typically employs the concept when there are conflicting identities or identity crises at work, such as in the fields of mobilization and conflict, social movements and collective action, nationalism and nation building, or resilience and stability of governments, just to name the most important examples.

Identity has not been sufficiently conceptualized; it remains vague and requires contextualization. The current mainstream literature suggests that identity is a construction of one's self and its persistence, occurring at both an individual and collective level. The way to build identity is by the construction of belonging. Individual identity is based on a person's series of social roles and cultural categories, whereas collective identity means the affiliation with certain groups (Smith 1991:3). Collective identity is shared belonging that unites individuals by creating (a feeling of) membership. In this sense, identity does not exist objectively. It is subjectively constructed or built by the individual or the collective self under the direct or indirect influence of other individuals and collectives.

Actually, identity is a plurale tantum, as there is not the one identity but several competing, sometimes even conflicting identities. Reflecting this phenomenon, the literature suggests the terms "multiple" (Smith 1991:3) or "hybrid" (Iyall Smith/Leavy 2008) identity. Also, identity is not stable over time, but fluid—and may change during an individual's life time (Touraine 1981; Melucci 1989). These implications do not undermine the political impact of identity but strengthen it. Both individual and collective identities have been substantially affected by societal and political changes in recent decades. Emancipation, globalization, industrialization, migration, modernization, and the proliferation of technology all challenge existing identities. Identity building, which is literally the making of identity, is therefore an ongoing process for both individuals and groups

For political science and hence for this study, the focus is on collective identity, because political actors—parties, elites, governments, nation states, and international organizations—are typically collectives. State identity can be considered a collective or group identity that is connected to the state as the dominant form of political organization. In order to explore state identity, the focus must be on how states are organized. In modern times, states have been organized as national states. Even though nation states in the age of multilateralism seem to increasingly transfer their sovereignty to alliances and supranational organizations, they remain the norm of political order. Any state or group needs identity to maintain its existence. Identity serves as a tool or instrument, as the glue that unites individuals among themselves, and between citizens and the state. Both dimensions of state identity (solidarity between citizens, and loyalty between citizens and the state) are subject to the building of identity. Identity is hence a policy field just like others. Nevertheless, it plays a crucial role for the integration of society under the roof of the state. Global trends suggest that states are presently experiencing weaker social cohesion. This seems to be true for the relationship or solidarity among individuals, as well as for loyalty between citizens and the state (Kamens 2012). State identity-building in this sense is challenging and a "fundamental process of political work" around the globe (Kaufmann 1990).

The new Russian state emerging in 1991 was not provided with state identity. All former state identity had ceased to exist. There were several lost state identities or identity traditions, and at the same time, resurgent or newly emerging conflicting identities, resulting in the dissolution of the Soviet Union. The New Russia was built on a construction site of changing and conflicting identity traditions, including various Tsarist, imperial, communist, and sub-national identities (Warhola 2007:81).

Policies, including state identity-building, are generated and practiced by political actors or—more precisely—by political elites. In this sense, state identity-building is a top-down policy-making process led by political elites. It aims to create a sense of belonging to the state by constructing commonalities that people share. Ideally, identity building produces not only solidarity between individuals and loyalty towards the state, but also participation within the community in the vein of the state's identity (Cerutti/Lucarelli 2011:18).

Identities are constituted through narratives; stories about the collective self (Bruner 2001:25). In state identity-building, political elites become the narrators. Somers proposes four dimensions of narratives relevant for identity building: The ontological dimension defines who we are and what to do. Its function is to make sense of the personal being. The public dimension gives a mainstream plot that aims to unite a number of people around something shared. Shared goods can be found at either micro or macro levels. Metanarratives use abstract master stories (capitalism, communism, modernization, etc.) to constitute identity. Typically, they legitimize certain actions that are not legitimized through other story dimensions. The conceptual dimension formulates vocabulary (concepts and explanations) used in narratives (Somers 1994:617–620). These four notions help to analyze narratives as tools for state identity-building.

Narratives are not stable but change over time. Political actors use them consciously for constructing identity, meaning that stories that do not automatically fit the political context can—and will—be made to do so. The narrativity of state identity-building identifies it as an act of political communication and its various channels. Just telling a story is not enough: to build identity, actors need to convince the audience, to make them share something. Reaching hegemony in public discourse is a step to creating hegemonic narratives. Everhard Holtmann and Werner J. Patzelt suggest that, in order to gain support for their narrative of state identity, political actors must meet the three requirements of responsiveness, legitimacy, and performance (Holtmann 2008:8; also Sarcinelli 2011:89). Responsiveness means that all political action, including state identity-building, should ideally match with the citizens' needs and demands. This is why elites in democracies pay specific attention to public polls in the process of decision-making. Talking about identity policy, the reference points of belonging should at least attract the majority of citizens. Legitimacy requires political action to be justified, implying that both formal and informal institutions must be respected. Furthermore, there can be a need for authenticity and truthfulness (Taylor 1994:28, 30). Whatever seems inappropriate or odd in identity-building narratives will be quite unlikely to promote state identity. Elites who manage to draw on historical and social events that are considered seminal are more likely to successfully build state identity because they are perceived as authentic. Performance reflects that political progress is expected. Successful narrators manage to draw a line from the state identity they built to the political progress they achieved. Ideally, the promoted state identity, the political program, and performance are convergent

In the contemporary political order, nation states are the global norm, hence state identity is typically connected to the nation—or what nationalism has constructed as the nation. There is no consensus on the concept of a nation or its origin. However, in the 21st century, primordialist approaches which understand nation as a natural and organically grown group of people are overcome in social sciences (Brubaker 2009:28), yet not necessarily in politics—as we can learn from contemporary violent conflicts in the name of nationality. National belonging can be instrumentalized for political mobilization, both peacefully and violently. However, nations are products of social imagination and political creation (Andersen 1983). In this respect, narratives are needed that ensure solidarity within the national community. The narrative can emphasize any commonality shared by the majority. Theories on nationalism often differ between the types of the cultural and the political nation. Narratives of cultural nation states (Kulturnationen) rely on shared cultural goods and experiences whereas political nation states (Staatsnationen) tend to refer to shared political history that includes a certain type of rule or de facto political system that contributes to build, or is an expression of, collective identity (Meinecke 1922:3ff.)[5]. In reality, many countries reflect features of both ideal types, and only a few nation states fit into either one of the categories. The New Russia has inherited both traditions in various ways. While imperial Russia tended towards features of the cultural nation, the Soviet Union drew more on elements of the political nation, inspired by salvation through communism. Both cultural and political nations can make religion an element of state identity—it all depends on the narrative. For cultural nation states, religion typically serves as shared cultural capital. This can be studied in the case of Poland. For political nation states, religion can be employed as the reference point in the founding narrative. Examples include Iran and Israel. The New Russia relies on both concepts, and represents a synthesis of a cultural and a political nation. The analysis of Orthodoxy and state identity-building in the New Russia (section 5) will explore what this means for the employment of religion in state identity-building

Tracing Changing State Identities

Religious/political relations, particularly the role of Russian Orthodoxy and the ROC in the state, have been a key element of the changing state identities in the Russian Federation and its predecessor states. Tracing the changing relationships via central events and historical phases contributes to the understanding of the various state identity traditions that the New Russia inherited. These traditions can be understood as multiple institutional layers. The theoretical approach of institutional layering borrowed from historical Neo-Institutionalism argues that older layers of institutions do not disappear but are overlaid with younger ones (Van der Heijden 2011:9ff.), and that they may therefore continue to produce meaning. The main question in this case is whether different layers produce conflicting or convergent meaning, and whether they are capable of coexistence or not (Liebermann 2002:703). In the

5 The differentiation between *Kulturnation* and *Staatsnation* was introduced by Friedrich Meinecke in 1908. The edition of his study used here was published in 1922.

framework of this study, the lesson learnt from institutional layering is that historical relationships between religion and politics / ROC and the state may well have an impact on the current building of state identity. Other than the model of path dependency, that understands change as a deterministic and predictable process, institutional layering suggests only the possibility that older layers could influence later developments. This means that older state identity traditions can be employed or revitalized in narratives for current state identity-building. Still, a rational political decision is needed as a premise, because the reemergence of older layers does not happen naturally\

The timeline that connects Orthodoxy and Russia starts in the late 980s, when Vladimir I introduced Eastern Orthodoxy by mass baptism to the Kievan Rus'[6]. The link between state and Orthodoxy was initially influenced by the Byzantine ideal of symphonia, which understands the relationship as being complementary and mutually dependent: the church being the ecclesiastical and the state the temporary authority (Knox 2005b:5). In the following centuries, this harmony was contested several times. Tsar Peter I abolished the Patriarchate in 1721 in favor of a committee of appointed laypersons, the Ecclesiastical College, which was soon renamed the Holy Governing Synod. Hence, he made the Orthodox Church more dependent, and introduced a hierarchy that placed the state over the church. The intention was to foster autocracy, the political system in which all power and wealth was distributed by the tsar: without checks and balances by law, authorities—or the church. Nevertheless, even under state control, the Orthodox Church continued to play a significant role

In the context of the Decembrist uprising of 1825 and rebellions against monarchs in Europe, Nicholas I[7] built a counter-state identity in order to meet the systemic challenges to his regime. This is reflected in a statement from 1833 by the minister of education, Count Sergei Uvarov[8]: "It is our common obligation to ensure that the education of the people is to be conducted, according to the Supreme intention of our August Monarch, in the joint spirit of Orthodoxy, Autocracy, and Nationhood (Pravoslavie, Samoderzhavie, Narodnost')" (Quote taken from Hosking 1998:146). The quote offers at least two branches of interpretation. First, education is defined the main tool of raising loyal citizens and elites. The core of this education comprises intertwined political and spiritual elements. Second, religion, state, and nation are identified as inseparable pillars of Russia. As for state identity, the sacred is to melt with the actual; religion with politics (or even a certain type

6 Vladimir I (958–1015) ruled the Kievan Rus' from 980 until 1015.

7 Nicolas I (1796-1855) emperor of Russia from 1820 until 1855.

8 Sergei Uvarov (1786-1855) scholar in classical studies, served in politics under Nicolas I.

of government: autocracy). The original ideal of symphonia was revised: the two separate spheres became one

The role of the Orthodox Church increased again from the 1830s until interrupted by the 1917 Bolshevik Revolution (Knox 2005b:5). Bolshevism stood, among others, for internationalism and atheism. The consequence was to dissolving the attachment of citizens from ethnic identity and religion (Service 2003:190). Atheism, or the negation of religion, was promoted as part of the official state identity. Religion was banned from the public sphere during Soviet times, except for the years in which the Red Army fought in World War II (Agadjanian 2001:351). More than simply the neglect of religion and religious institutions, during some periods the ban on religion implied persecution and violent suppression. In the 1930s, out of 20,000 churches, only a few hundred remained in existence (Marsh 2011:247). Practicing religion became something secret and private, and for many citizens, a form of "inner emigration" to political reality (Deutsch Kornblatt 2004: 69, 82). The Soviet state identity banned traditional religion; nevertheless, spirituality played an important role. For many years, state socialism served as a surrogate for religion by inheriting systems of belief including "holy books" and "saints", as well as sacralization in architecture and public rituals. These striking similarities between religion and totalitarian anti-religious movements have been referred to as "secular religion" or "political religion" (Maier 2007:5 ff.)

The political attitude towards religion changed during the period of perestroika in the 1980s. In the framework of overall liberalization, religion was granted a return to the public sphere. In 1988, both Kiev and Moscow held publicly organized celebrations for the millennium of the baptism of the Kievan Rus'. Religious suppression ceased, and religious freedom was enshrined in the law On Freedom of Belief and Religious Organizations (1990). After the dissolution of the Soviet Union, the Constitution of the Russian Federation (1993) provided the equality of all religions before the law, and the separation of church and state. However, the law on Freedom of Conscience and Religious Associations (1997) implies several changes. The law defines the role of the ROC as particularly salient, elaborating in the preamble on the "(…) the special contribution of Orthodoxy in the history of Russia and in the establishment and development of its spirituality and culture". At the same time, "(any other denomination of) Christianity, Islam, Buddhism, Judaism, and other religions" are described as "respected". The law defines an explicit preference towards Russian Orthodoxy. In this sense, there is no neutrality or equidistance towards religion. Furthermore, Orthodoxy is said to have historically supported the state's development, and to have stabilized the country.

In summary, the role of religion in Russia and its predecessor states has been crucial for state identity-building. Two conflicting traditions merge: In some periods, it has been the explicit inclusion and control of Russian Orthodoxy; in other periods, the explicit exclusion and persecution of any religion that formed a core feature of state identity. While the commitment to Orthodoxy was perceived as a commitment to the state in Tsarist times, in Soviet times commitment to religion meant the denial of the state or to dissent from the mainstream state's identity. Commitment to religion had different meanings in different periods, but would still define patterns of identity in relation to the state. In this sense, public confession of faith had both religious and political implications. In a broader sense this means that, at least informally, there was no separation between politics and religion / church and state.

Orthodoxy and State Identity-Building in the New Russia

The dependent variable of this study is the religious (Orthodox) core of state identity-building in the New Russia through the creation of political narratives. Tracing changing state identities in Russia reveals that religion has played significantly different roles over time. However, both the inclusion and exclusion of religion have had a substantial impact in shaping the state's identities. This section analyzes the role of Orthodoxy and the ROC in state identity-building in the New Russia as of 2013. I argue that the way in which Russian Orthodoxy is employed in narratives draws a bow from culture to politics, embracing both the domestic and the international political arenas. Orthodoxy is not only used as the glue uniting the people of Russia, but also links cultural with political features. This reflects a synthesis of a political and cultural nation state (s. Meinecke 1922:3ff.). According to Somers (1994: 617–620), the narrative technique employed connects the ontological dimension of who we are with the meta-dimension of political visions of and missions to the world.

For Vladimir Putin, Russian Orthodoxy and the values promoted by the ROC are the bond that unites not only the Russian Federation but also other Orthodox Soviet successor states, as he highlights in a TV interview on the film "The Second Baptism of Rus": "Essentially, it was after adopting Orthodox Christianity as a religion that the Russian nation began to emerge as a unified nation and began building a centralized Russian state. At the foundations of the Russian nation and the centralized Russian state are the same spiritual values that unite the whole of that part of Europe now shared by Russia, Ukraine, and Belarus. This is our common spiritual, moral and values space, and this plays a very big part in uniting the people" (Putin 2013p). In addition to the uniting factor of Orthodoxy, Putin promotes Russian Orthodoxy in narratives as the standard cultural and civilizational model of the New Russia, the core and driving force of what the New Russia has ultimately become. On the occasion of the 1025th anniversary of the mass baptism of the Kievan Rus' in 2013, Vladimir Putin outlined the Orthodox model: "The acceptance of Christianity determined Russia's fate and choice of civilization; it became a decisive turning point in the Russian state's ecclesiastical and secular history. The moral foundations of the Orthodox faith played a major role in the formation of our national character and the mentality of Russia's peoples, revealing the best creative qualities of our nation, helping Russia hold a dignified place among the European and global civilizations" (Putin 2013c). According to Putin, Orthodoxy marks the beginning or hour of birth of Russia. Orthodox religion in this sense can be understood as the genome ("moral foundations") of the Russian civilization. Identification with and commitment to Orthodoxy form what can be referred to as "Russianness" ("national character and mentality"). Russianness is here, following Arto Mustajoki and other scholars, explicitly not connoted ethnically, but culturally and civilizationally (Alapuro et al. 2012:xiii). It brings together people of different ethnic backgrounds around a shared idea. This idea, which is not political in the first stance but more of a general approach or attitude of belonging, makes up the core of the state identity a la Putin.

In most of his statements on religion, Putin emphasizes the relevance of its spirituality, morality, or set of values for the state. In this sense, the meaning of Orthodoxy for the state is shared principles and abstract belief systems—the Orthodox model. When he addresses religion in public, Putin never speaks about the content of religion or theological issues. He tends to look at religion from the perspective of how it can serve the state, both in abstract terms and tangible policy issues. In abstract terms, values promoted by the ROC can help to unite people and to found a common ground for Russian statehood. In tangible and domestic measures, Putin repeatedly invites religious actors to get involved in social services linked to family issues, which he defines as "nationwide tasks"(Putin 2004b) and to foster what he calls the interfaith dialogue (Putin 2013m; Medvedev 2011b). Both are obviously problematic policy fields in the New Russia, when considering the demographic crisis and the separatist conflicts and terrorism employed by fundamental Islamists. Whenever the state faces limits of influence, it is the ROC's turn to support.

This is also due to Putin's perception of the role that the ROC and Orthodoxy have played for the country historically. For Putin, the Orthodox turn has an impact on both the domestic and the international arena. It is causal not only for the establishment of Russian statehood, but also for all positive achievements in Russian history. This includes explicitly the making of Russia's status in the world, and also the country's competitiveness—not only with European neighbors but also on a global scale (Putin 2013c). Beginning with the Russian statehood, Russian Orthodoxy respectively its "moral foundations" unites the people of Russia. At the same time, Orthodoxy draws borders to most neighbors, particularly to the European ones or, frankly spoken: to "the West". For Putin, commitment to Orthodoxy implies the rejection of Western traditions, both culturally and politically. Religious borders for him mark a civilizational and a political divide. The civilizational divide is not only about the denomination to which people are committed, but also the role religion plays in state identity. Putin elaborates in his speech at the Valdai International Discussion Club in 2013: "We can see how many of the Euro-Atlantic countries are actually rejecting their roots, including the Christian values that constitute the basis of Western civilization. They are denying moral principles and all traditional identities: national, cultural, religious, and even sexual" (Putin 2013a). The main message is: Russia is different: Russia sticks to its moral foundation and Orthodox traditions. The West stands for arbitrariness and degradation where "they are implementing policies that equate large families with same-sex partnerships, belief in God with the belief in Satan" (Putin 2013a), whereas Russia is on the morally correct track. Putin drives the comparison between East and West, Orthodox and non-Orthodox to the very extreme, the friend/foe distinction with a religious connotation. He portrays the different civilizations like a decision between God and Satan, good and evil, moral and immoral, right and wrong. This view of the world hardly includes gray zones, only black and white.

According to Putin, the New Russia's otherness that is rooted in the Orthodox model also has political implications. The nature of Russian statehood derives from this culture: "Russia is characterized by a tradition of a strong state. Democracy is the only political choice for Russia. I would like to stress that we share the universal democratic principles adopted worldwide. However, Russia's democracy means the power of the Russian people with their own traditions of self-rule and not the fulfillment of standards imposed on us from the outside" (Putin 2012c). Western-style democracy is not a matter of choice for the New Russia. Putin argues for a Russian Sonderweg, which in earlier speeches (most prominently at the Munich Conference on Security Policy in 2007) he entitles sovereign democracy[9]. He does not clarify exactly what he means by the Russian "traditions of self-rule" except for a strong state and a commitment to basic democratic principles. In this respect, the narrative of the Orthodox model and unique Russian traditions create the basis for the narrative that only a strong state corresponds with Russianness. The New Russia has its own way, its own model, and its own standards, and does not need to be measured through the lenses of other standards. Putin sums up: "At the same

9 The concept of *sovereign democracy* originates from Vladislav Surkov, chief deputy of the presidential administration from 1999 until 2011. First mentioned in a speech delivered in February 2006 to the students of "United Russia's Center for Party Personnel Training", he elaborated on the concept more closely in his article "The Nationalization of the Future", published in November 2006.

time we see attempts to somehow revive a standardized model of a unipolar world and to blur the institutions of international law and national sovereignty. Such a unipolar, standardized world does not require sovereign states; it requires vassals. In a historical sense this amounts to a rejection of one's own identity, of the God-given diversity of the world" (Putin 2013a). In simple words, God wants the New Russia to be different and unique, and to remain on its historical path.

Closely connected to Russia's internal sovereignty is its external status. Putin has a decisive vision of the New Russia's status in the international arena: "In the 21st century amid a new balance of economic, civilizational and military forces Russia must be a sovereign and influential country" (Putin 2012c). The mission implied by this vision of a strong, superior state describes the status of a great power that plays a crucial role in the international arena. Putin's key argument is that it is the spiritual–religious foundation that is the basis of state identity, and which makes a country strong and superior to others: "It is evident that it is impossible to move forward without spiritual, cultural, and national self-determination. Without this we will not be able to withstand internal and neither external challenges, nor we will succeed in global competitions" (Putin 2013a). Russia has proved its strength and supremacy in history, beginning from the Kievan Rus'. "The Baptism of Rus was a great event that defined Russia's (…) spiritual and cultural development for the centuries to come" (Putin 2013n). The implication, then, it that the status of a great influential power has been lost and must be restored. The way to achieve it is from within. A state identity based around the core of the Orthodox model is the key.

State identity-building under Vladimir Putin prominently employs Russian Orthodoxy and the values promoted by the ROC as the core that determines both domestic politics and international status (strong state and great power). Nevertheless, political actors also mention other religions, mostly calling them "other traditional faiths" (Putin 2013k), analogous to the 1997 law on religion. Yet, the role of Orthodoxy is unchallenged. Vladimir Putin highlights not only the special role of the ROC and Orthodoxy for Russia, basically as an imagined continuum since the baptism of the Kievan Rus'; he also emphasizes the cooperation between state and church. On the occasion of Patriarch Kirill's birthday, he declares: "Under your guidance, the Russian Orthodox Church is developing constructive cooperation with the state authorities (…)" (Putin 2013m). The special role of the ROC and Orthodoxy for his state identity-building project does not prevent him from demanding the same contributions to the state from other religions as well. All religious actors, particularly Muslim leaders and authorities, are expected to support the state's unity (Putin 2013o).

Responsiveness and the "Vitality of Religion"

The first independent variable to be analyzed is "responsiveness and the 'vitality of religion'". Assuming that identity narratives are more likely to reach, convince, and integrate people when they reflect their demand and needs, I argue that the "religious turn" in state identity-building was taken because religion had become more vital and relevant among the public. The more relevant that religion is in public, the more likely political actors use religion in state identity-building. To test this hypothesis, the bottom-up trend of "religious vitality" must presume and coincidently correlate with the top-down "religious turn" in state identity-building.

The (increasing) relevance of religion in Russia is often referred to as the "religious revival". The theorem of religious revival has been prominently represented in the social sciences since the mid-1980s, introduced through the work of José Casanova (Casanova 1984). Other than the secularization or modernization theses that conclude in the gradual erosion of the role of religion or even the "death of religion" around the globe (Marx 1844; Weber 1904/1905), the revival theorem claims there are trends that suggest the resurgence of religion under certain preconditions. It can be either negative economic or political development or, more generally, increasing human need for orientation in times of uncertainty, that provoke an increasing relevance of religion (Inglehart/Norris 2004). This may refer to the revival of traditional faiths, but also to the emergence of new religions or syncretistic belief systems (Luckman 1967). Casanova's indicators of the religious revival refer to new religious movements, new forms of individual religiosity, the proliferation of religious fundamentalism, and the renewal of established churches (Casanova 1984:15 ff.). In the past two decades, the theorem played a crucial role in explaining the new impact of religion in the post-Soviet space and generally, in world politics after 9/11 (Huntington 1993).

With regard to Russia, scholars have almost unanimously cited a religious—especially Orthodox—revival (Mitrokhin 1993), usually vaguely and without clarifying the indicators. Only a few studies rely on robust statistical analysis (Greeley 1994; Kääriäinen 1998; Norris/Inglehart 2004). Generally, the data on religion in Russia is limited, and there are no reliable figures for the Soviet period. In this sense, science lacks empirical evidence to support clams of a revival of religion. More precisely, resurgence could only be claimed for public religion (Agadjanian 2001:351ff.), using the anti-religious policy of the state and the suppression of religious activities and actors as evidence for its disappearance from the public sphere. If, or to what extent, religious attitudes and affiliations remained in private, is a matter of speculation. There are theoretical approaches making sense of the disposition of religion in secular and/or anti-religious times. The concepts of political religion (Voegelin 1938; Maier 2007), civil religion (Bellah 1967), and invisible religion (Luckman 1967) share the assumption that religion would not disappear completely, but instead change its form, appearance, or merge with politics. These approaches can be employed to explain the role and practice of religion during the Soviet period

Considering the lack of data, the framing of religious change in the New Russia as a "religious revival" is eye-catching but misleading. In addition, there is no definitive concept of the revival of religion. Following Andrew Greeley's definition, religious revival means a substantial increase in both religious belief and affiliation (Greeley 1994:253). The two dimensions Greeley suggests—belief and affiliation—are useful for the operationalization of the relevance of religion. Nevertheless, it seems more appropriate to speak about (new) religious vitality (Pickel/Müller 2009:7) instead of religious revival, reflecting the lack of data for the Soviet period. As for the vitality of religion, Greeley's theoretical approaches can be borrowed. Subsequent research on Russia has followed his dimensions in general, but specified them. This study applies the framework introduced by Timmo Kääriäinen (Kääriäinen 1998 and 2009), because it corresponds best with the limited data available. It measures religious vitality by five indicators: the institutional dimension, the importance of religion in life, the belief dimension, the ritual dimension, and the moral dimension. Kääriäinen's concept will be used for the subsequent analysis.

In the New Russia, people do not register as members of churches or pay taxes. There is no data that could clearly identify 'membership', which means that the institutional dimension must rely on surveys. The Academy of Finland and the Russian Academy of Science (subsequently Academies) have collected data from 1991 to 2005 on how people consider their relation to religion in general, by asking whether people "believe", "seek", "do not believe", consider themselves "atheists" or "cannot say". It is striking that the number of believers in the Russian Federation increased gradually from 23% in 1991 to 53% in 2005. This development correlates with an increasingly heterogeneous age distribution among believers. While the typical believer in 1991 was an elderly female, in 2005 younger people were also visibly represented in the group of believers. Still, believing is more prevalent among woman than among men (64% versus 41%). During the same period, the number of atheists and non-believers dropped significantly. In 1991, 35% considered themselves atheists. Two years later, only 5% of the respondents were atheists. This has subsequently remained the most stable category in the entire data set. The percentage of atheists 'converted' to the number of non-believers. In 1991, 7% were non-believers, while two years later 30% of the respondents considered themselves non-believers. The different framing may reflect the ideological turn at the end of the Soviet Union. However, it is interesting that the number of non-believers declined gradually after 1993 until it reached 14% in 2005 (Academies 1991–2005).

Further statistics support the Academies' findings. The Russian research institute Levada collected more detailed data from 1991 until 2012, asking for specific religious affiliations, such as commitment to the Russian Orthodox faith, Islam, or other denominations. During this period, the number of Orthodox believers increased from 31% to 70%, which seems to be the zenith, having remained stable since 2010. In the same period, the number of Muslims rose from 1% to 7%. All other religious affiliations represented in the data set seem to be stable at a low level (< 1% reported for Judaism, Protestantism, Catholicism, and Hinduism). While religious affiliations with the two major denominations rose significantly, the New Russia faced a decline in non-believers from 61% to 21% according to the Levada polls (Levada 2011). The Russian research institute Sreda presents contradictory findings in its 2010 survey (published 2012) on religious affiliations. According to Sreda, 41% consider themselves Russian Orthodox. Sreda is uses one category that is not used by Levada: "believing without religion". This group comprises of 25% of the respondents (Sreda 2012). By adding the numbers of Orthodox believers and believers without religion, the sum is close to what Levada estimates as the percentage of people committed to Orthodoxy. Mainstream literature suggests that in the New Russia, religious commitment is connected to Russian identity (Kääriäinen 2009:56; Richters 2013:63). This could explain why the Levada polls suggest such a high number of people affiliated with Orthodoxy while some of them would specify their commitment when the survey categories allow them to.

According to the findings of the Academies and Levada, the perception of the importance of religion in life increased somewhat, but not significantly. Both use exactly the same categories to measure the importance, "very important", "fairly important", "fairly unimportant", "not important", and "cannot say". The highest importance has been relatively stable according to both surveys. However, the Academies suggest a higher approval (between 11% and 15% from 1991 to 2005) than Levada (5% or 6% from 2007 to 2013). Most interesting is the fluctuation of the categories "fairly important" and "not important at all". While the former increases gradually from 20% in 1991 until 30% in 2005, the latter decreases from 30% to 20%. At the same time, the category "fairly unimportant" is relatively stable (between 37% and 33%). Overall, the importance of religion seems to increase in the less observant categories ("fairly important") while people increasingly tend to perceive religion at least as "not unimportant" in their life (Kääriäinen 2009:58). These trends are supported by Levada's polls from 2007 to 2013 (Levada 2013).

As for the dimension of belief, it is interesting to observe that the belief in God (from 34% to 66%), in Satan (from 12% to 38), in Heaven (from 15% to 39%), and in Hell (from 13% to 36%) gradually and significantly increased between 1991 and

2005 according to the Academies' findings (Kääriäinen 2009:58). Levada supports the trend, but on a lower scale (Levada 2010a and 2010b). This means that especially the personalization and localization of belief has been strengthened.

The growing dimension of belief does not correspond with changing collective ritual behavior. The practice of religious rituals such as attending church services on a regular basis or celebrating religious holidays is relatively stable at a low level. The number of people attending church services on a regular weekly or monthly basis was between 1–2%, and 3–4% from 1991 until 2007 (Levada 2011). The only groups that changed their behavior were those who never attended church services: The percentage declined from 67% in 1991 to 59% in 2007. The Academies suggest an even more significant drop, from 59% to 38% of respondents who attend service once a year or less (Kääriäinen 2009:59). It is interesting that the individual ritual dimension became stronger. More people are being baptized, and more people pray on a regular and frequent basis (Levada 2011). The data suggest that growing commitment to religion and religious belief has little or no influence on the moral dimension. In particular, the non-acceptance of acts that are also criticized or even condemned by most churches, like abortion, euthanasia, divorce, or homosexuality, has dropped markedly between 1991 and 2005 according to the Academies (Kääriäinen 2009: 61).

Overall, the vitality of religion in the New Russia increased gradually since 1991. This is true for both of Greeley's dimensions: affiliation and belief; and for three of Kääriäinen's indicators: the institutional dimension, the importance of religion, and the belief dimension. Both collective ritual and moral dimension seem not to be influenced by growing belief, relevance, or affiliation. In particular, the general commitment to religion and religious faith became significantly stronger. This does not seem to have practical implications; it appears to be more of a mindset. This study does not examine why religion became more vital in the New Russia, but only why religion became part of the core of state identity-building. Apart from personal preferences among political elites, the growing vitality of religion has made the incorporation of religion not only a responsive and popular political action, but also a political asset, speaking about its legitimizing political affect.

Legitimacy and the "Legitimizing Effect" of Religion

The second independent variable to be analyzed is "legitimacy and the 'legitimizing effect' of religion". Assuming that all political action including state identity-building is more likely to find popular and mass support when it is perceived to be both legally and politically legitimate, I argue that the "religious turn" in state identity-building was taken because of the perceived legitimizing effect of religion. The more religion can contribute to political legitimization, the more likely political actors are to use religion in state identity-building. To test this hypothesis, it is necessary to explore how political elites use religion to create legitimacy, and whether this correlates with the "religious turn" in state identity-building.

Legitimacy is central to the creation of political community and hence for state identity-building. Any political regime, no matter whether democratic, authoritarian, or totalitarian, seeks legitimacy. The concept of legitimacy pertains to how political power can be used in ways that citizens consciously accept (Gilley 2006:499). The absence of legitimacy not only reduces popular mass support but also increases the vulnerability to government or regime change (Gilley 2006:499). To ensure legitimacy is therefore a key political project. Sources of political legitimacy can be virtually anything of "common interest" (Easton 1965:312-319). This shows how closely responsiveness and legitimacy are connected.

One source of political legitimacy can be found in religion. Its legitimizing effect has not been systematically conceptualized yet, but general concepts of legitimacy can be applied. Bruce Gilley develops three indicators of legitimacy along the legal and the political sphere: Views of legality, views of justification, and acts of consent. He operationalizes them through the dimensions of attitudes and actions (Gilley 2006:505). This section seeks to make sense of why religion in state identity-building may enhance political legitimacy. This means that the indicator reflecting legality can be neglected. The conceptualization of the political sphere—consent and justification—will be borrowed. Hence, the legitimizing effect of religion will be measured using two indicators. The first indicator reflecting consent is public trust in religion, especially in Orthodoxy. Whenever people trust in religion and religious actors (maybe even more than in politics and political actors), it can be rational for political actors to enhance their own legitimacy by complying with religion with respect to their relations with religious actors. The scope of compliance may range from symbolic politics to dense cooperation.

The second indicator reflecting justification links religion with the political history of the state. Through the ways in which political actors employ certain interpretations of religion and its role in the history of the country, they attempt to make sense of and give reason to the present; justifying, legitimizing. This mechanism is referred to as the "reinvention of tradition". The theorem of the reinvention of tradition—or invented tradition—has been prominently represented in the humanities and social sciences since the mid-1980s, introduced through the work of Eric Hobsbawm and Terence Ranger (Hobsbawm/Ranger 1983). This constructivist approach claims that recent or even imagined events can be promoted as historical tradition. The authors conceptualize invented tradition as a set of practices that claims to reflect continuity with the past and promotes certain values and norms.

The link to the past represents a response to present novelties, which are used to make reference to the past. Hence, the present is legitimized via the past.

Data on citizens' trust in public actors in the New Russia has been collected regularly by Levada since 1994. Recently, the Russian research holding Romir, affiliated with Gallup International, has also conducted research. Figures are available for the years 2004, 2011, and 2013. Also, Timmo Kääriäinen and Dmitri Furman contributed data to the study of trust for the 1990s and for 2002. The guiding question of the data evaluated is to what extent people trust in public actors

There is one data feature that may cause bias for this study, and this is connected to the choice of public actors by the surveys. The public actors chosen come from the spheres of politics, media, military and intelligence, law, and religion. The sphere of politics is presented in great detail, i.e. it includes the president, the prime minister, the government, the parliament, political parties, unions, and even regional authorities. The sphere of religion is represented by "the church" (tserkov'), meaning solely the ROC. The Patriarch or other religious actors, including those representing other faiths, are not included. The evaluation of the data on politics suggests significant variations in trust among different political actors. While the president was fully trusted by 64% of the respondents in 2007, trust in the parliament was only 7% (Levada 2013b). It is a matter of speculation whether there might be similar variations within the sphere of religion, but a more analogous choice of actors for the surveys would exclude biases.

It is striking that all the surveys indicated that the Orthodox Church was undisputedly the most trusted public actor during the politically turbulent 1990s. Following Levada (which employs the three categories of full trust, not full trust, and no trust at all), between 46% and 32% of the respondents fully trusted the church. Overall, the trust in non-political actors was markedly higher than in political actors. After the church, respondents expressed trust in the army (26–36%), the media (20–26%), and the Federal Security Service (FSB) (12–20%) (Levada/Intercenter 2012:43). The rating for the president (at that time Boris Yeltsin) ranged between 2% and 22%. During the last years of Yeltsin's term, his public trust rating declined to 2% in 1998 and 1999. In these years, 72% and 75% said that they would not trust him at all. No other public actor had such a low rating. Respondents also expressed very low levels of trust in the parliament, the government, and political parties (most of the time < 10%) (Levada/Intercenter 2012:43). In this context, the church was without doubt a successful exception among all public actors. This great divide in trust between the church as a religious actor and political players must have been observed by the political elites.

When Vladimir Putin took office in 2000, the church retained a relatively high level of trust. In the 2000s, public trust in the church was most stable out of all actors, with ratings usually exceeding 40%. In the 2010s, trust in the church even exceeded 50%. However, most interesting is that some political actors dramatically improved in trust surveys. Most significant is the increase in trust in the president. In 2000, his first year in office, Putin achieved a 45% trust rating compared with Yeltsin's 2% in 1999. The level of trust in Putin gradually increased to 70% in 2007 and 2008, and he became the most trusted public actor even during his popularity crisis that started in 2010, always followed by the church as the eternal bridesmaid. Most political actors benefited from the growing trust in the president (and, from 2008, the increasing trust in the prime minister), but on a relatively low scale that would rarely meet 20%, as Levada suggests (Levada/Intercenter 2012:43f.). Romir supports the trends for recent years. Though employing five categories instead of three[10], the data suggest a greater expression of full trust in the church than in the president for 2013 (Romir 2013). This study cannot explain whether the growing trust in the president and other political actors from 2000 was caused or at least influenced by the "religious turn", and therefore whether the incorporation of religion within state identity-building provoked the improvement of the (in the president's case, more or less personal) trust ratings.

What can be concluded is that at the beginning of Putin's term, it was decided that religion and religious actors were to be treated as a serious political force because the church was the only widely trusted public actor. In this respect, it was a rational decision to employ both religion and the church (as its most important actor) in political narratives on the building of state identity. As for trust, initially there was virtually nothing to lose—only to gain—by co-opting the trust accorded to the church. Once in office as president and premier minister, it was rational to maintain or even deepen what had been imposed, not only to benefit from public trust in the church, but also for the sake of control over the church, which, due to its popularity and trust, had potential influence over the people. Evaluating the figures, no public actor other than the church has been trusted as stable and reliable over time. Rationally, this could not and still cannot be ignored in political decision making.

The second factor that made religion and church prone to play a crucial role in state identity-building is the transition period faced by the New Russia, especially the political and economic hardships of the 1990s. All state identity was lost with the end of the socialist experiment and the break-up of the Soviet Union. Separatist movements challenged the New Russia. In this respect, there was a state identity gap that needed to be filled. Just like all other 14 successor states of the Soviet Union, the New Russia enforced the "reinvention of tradition" to build and legitimize its

10 The categories employed by *Romir* are full trust, partial trust, partial distrust, no trust at all, and no opinion.

new state identity. For this reason, religion has been employed in political narratives as the missing link between the vague past and the present (historicization), and at the same time has been made the cultural core of tradition (culturalization). The data to be analyzed are political statements reflecting the master narrative.

Except for the commemoration of World War II and the victory over the Third Reich, political narratives in the New Russia tend to reference periods of history that are vague and lack contemporary witnesses. The Kievan Rus' and Tsarist (rather than Imperial) Russia seem to be the most common references. Inevitably, the lack of data for these periods makes the use of history in narratives appropriate for current political reinterpretations, including the utilization of religion in narratives. It is striking that both the Rus' and Tsarist Russia mark exactly the periods in Russian history in which religion and politics, church and state were connected in symphonia. Orthodoxy was part of state identity, unlike in revolutionary or Soviet times.

The historicization of religion—or the religionization of history—starts in rather symbolic and sometimes subtle ways. In Putin's first term, religion and Orthodoxy did not yet make it to the top of the narrative agenda, though the root of what was later promoted as state identity can be traced. The first inauguration ceremony and its non-public component held in the cathedral illustrate the symbolic but yet semi-public dimension. In his inauguration speech in May 2000, Putin employs the history of Russia several times, connecting it to the present, contrasting the country's grandiose past with the difficult times it was facing in 2000. The Kremlin as the historical center of Russia shall become the starting point for his historical mission as president, leading the New Russia into a better future. The language he uses to describe his future presidential tasks is inspired by religious terminology. For Putin, the presidency, which in the first instance focuses on calming the troubled country, is his "sacred duty" (Putin 2000a).

With the beginning of his first term, Putin starts to pay visits to various sites all over the New Russia, many of which are Orthodox monasteries and cathedrals[11]. All statements during and after these visits include the same line of topoi: The site just visited represents the grandiose but yet difficult history of Russia. The history of Russia is linked with Orthodoxy. Orthodoxy has promoted Russian statehood and

11 Putin's visits during his first two years in office included the Pechersk Lavra Monastery (Kiev, April 2000); the Isakyevsky Cathedral (St Petersburg, April 2000); the Christ the Savior Cathedral (Moscow, April 2001); the Dormition of the Most Holy Theotokos/ Pskov-Pechersky Monastery (Pskov, August 2000); the Archimandrite John Monastery (Kriestyankin, August 2000), the Trinity-St Sergius Monastery (Sergiev Possad, January 2001) the Solovetski Monastery (Solovetski Archipelago, August 2001); the Cathedral of the Transfiguration of the Savior (Pereslavl- Zalessky, January 2002); the Cathedral of the Assumption (Vladimir, January 2002).

hence, needs to play a crucial role in Russia today[12]. These occasions certainly serve Putin's personal image-building, but they also announce the emerging historicization of religion, respectively Orthodoxy, in state identity-building. In narratives, Russian Orthodoxy becomes a special and inseparable feature of Russia's political history. Russian and Orthodox history gradually merge into one. As of 2013, Russian history equals Orthodox history according to the master narrative. This can be referred to as the "one-history-paradigm".

The one-history-paradigm, first and foremost introduced by Vladimir Putin, became prominent among senior political actors in the New Russia. In 2011, then President Dmitri Medvedev reflected on the role of Orthodoxy in history: "And at that time I realized that the history of our country—Russia, the history of Rus'—is at the same time the history of Orthodoxy. For me it really was a period of discovery, particularly because of the well-known ideological dogmas imposed during the Soviet period" (Medvedev 2011). Apart from the adaption of the paradigm, Medvedev assumes the role of an ordinary citizen of the New Russia who only starts to understand the relevance of Orthodoxy—unlike Putin, who claims he was secretly baptized in Soviet times and has always worn a cross—even when serving as a KGB officer in the former East Germany. These two stereotypical approaches to religion represented by two key political actors allow all citizens to identify with religion, no matter whether they had done so even during Soviet times or are just about to.

Making the historical Kievan Rus' the cradle of both the Russian state and Russian Orthodoxy implies exceeding current state borders. Senior Russian political actors tend to make more-or-less subtle claims towards Ukraine and Belarus using the narrative of shared Orthodox history. On the occasion of the 1025th anniversary of the baptism in 2013, Putin explains the historical Orthodox brotherhood between the three states and its political impact: "Orthodoxy has become a spiritual buttress for the Russian state and for our national consciousness, uniting Russia, Ukraine, and Belarus through strong bonds of brotherhood. It is symbolic that a joint steering committee headed by Patriarch Kirill of Moscow and All Russia was formed to organize the combined celebrations of the 1025th anniversary of the Baptism of Rus in our three nations" (Putin 2013c). The New Russia is, in this imagined brotherhood at least, prima inter pares.

Paying political tribute to the imagined "spiritual unity", Putin awards Russian state decorations to the highest representatives of the Ukrainian Orthodox Church, which had already been granted to ROC officials (then Patriarch Aleksii II: Aleksei

12 See Putin's visit to the monastery in Pskov in August 2000, http://www.newsru.com/arch/religy/03aug2000/putincerk.html.

Ridiger) in January 2001. The award for the Ukrainian clerics is justified by employing Orthodox history: "Please let me sincerely congratulate you on receiving Russian state decorations and allow me to recall, as was said earlier, our common history, which began so long ago. Our spiritual unity began with the Baptism of Holy Rus' 1025 years ago. Since then, much has happened in the lives of our peoples, but our spiritual unity is so strong that it is not subject to any action by any authority" (Putin 2013d).

The focus on Russian Orthodoxy for the history of Russia has been accompanied by statements on the relevance of other religions. Some of the statements are reminiscent of the conceptualization of the hierarchies of religious denominations in the 1997 law on Freedom of Conscience and Religious Associations, wherein the special role of Orthodoxy is defined while other faiths are mentioned in subordinate clauses. Among other faiths, the greatest attention is given to Islam as the second-largest religious denomination. Unlike the narratives on Orthodoxy, those on Islam are ambiguous. On the one hand, Putin has sent his congratulations to the Muslim community on religious holidays and highlighted the social relevance of Islam (Putin2013e; Putin 2013f). On the other hand, he uses meetings with Muslim spiritual leaders to warn about Islamism and terrorism (Putin 2013g; Putin 2013h).

Apart from promoting shared history, the one-culture-paradigm makes Orthodoxy an inseparable and unique part of Russian culture and the church its advocate. In 2006, describing the historical role of the ROC, Putin states that: "It helped to not only preserve faith but also national identity, (…) native culture, language and the spirit of Russia" (Putin 2006a). As such, the church is perceived not only as a religious or spiritual institution, but also as a proactive cultural institution supported by the state. On the occasion of the Day of Slavic Writing and Culture in 2012, Putin emphasizes the church's wide-ranging contribution to culture and education for the New Russia: "The Russian Orthodox Church plays a special role in organizing the celebrations in honor of the great educators Cyril and Methodius. Together with the state, it actively promotes respect for Slavic languages and cultures, strengthening the fundamental moral values and unity of Orthodoxy" (Putin 2012b). In such narratives, Russian cultural traditions merge with Orthodox traditions. One example is the promotion of Orthodox Easter as Russian culture by Vladimir Putin in May 2013: "Easter brings hope and joy to millions of people, inspiring them to do good and turning them towards the fundamental spiritual values that have played such an important part in Russia's history and feed our national culture" (Putin 2013i).

Although it becomes clear that religion is employed as the cultural capital of the country that links the past with the present, the culturalization remains vague. Dmitri Medvedev elaborates on the ROC's contribution to the country: "The Russian Orthodox Church has always been the guardian of our people's cultural traditions, defending our holy places over the centuries and serving our country's unity and togetherness" (Medvedev 2012a). Similarly, Vladimir Putin argues: "You do much for patriotic education, so that even when abroad, our people do not lose their spiritual ties to their homeland" (Putin 2013j). The main contribution, according to the master narrative, is a certain spirit and a certain set of values, which create civic attitudes—in particular, a sense of unity and patriotism. This, again, is not bound to national borders.

Overall, religion—respectively Orthodoxy and the ROC—has been employed to enhance political legitimacy on the levels of acts of consent and justification. Public trust in the church has been relatively high and stable since 1991, whereas political actors ranked lowest in the 1990s. The reinvention of tradition uses the historization and culturalization of Orthodoxy to create a master narrative. The one-history-paradigm merges Russian and Orthodox history into one shared history. The one-culture-paradigm amalgamates Orthodox and Russian cultures into one common culture. By making the most trusted public actor a reliable historical partner and advocate of culture over centuries, political actors use the legitimizing effect of religion and church in state identity-building. Primarily, this serves the domestic dimension, but the outreach—at least in the cases of Ukraine and Belarus—transcends territorial borders.

Performance and the "Creation of Unity"

The third independent variable to be analyzed is "performance and the 'creation of unity'". Assuming that state identity-building is more likely to create a feeling of "belonging" to the state when political performance is evaluated positively, I argue that the "religious turn" in state identity-building was taken because it was perceived to enhance political performance. The more that religion can contribute to political performance, the more likely political actors are to employ religion in state identity-building. To test this hypothesis, it is necessary to explore how political performance can be enhanced by employing religion or religious actors, and whether this correlates with the "religious turn" in state identity-building.

Political performance has been a blurry but nevertheless popular concept in political science and public management for measuring the achievements of political actors, especially for comparative purposes. Most of the research has been conducted on the question of who is performing best (e.g. among various sub-types of democracy or among democracies and non-democracies) and what factors can enhance performance. According to the mainstream literature, political performance refers to the evaluation of the outcomes of the political process (Fuchs 1997:2). In this sense, performance is the perceived result of political action. The main focus is on what emerges from the political process, not on the political process itself. Yet, the concept lacks key dimensions: who is the evaluating group, and on what criteria is the evaluation based? Scholars propose various sets of indicators for measurement, based on "political productivity" (Almond/Powell 1996:144f.), "measures of the political process, policy outputs and policy outcomes" (Lijphart 1999), or the "socio-economic outcome" (Roller 2001). These different approaches reflect the variety of political science-based analyses of performance, and imply the need to define carefully who is evaluating what out of the aim of the research and the respective political context.

For the present study on state identity-building, the performance-evaluation criteria are borrowed from the formulation of key political objectives that target state identity. Political objectives will be identified by interpreting presidential inauguration speeches. We then explore what religion—respectively Orthodoxy—can contribute to enhance political performance, as perceived and expressed by political actors. This narrative analysis employs speeches and public addresses on religion or the role of religious actors with respect to the state.

In his first inauguration speech in May 2000, Vladimir Putin was rather vague about the policy objectives of his presidency. However, he addresses both the formal and informal institutions on which he intends to focus as president. The formal institutions that he wishes to strengthen can be summarized as an accountably "modern democratic state" that serves the people according to the legislation (Putin 2000a). The informal institutions almost invariably refer to state identity-building. He defines his main political objective as follows: "I consider it my sacred duty to unite the people of Russia and to gather citizens around the clearly-defined tasks and aims to remember, every minute of every day that we are one nation and we are one people. We have one common destiny" (Putin 2000a). Putin aims to create unity (edinstvo). This policy objective remains his priority, even after more than a decade in leading political positions (Putin 2013a). However, the sense of the narrative of unity has been changing over time. In 2000, the idea of unity was relatively vague. From the political context, unity must be understood as a synonym for territorial integrity and as an antonym for secession. In this respect, unity refers to shared territory. From this very existential meaning, it has been gradually moving away—via a unity of shared history of a great nation and its revitalization through policy both domestically (Putin 2004a) and internationally—towards a unity of shared values and spirituality (Putin 2012a). As of 2013, the narrative of unity asks for more actual commitment to the state than in 2000. It is not only the commitment to shared territory, but also to shared history and shared values. Also, the radius of unity expanded from the domestic to the international dimension. Unity refers not only to preserving territorial integrity, but also to demonstrating the strength of

Russia to the world. While the narrative of unity is expanding, the preservation of what has been achieved politically becomes more prominent and a linked policy objective. This is labeled stability (stabil'nost').

Political actors in the New Russia have employed religion and religious actors, especially the ROC, to enhance their performance in a twofold way: Firstly, they have created narratives that link policy objectives—mostly historically—to Orthodoxy or directly to the ROC. This is to underline political and religious isomorphism, or to imply convergence of ideas. Secondly, they have publicly called for religious actors, particularly the ROC, to engage in achieving certain joint policy objectives; with the recent implementation of compulsory religious education courses in public schools, this even takes an institutionalized form (Shnirelman 2012:263ff.). What started as a "dialogue" (Putin 2005b) about current issues, is now openly called "cooperation" (historicized, symphonia) by both political and religious actors (Putin 2013k and Gundaev 2013a).

The creation of the narrative on the convergence of ideas started early during Vladimir Putin's first term and has been prominent ever since. One of the most decisive statements on shared objectives was made by Dmitri Medvedev in 2012: "The Russian Orthodox Church has always been the guardian of our people's traditions, defending our holy places over the centuries and serving our country's unity and togetherness.“ (Medvedev 2012b) According to Medvedev, not only the state, but also the ROC has traditionally promoted Russia's unity. From the political perspective, the church has been supportive in creating the spirit of belonging: identity. As early as 2000, Putin specifies the actual contribution by the ROC to the unity and future of the country: "Russia's revival, the growth of its power, is impossible without strengthening the moral foundation of the society. The role of the Russian Orthodox Church for this is enormous" (Putin 2000c). The church's tool to unite people is the proliferation of certain values that provide society with a "moral foundation". On top of this set of values, the New Russia can, according to Putin, regain strength and influence. For him, a certain moral foundation is the precondition to achieve political objectives.

The ability to promote values and to reach people spiritually is obviously something that Putin believes only religious actors possess; by implication, political actors lack this skill, even though they need it politically in order to unite people. In other words, churches have something to offer to the people that the state cannot provide. Putin has noted this on several occasions, most decisively in 2005: "The Church, like no other organization (…) is probably closer to people, works with people and gives them hope. This emphasis on moral support is very important for Russian citizens" (Putin 2005a). It becomes clear that the political demand of what Putin calls the "moral foundation" creates a state-dependency from the church. Unity cannot be achieved by political efforts alone. The political sphere needs the spiritual or religious sphere to achieve unity as the main policy objective—as a stepping-stone towards what Putin calls "Russia's revival". The exact meaning of this revival remains undefined, except that it reflects a positive development by applying the best from the past in order to benefit the future. The openness and ambiguity of the term allows people, political and religious actors to use their imagination, and to project their own wishes and hopes onto it.

The role of religion in building unity has been prominent, according to Putin. He warns of what might happen to the unity of the New Russia if religion was neglected in politics, employing his interpretation of the past: "It was in large part the erosion of our spiritual and national foundations and the real persecution of the Russian Orthodox Church and our other traditional faiths that set our unified country on a course of destruction and precipitated it into revolution, upheaval and fratricidal conflict and war" (Putin 2013k). According to Putin, the suppression of religion and loss of the religious and spiritual values promoted by churches caused what he refers to as the dark side of Russian political history, including violence, bloodshed, and radical political change. Remarkably, the Soviet period is not explicitly mentioned or condemned, even though religion was officially banned during those times. Instead, the events of revolution and upheaval are demonized. This evaluation of uprisings most probably refers to the protests in the aftermath of fraudulent elections in 2011/2012, and in this respect, it also reflects self-protection. The quote further indicates how different political narratives—those on the "loss of religion" and the narrative of "turmoil"—are combined into one of cause and effect, irrespective of any empirical evidence.

The potential of religion and the ROC for enhancing political performance in uniting the New Russia has not only been stated verbally, but also employed politically. During his second presidential term, Putin institutionalized meetings with religious actors, particularly with representatives of the ROC. In September 2004, he outlines how he is planning to continue the collaboration with religious actors: "I also think that it is extremely important now to further develop cooperation between religious groups and the state, to cooperate in the interests of solving nationwide tasks" (Putin 2004b). By cooperation, Putin means that religious organizations are supposed to serve the state in what he calls "nationwide tasks". These are obviously objectives defined by his political agenda.

Putin outlines a number of social services that he wants the ROC and other churches to conduct, thereby relieving pressure and responsibility from the state: "The Russian Orthodox Church plays a major role in bringing people together around common spiritual values. Today, in close cooperation with other faiths, community organizations and the government, it is doing much to strengthen civil accord and moral principles, support the institution of family, protect motherhood and childhood, and educate young people in the spirit of patriotism and respect" (Putin 2004b). The enumeration of duties that go beyond spiritual services includes various tangible policy objectives of the Putin administration, most of them connected to demography and education.

One of the main social issues Putin has been trying to cope with is easing the demographic crisis, particularly by increasing birth rates (Rotkirch et al. 2007:349ff.). The policy offensive has been introduced in several steps. Starting from 2007, families were granted significant financial support from the state. Producing and raising children has been rewarded by the state with social benefits, cash bonuses and credits representing as much as $13,500 US in 2013. In addition, maternity leave has been significantly increased (Putin 2013l). The year 2008 was announced the "year of family", 2009 the "year of the youth". Families have been encouraged by Putin to have an average of three children (Putin 2012c). Apart from demographic issues, education has made it to the top of the political agenda in recent years. Higher education has undergone particularly extensive reforms, including the merging of educational institutions and the introduction of federal universities (The Concept of Establishing and Funding the Development of Federal Universities 2009:1ff.). The curriculum for public schools has been broadened by making religious education compulsory from the school year 2012/2013 (Shnirelman 2012:263ff.). The Armed Forces of the Russian Federation have been recently joined by Orthodox priests, who serve an educational role as military chaplains (Herspring/McDermott 2010:51ff.).

Putin asks for the engagement of religious actors in the policy fields of both demography and education. With respect to family issues, Putin believes churches share similar views, including his policy objective of increasing the birth rate, as evidenced by the church's promotion of family values. There is evidence for a high degree of convergence between state and church objectives. In the Basis of the Social Concept, the ROC's fundamental statement on political and social issues, the family is defined as the "initial cell of human society", which demands special protection (Russian Orthodox Church 2000). It is within the realm of education that Putin believes the ROC and other churches can best target and promote spirituality and convergent values. The political objective is building patriotism—a positive attitude that creates commitment to the state—out of general spirituality. This clearly refers to his general objective of uniting people, and of strengthening their identity with the state—the New Russia. The religious sphere is employed to serve the political sphere. For this service in favor of the state, the state permits churches to enter the public sphere and to conduct "church business" within the scope of the state's control. The informal cooperation agreement in this sense reflects a mutual do ut des-relationship—or symphonia of the 21st century.

The ROC takes the opportunity of conducting social services for the state, and thus enhances the political performance of the state by supporting policy objectives. In February 2013, Patriarch Kirill explicitly enumerates the ROC's socio-political engagement and thanks Putin for "the cooperation that we are carrying out with many state institutions" (Gundaev 2013a).

The collaboration between state and ROC has been criticized regarding the constitutionally guaranteed secularity of the state. Putin reluctantly addresses the criticism in February 2013: "There is greater demand than ever today for the state authorities and all of the traditional faiths to work together in cooperation and partnership. We are a secular state of course, and cannot allow state life and church life to merge, but at the same time, we must avoid too, a vulgar and primitive interpretation of what being secular means" (Putin 2013k). Putin makes secularity not only an elastic clause, but also accuses criticism of the actual church-state relationship as being "vulgar" and "primitive". He clarifies the role of religious actors for the state and his support as follows: "The Russian Orthodox Church and our other traditional faiths must have all the possibilities for carrying out full and real service in important areas (…)" (Putin 2013k).

Apart from the contribution to the unity of the country, the ROC also promotes Putin's policy objective of stability, which headlined his recent presidential campaign. Ironically, the mass protests of 2011/2012 took place exactly when the narrative of stability was most prominent. During these times, representatives of the ROC explicitly supported not only stability but also Putin, respectively his image as the guarantor of stability. In May 2012, Kirill reflects on the collaboration with the Putin administration: "I hope that the wonderful progress we have made over these years will not be stopped by any political upheavals and that Russia will continue to advance, continue to gather spiritual and material strength (…)" (Gundaev 2012b). Like Putin, the Patriarch perceives protests as politically harmful and warns that if they continue, the New Russia could lose track and even lose what has been achieved. Overall, leading ROC representatives have been supportive of Putin's political course and his way of ruling the country. The most prominent statement of endorsement was made by Kirill in February 2012, when he described Putin's terms as a "miracle of God". Considering Putin's starting point after Boris Yeltsin's presidency, Kirill stated that Putin had "rectified the crooked path of history" (Gundaev 2012a).

The current state of convergence and collaboration in social policy fields between political and religious actors is reminiscent of the historical relationship between the ROC and state that was created in the 1830s. The contemporary slogan "Autocracy, Nationality, Orthodoxy" introduced a policy of joint efforts of state and church (particularly in education) to build a generation of citizens who felt a religious and political double-identification, and seems to reflect today's situation. In the symphonia of 2013, the ROC steps outside the religious sphere and becomes a political actor by serving policy objectives. In doing so, the ROC contributes to enhancing political performance

Conclusions

This chapter focused on why Vladimir Putin made a political decision to incorporate religion in state identity-building, employing Russian Orthodoxy as its core narrative. State identity-building is a top-down political project in which political actors employ narratives in an attempt to create a form of belonging among citizens, and between the citizens and the state. The making of identity is a key political challenge that ideally provides an idea that is shared by the majority, around which identification takes place. This study was based on the assumption that the inclusion of religion is by no means a consequence of historical determinism, i.e. that the Soviet era of promoting state atheism must automatically be followed by a period of endorsing religion. Instead, the meta-theoretical approach of the rational actors' paradigm was used to explain the emergence of religion. Political decisions are therefore seen as rational, focusing on benefits and avoiding both cost and risk. In the context of the dissolution of the Soviet Union in 1991 and the emergence of the New Russia, formal institutions obviously failed to guarantee the country's territorial integrity, political stability, and economic development. This challenge was left to informal institution-building in the form of a new state identity-building project. The Russian Federation initially lacked a state identity, and had lost several state identity traditions. The building of state identity headed Vladimir Putin's political agenda around the turn of the millennium, when his inauguration speech highlighted his "sacred duty" to unite the people of Russia.

The research design is based on an x-centered variable system. The dependent variable or explanandum is the inclusion of Russian Orthodoxy in state identity-building. For the independent variables or explanantes, a rational-actor approach was borrowed from Everhard Holtmann and Werner J. Patzelt, which focuses on how political actors seek popular support for their decisions and actions. It explains the perceived success of political decisions on three levels: They need to be responsive and serve the peoples' demands and needs; they must reflect legitimacy, both legally and politically; and they must dispose a performance that is perceived positively.

Russian Orthodoxy is the most prominent feature of Putin's state identity-building. In narratives, Orthodoxy appears as the lowest common denominator that unites the people of Russia—explicitly not only ethnic Russians. The values promoted by the ROC's Orthodox model impose Putin as both the genome of all Russianness, and also the "moral foundation" not only of Russia's statehood but also of all the countries that share the baptism of the Kievan Rus' (Belarus, Ukraine). According to Putin, these spiritual values have created the enormous strength and the grandiose achievements of Russia over the centuries. The Orthodox model unites all believers and at the same time differentiates them from "the West". While Orthodoxy demands commitment not only on a private but also on a public (state) level, non-Orthodox societies tend to lose their spiritual core and drift towards arbitrariness and degradation. The Orthodox model is the God-given root of Russian otherness, both civilizational and political. Putin claims a Russian Sonderweg (sovereign democracy) and links this to the tradition of a strong state: Russia's inner strength defines its natural destiny as a great power, and the inevitable restoration of its leading status in the international arena. Despite Russia's ethnic and religious diversity, Orthodoxy is promoted in a much more prominent way than so-called "other traditional faiths".

One factor influencing the political decision for the inclusion of Orthodoxy is rooted in responsiveness. Starting from the perestroika period, public religion increases in relevance and vitality. The institutional dimension is strengthened by a growing number of believers and a shrinking number of non-believers and atheists. Affiliations with the church increase significantly. Figures show a slight growth in the perception of the importance of religion in life. More people consider themselves as believers (in God, in the Devil, etc.). Collective ritual behavior remains relatively uncommon, which means that people would rather not attend church services on a regular basis. However, individual ritual behavior such as baptism or marriage becomes more popular. Moral attitudes are not influenced by the growing vitality of religion. In summary, there is greater general commitment to religion and religious faith, which corresponds with its inclusion in state identity-building. Due to the growing popularity of personal religious identity, the inclusion of Orthodoxy becomes a rational political strategy for state identity-building.

A second factor explaining the political relevance of Orthodoxy is rooted in the way religion can be used to construct legitimacy for political decisions and actions. Through narratives, religion can enhance legitimacy. Under the leadership of Vladimir Putin, the instrumentalization of Orthodoxy had a legitimizing effect through the public's trust in religion and religious actors. According to various data sources, the ROC was the most trusted actor during the politically turbulent 1990s. All political actors had extremely poor ratings, lower even than the army, media, and FSB. After 2000, the ROC continued to increase in popularity, achieving more than 50% trust. The only actor to overtake the church's popularity was the new President Putin, who rapidly overturned Boris Yeltsin's 2% rating to achieve more than 70% in 2007 and 2008. The ROC has since been second-best, but remains the most consistently trusted public actor over time. The legitimizing effect of religion has also come into play because of an enforced "reinvention of tradition" that includes the one-history and the one-culture paradigm. Orthodoxy amalgamated with both history and culture. Russian political history becomes Orthodox history, Russian culture becomes Orthodox culture. As a consequence, Orthodoxy substitutes history and culture. The New Russia—as well as brother and sister Belarus and Ukraine—can be explained by Orthodoxy. The incorporation of religion into politics therefore makes rational sense: riding the crest of the ROC as the most trusted actor, and making Orthodoxy serve both history and culture as a means of constructing legitimacy and national identity.

A third factor facilitating the choice for the Orthodox turn is rooted in how religion can enhance the perception of political performance. With Vladimir Putin taking office, political actors have promoted political and religious isomorphism and highlighted the convergence of ideas between state and church. This starts from the "moral foundations" which the ROC promotes and which the state is in need of, and draws the bow all the way via the shared idea of national/Orthodox unity to the restoration of Russia's lost status in the international arena. Out of the imagined convergence derives the call for cooperation between state and ROC. Putin invited the ROC and other religious actors to contribute to his policy objectives by assuming a role in the provision of social services. The most prominent ones are to educate young people in a "patriotic spirit" in order to strengthen the "moral foundation" of the country, and to support families as the nucleus of the state. They reflect two major challenges for the New Russia: tackling the demographic crisis, and achieving territorial integrity through unity. As a popular and trusted partner, it makes sense to involve the ROC (and other churches) in serving the state and thus enhancing perceptions of political performance. At the same time, state/church cooperation based on imagined convergence of objectives is a useful tool by which to control religious actors.

Overall, making Orthodoxy the core of state identity-building reflects a rational political decision, within which religious sentiment is not the cause but is possibly the consequence that can also be used to convince and attract people on an emotional level. Despite—or maybe particularly because of—the political rationality behind this decision, the emergence of the new relationship has led to criticism far beyond the measures of secularity. The newly established symphonia has to be contextualized within a state in which wider issues, such as separation of powers and pluralism, have been in free-fall. The Putin administration has done a lot either to ban potential opponents or capture them via "joint ventures", and has influenced areas that by democratic means should not be interwoven with politics. Religion and state identity-building in the New Russia perfectly fit within this pattern.

References

Data Sets

Academy of Finland; Russian Academy of Sciences (1991–2005) Religion and religiousness in Russia 1991–2005. http://www.fsd.uta.fi/en/data/catalogue/all_archived_by_series.html#uuv

Levada-Center: Yuri Levada Analytical Center (2010a) Do you believe in the existence of hell? (Berite li vy v sushstestvovannie Ada?). http://www.levada.ru/archive/religiya/verite-li-vy-v-sushchestvovanie-ada

Levada-Center: Yuri Levada Analytical Center (2010a) Do you believe in heaven? (Berite li vy v Tsarstvo Nebesnoe?). http://www.levada.ru/archive/religiya/verite-li-vy-v-tsarstvo-nebesnoe

Levada-Center: Yuri Levada Analytical Center (2011) Religious belief in Russia (Religioznaya vera v Rossii). http://www.levada.ru/26-09-2011/religioznaya-vera-v-rossii

Levada-Center: Yuri Levada Analytical Center; Interdisciplinary Academic Center of Social Sciences (Intercenter) (2012) The Russian public opinion herald (Vestnik Obshstestvennogo Mnenia) 17. http://www.levada.ru/sites/default/files/vom2_2.pdf

Levada-Center: Yuri Levada Analytical Center (2013a) Religion and church in social life (Religia i tserkov' v obshshestvennoi zhizni). http://www.levada.ru/18-04-2013/religiya-i-tserkov-v-obshchestvennoi-zhizni-0

Levada-Center: Yuri Levada Analytical Center (2013b) Trust in state authorities (Doverie institutam vlasti). http://www.levada.ru/07-10-2013/doverie-institutam-vlasti.

Research Service "Sreda" (2012) Arena – atlas of religion and ethnicity (Arena – Atlas religii I natsional'nostei Rosii). http://sreda.org/arena

Romir Research Holding (2013) For belief, tsar, and fatherland (Za veriu, tsar i otechestvo). http://romir.ru/studies/499_1378238400

Policy Papers and Law

The Russian Orthodox Church: The basis of the social concept: church and state (2000) https://mospat.ru/en/documents/social-concepts/iii/

Ministry of Education and Science: The concept of establishing and funding the development of federal universities (2009)

http://xn--80abucjiibhv9a.xn--p1ai/%D0%B4%D0%BE%D0%BA%D1%83%D0%BC%D0%B5%D0%BD%D1%82%D1%8B/2005/%D1%84%D0%B0%D0%B9%D0%BB/107/41d3da2569937282f1f3.pdf

Law on Freedom of Conscience and Religious Associations (1997) http://www.cesnur.org/testi/Russia.htm\

Literature

Agadjanian A (2001) Public religion and the quest for national ideology: Russia's media discourse. Journal of the Scientific Study of Religion 40:351–365
Alapuro R, Mustajoki A, Pessonen P (2012) Understanding Russianness. New York
Anderson BR (1983) Imagined communities: Reflections on the origin and spread of nationalism. London
Bellah RN (1967) Civic religion in America. Daedalus 96:1–21
Brubaker R, Cooper F (2000) Beyond "identity". Theory and Society 29:1–47
Bruner J (2001) Self-making and world-making. In: Brockmeier J; Carbaugh DA (eds) Narrative and identity: studies in autobiography, self and culture. Amsterdam, pp 25–38
Casanova J (1984) The politics of the religious revival. Telos 20:3–33
Cerutti F, Lucarelli S (2011) The search for a European identity. New York
Daniel WL (2006) The Orthodox Church and civil society in Russia. Texas A&M University Press
Easton D (1965) A systems analysis of political life. Chicago
Erikson EH (1968) Identity: youth and crisis. New York
Fagan G (2012) Believing in Russia—religious policy after communism. New York
Fuchs D (1997) Kriterien demokratischer Performanz in liberalen Demokratien. Berlin
Gilley B (2006) The meaning and measure of state legitimacy: Results for 72 Countries.
European Journal of Political Research 45:499–525
Greeley A (1994) A religious revival in Russia? Journal for the Scientific Study of Religion 33:253–272
Herspring DR, McDermott RN (2010) Chaplains, political officers, and the Russian armed forces. Problems of post-communism 57:51–59
Hobsbawm E, Ranger T (1983) The invention of tradition. Cambridge
Holtmann E (2008) Einleitung. In: Holtmann E, Patzelt, WJ (eds) Führen Regierungen tatsächlich? Zur Praxis gouvernmentalen Handelns. Wiesbaden
Hosking G (1998) Russia: people and empire. Harvard, pp 1552–1917
Huntington SP (1993) The clash of civilizations? Foreign Affairs 72:22–49
Iyall Smith KE; Leavy P (2008) Hybrid identities: theoretical and empirical examinations. Leiden

Kääriäinen K (1998) Religion in Russia after the collapse of communism. religious renaissance or secular state? London
Kääriäinen K (2009) Religion in Finland and Russia in comparative perspective. In: Pickel G,
Müller O. Church and religion in contemporary Europe: results from empirical and comparative research. Wiesbaden, pp 49–64
Kamens DH (2012) Beyond the nation-state: the reconstruction of nationhood and citizenship. Bingley
Kaufman LA (1990) The anti-politics of identity. Socialist Review 90:67–80
Knox Z (2005a) Russian Orthodoxy, Russian nationalism and Patriarch Aleksii II. Nationalities Papers 33:533–545
Knox Z (2005b) Russian society and the Orthodox Church: religion in Russia after communism. New York
Knox Z (2008) Religious freedom in Russia: The Putin years. In: Steinberg MD, Wanner C (eds) Religion, morality, and community in post-soviet societies, pp 281–314
Lieberman RC (2002) Ideas, institutions, and political order: explaining political change. The
American Political Science Review 96:697–712
Luckman, Th. (1967) The invisible religion: the problem of religion in modern society. New York
Maier H (2007) Political religion: a concept and its limitations. Totalitarian Movements and Political Religions 8:5–16
Marsh, Ch. (2011) religion and the state in Russia and China: suppression, survival, and revival. New York
Marx K (1844) Philisophisch-oekonomische Manuskripte. Paris
Meinecke F (1922) Weltbürgertum und Nationalstaat: Studien zur Genesis des deutschen Nationalstaates. Munich
Melucci A (1989) Nomads of the present: social movements and individual needs in contemporary society. Berkeley
Mitrokhin L (1993) post-communist Russia: spiritual renaissance and religion. In: Pishchik YB (Ed.) Russian culture at the threshold of the third millennium of Christianity. Moscow
Norris P, Inglehart R (2004) Sacred and secular: religion and politics worldwide. Cambridge
Panov P (2010) Nation-building in post-soviet Russia: what kind of nationalism is produced by the Kremlin? Journal of Eurasian Studies 1:85–94
Pickel G; Müller O (eds) (2009) The comparative empirical view on religion and religiosity. Church and religion in contemporary Europe: results from empirical and comparative research. Wiesbaden, pp 7–12

Richters K (2013) The post-soviet Russian Orthodox Church: politics, culture and greater Russia. New York
Rotkirch A, Temkina A, Zdravomyslova T (2007) Who helps the degraded housewife? comments on Vladimir Putin's demographic speech. European Journal of Women's Studies 14:349–357
Sarcinelli U (2011) Politische Kommunikation in Deutschland. Medien und Politikvermittlung im demokratischen System. Wiesbaden
Service R (2003) A history of modern Russia: from Nicholas II to Putin. New York
Shnirelman VA (2012) Russian Orthodox culture or Russian Orthodox teaching? Reflections on the textbooks in religious education in contemporary Russia. British Journal of
Religious Education 34:263–279
Smith AD (1991) National identity. London
Somers MR (1994) The narrative constitution of identity: a relational and network approach. Theory and Society 23:605–649
Taylor, Ch. (1994) Multiculturalism: examining the politics of recognition. Princeton, pp 25–73
Touraine A (1981) The voice and the eye: an analysis of social movements. Cambridge
Van der Heijden J (2011) Institutional layering: a review of the use of the concept. Politics 31:9–18
Voegelin E (1938) Die politischen Religionen. Wien
Warhola JW (2007) Religion and politics under the Putin administration: accommodation and confrontation within "managed pluralism". Journal of Church and State 49:75–95
Weber M (1904/1905) Die protestantische Ethik und der Geist des Kapitalismus. Archiv für Sozialwissenschaft und Sozialpolitik 20/21, 1-54/1-110)
Willems J (2013) Pussy Riots Punk-Gebet: Religion, Recht und Politik in Russland. Berlin

Statements, Speeches, and Public Addresses

EU Statement on Freedom of Expression in the Russian Federation (2012) http://eeas.europa.eu/delegations/vienna/documents/eu_osce/permanent_council/2012/pc_923_eu_on_fom_in_russia.pdf
Gundaev VM (2012a) http://www.interfax-religion.com/?act=news&div=9049
Gundaev VM (2012b) http://eng.kremlin.ru/news/3381, 2012
Gundaev VM (2013a) http://eng.kremlin.ru/news/4925
Medvedev DA (2011) http://eng.kremlin.ru/news/3032, 2011

Medvedev DA (2011b) http://eng.kremlin.ru/news/1765
Medvedev DA (2012a) http://eng.kremlin.ru/news/3670
Medvedev DA (2012b) http://eng.kremlin.ru/news/3670, 2012
Putin VV (2000a) http://news.bbc.co.uk/2/hi/world/monitoring/media_reports/739432.stm
Putin VV (2000b) http://www.religion-online.org/showarticle.asp?title=2099
Putin VV (2000c) http://www.newsru.com/religy/03aug2000/putincerk.html
Putin VV (2004a) http://archive.kremlin.ru/eng/speeches/2004/05/07/0100_type-82917type127286_64200.shtml
Putin VV (2004b) http://archive.kremlin.ru/eng/speeches/2004/09/29/1946_type-82912type
82913type84779_77365.shtml
Putin VV (2005a) http://archive.kremlin.ru/eng/speeches/2005/06/10/1937_type84779_89383.shtml
Putin VV (2005b) http://archive.kremlin.ru/eng/speeches/2005/09/15/0232_type84779_93895.shtml
Putin VV (2006a) http://archive.kremlin.ru/eng/speeches/2007/05/19/1950_type-82912type84779
type127286_129746.shtml
Putin VV (2012a) http://eng.kremlin.ru/news/3749
Putin VV (2012b) http://eng.news.kremlin.ru/news/3892
Putin VV (2012c) http://eng.kremlin.ru/news/4739
Putin VV (2013a) http://eng.kremlin.ru/news/6007
Putin VV (2013b) http://eng.kremlin.ru/news/3672
Putin VV (2013c) http://eng.kremlin.ru/news/5758
Putin VV (2013d) http://eng.news.kremlin.ru/transcripts/5790
Putin VV (2013e) http://eng.kremlin.ru/news/6121
Putin VV (2013f) http://eng.kremlin.ru/news/5825
Putin VV (2013g) http://eng.kremlin.ru/transcripts/6155
Putin VV (2013h) http://eng.kremlin.ru/news/4334
Putin VV (2013i) http://eng.news.kremlin.ru/news/5360
Putin VV (2013j) http://eng.kremlin.ru/news/4925
Putin VV (2013k) http://eng.news.kremlin.ru/news/4926
Putin VV (2013l) http://eng.kremlin.ru/news/5049
Putin VV (2013m) http://eng.kremlin.ru/news/5475
Putin VV (2013n) http://eng.kremlin.ru/news/5783
Putin VV (2013o) http://eng.kremlin.ru/transcripts/6157
Putin VV (2013p) http://eng.kremlin.ru/news/5747

Resurrection of the Temple. The Role of the State in Shaping Regional Political Identity

Nadir Kinossian

Introduction

The disintegration of the USSR in 1991 left Russia's new leaders without a "defining idea" (Gill 2005:494); recently, the Russian political leadership has clearly demonstrated that religion should play a stronger role in the search for such. For example, at the 2012 pre-election meeting with the leaders of the "traditional religious communities", Vladimir Putin—then the Prime Minister and a presidential candidate—stated that, "since the collapse of the Soviet Union, our country has lived through turbulent times and, in moral questions, could not rely on anything else except for religious values". Putin then added, that the "primitive" Soviet understanding of the norm of separation of church and state must be replaced by "a completely different regime of relations—that of partnership, mutual assistance and support". Putin called for "active, direct, effective, daily participation of religious organizations in the life of society and state" (Russian Orthodox Church 2012).

These partnership relations have manifested most visibly in various projects to restore religious buildings, historic sites, and monuments, which thereby transformed the symbolic landscape of the post-socialist city. The resurrection of the Cathedral of Christ the Savior in Moscow has become the most prominent resurrection of a religious building during the post-socialist period (Sidorov 2000). Political and business elites have taken an active part in restoring religious buildings, looking to shape the national identity and expand a base of popular support.

Regional elites also implemented various symbolic projects, although different in scale and nature to those implemented in the center. Region-based political identity projects aim to create an alternative ethno-national identity and therefore actively exploit ethnic, linguistic, and religious differences between the center and provinces. According to Graney (2007), the city of Kazan, the capital of the Tatarstan Republic, "has undergone a remarkable transformation and 'repackaging' to serve the republic's goal of extending its sovereignty and institutionalizing greater ethno-cultural pluralism in the Russian Federation" (p. 18).

Although the political motivation behind these processes has been acknowledged, the role of the state in shaping regional political identities has received relatively modest academic reflection. This chapter seeks to contribute to the current debates by addressing the question of why, during the post-socialist period, the local state actively participates in the reconstruction of religious buildings. The chapter focuses on the reconstruction of religious buildings inside the Kazan Kremlin during the period 1995 to 2005.

Nationalism and Political Identity

The collapse of communism in Eastern Europe produced dramatic transformations of urban symbolic landscapes, which involved erasing traces of the "unwanted past", often by destroying material legacies associated with it (Leach 2002), accepting a once-rejected past (Frierson 2010), and celebrating national and religious identities via monumental art and architecture (Adams 2008).

According to nationalist doctrines, the nation-state is a 'natural' outcome of ethnic political mobilization based on a shared sense of belonging, common language and culture, and a shared vision of the past and future of the nation. In contrast to the essentialist conceptualizations of nationalism, Roeder (2007) argues that new nation-state projects emerge from pre-existing segmental states (e.g., federations) and require state resources to succeed. Apart from resources, the successful implementation of a nation-state project requires the establishment of political-identity hegemony, which "consists of both the relative predominance of a national identity within 'the people' and the relative empowerment of a cohort of politicians associated with that project within 'the homeland'" (Roeder 2007:83). In order to establish and strengthen political-identity hegemony, secessionist political leaders foster national cultures and use their powers "to create research centers that develop and write national histories; to maintain archives, libraries, and museums that preserve and display the monuments of this history" (Roeder 2007:149–150).

Everyday social practices play a central role in the formation of the "socio-spatial consciousness" that marks the perception of spatial belonging, and we-ness and other-ness. The socio-spatial consciousness is reinforced through education, culture, politics, economy, administration, communication, etc. (Paasi 1996:66). Dominant groups promote specific interpretations of the past, which became known in heritage studies as "the authorised heritage discourse" (Smith 2006). Identity and heritage are mutually reinforcing concepts, as the latter supports claims over territories and borders, and implies the right to interpret and use the past for the purposes of contemporary politics (Graham et al. 2000).

Despite its potential political significance, heritage has very little intrinsic worth apart from the value people attach to it through lenses such as nationality, religion, or ethnicity (Graham and Howard 2008:2). Heritage as a discursive concept can help to analyze the transformation of symbolic landscapes, and to illuminate the relationship between political leaders, governing institutions, and ethnic and religious groups in interpreting the past and re-creating the meaning of cityscapes, monuments, and important sites (Harrison 2010; Littler and Naidoo 2005).

The role of the state in constructing the new political identity of the region has been particularly visible in Tatarstan, where the authorities have made considerable efforts to introduce a 'national component' into the cityscape (Hughes 2007). In Kazan, these efforts manifested most vividly in the post-socialist reconstruction of the Kazan Kremlin.

Reconstruction of the Kazan Kremlin

The Kazan Kremlin dates back to the pre-Russian period. In 1445, Kazan became the capital of the Kazan Khanate (1445–1552) following the disintegration of the Golden Horde. In 1552, Kazan was conquered by the Russian Tsar Ivan the Terrible; the Kazan Kremlin was ruined and most of the defenders and civilians were killed. The Russian period lasted until 1990, when Tatarstan declared its independence from the Russian Federation. In the early 1990s, Russia's ethnic republics started making claims for extended political and economic rights, first in the USSR and later in the Russian Federation. The main drivers of the 'sovereignty' movements were issues of political power, control of natural resources, and fiscal aspects of center–periphery relationships. During that period, regions and the federal center became engaged in a complex negotiation process, arranged on a one-to-one basis, to define mutually acceptable conditions of federalist relations (Dowley 1998).

The nationalist leaders of Russia's ethnic republics used national identity as a means to secure political support both inside the region and in front of the authorities of the central state. Nationalist elites in ethnic republics used ethnic and religious identification, in addition to memories of Russification and earlier deportation, to create new post-socialist identities (Johnson 2005:22). National identity was used "as a rallying banner to claim autonomy and threaten separatism in order to obtain special status and additional resources from Moscow" (Castells and Kiselyova 2000:177).

In Tatarstan, the authorities used several key components, including the discourses of ethnicity and post-colonialism, media and language policy, religion, architecture, and heritage to create the republic's new political identity (see Rolich 1999; Davies 2000; Yuzeev 2005).

Ambitions of secession gave rise to debates about rebuilding Kazan as the capital city of a 'sovereign' state. In November 1992, a group of Tatar nationalists and Muslim activists published an open letter to then-President Shaimiev, claiming that "the churches in the Kazan Kremlin were built "on the graves of Tatars and the foundations of their mosques", and demanded that the authorities rebuild mosques inside the Kremlin walls" (cited in Graney 2007:21). Later, a group of architects proposed to commemorate the restoration of Tatarstani statehood by 'resurrecting' the historical Kul-Sharif Mosque that was destroyed as a result of the Russian invasion of 1552. The idea initially received a mixed reception, but later gained numerous supporters (Khalitov 1997:234).

The Kazan Kremlin became a prime site on which new political identities of semi-sovereign Tatarstan were staged. In 1994, the "State historical, architectural, and arts Museum-Reserve Kazan Kremlin"1 was established for the "preservation and development of historical and cultural heritages of the peoples of Tatarstan and revitalization of the Kazan Kremlin as the historical, cultural, and administrative center of the Tatarstan Republic" (President of Tatarstan 1994). Initially, it was proposed to restore the Kremlin on the basis of preservationist principles, using archival data and archaeological surveys (Aidarov and Khalikov 1994).

The Tatarstani Academy of Sciences responded negatively to the proposed concept, due to its alignment with the Soviet historiography tradition that saw the Kremlin as a "product" of Russian architecture. Architecture historian Niaz Khalitov—then Deputy Director of the Museum-Reserve—explained that the concept entirely excluded the idea of new construction in the Kremlin (Khalitov 1997:235). According to Khalitov, the proposed conservation approach inevitably raised the question as to what exactly had to be preserved (p. 235).

Adherence to the conservation approach implied restoration of only those buildings that could be verified by historical data. Such an approach would imply reconstruction of Russian churches and monasteries, which previously populated the Kremlin. However, that would be inappropriate on political and moral grounds, because the reconstructed churches would become "monuments to the barbaric demolition of buildings sacred for the Muslim population of Kazan: mosques, tombs of khans and the saints" (Khalitov 1996, 1997a:237). To avoid this, Khalitov suggested that the whole approach to historical heritage should be critically reviewed, because "reconstruction of the Kremlin as a stronghold of state power and a symbol of its state history today is not a mere architectural task but also a political act, and its necessity could not be doubted" (Khalitov 1997a:238–239).

Eventually, the issue was resolved when Mintimer Shaimiev—then President of Tatarstan—endorsed new construction in the Kremlin. The Presidential Decree "On the concept of preservation, development, and use of the ensemble of Kazan

1 Museum-Reserve Kazan Kremlin web site: http://www.kazan-kremlin.ru/mzkk/

Kremlin" (1995) ordered the restoration of the Blagoveshchenskii (Annunciation) Cathedral (built 1556–1562) and the recreation of the Kul-Sharif Mosque (President of Tatarstan 1995).

In December 1995, the Tatarstani government announced a design contest for "the best project for the resurrection of the mosque (Kabinet Minisrov RT 1995). The design brief created many opportunities for design teams to interpret what ought to be built, but—at the same time—gave no clarity as to what the actual design would look like, and offered no information on possible sources of knowledge that might be used to collect information about the legendary mosque; it was left to the contestants to decide whether to align with the *conservation* approach and consider the Kremlin as predominantly Russian architectural ensemble, or to align with the *reconstruction* approach oriented more towards recreating the Kremlin as the center of the capital of the Tatarstan Republic.

The siege of 1552 left the Kazan Kremlin in ruins, making it difficult to find any reliable data about the pre-Russian period. The lack of information about the original mosque made its "resurrection" difficult. Not only was the appearance of the mosque unknown, but even its location within the Kremlin was yet to be found (Sitdikov 2006:110–111). The construction of a large mosque inside the Kremlin—already populated by Russian Orthodox churches and monasteries—raised questions about the impact of the new construction on the existing Russian heritage2. Finally, it was not clear what reaction the construction of a mosque at a predominantly Russian heritage site might cause in Moscow and among the Russian population of Tatarstan3.

Although the ambition was to make the Kremlin look "more Tatar", the Tatarstani political leaders were also cautious that Moscow might interpret the construction of the mosque as a sign of the region's growing Islamization. The proposal to restore both Christian and Muslim monuments was therefore intended to demonstrate a balanced approach. The language used in documents also emphasized preservation and restoration rather than new construction.

2 Interview with a professor at the Kazan School of Architecture, June 2007, Kazan.

3 Interview with a senior planner at a design institute, January 2007, Kazan.

Figure 6.1. The Kul-Sharif Mosque in the Kazan Kremlin. Destroyed in 1552, 'resurrected' in 1996–2005. Photo by the author, 2011.

After the grand opening on 24 June 2005, the Mosque became a part of the museum-reserve of the Kazan Kremlin, which had operational control of the building. To emphasize a broader cultural role of the building, a small museum of Islam was organized in its basement. The Muslim Religious Board of the Republic of Tatarstan opposed locating a museum in the Mosque building on the grounds that visitors to the museum might consume tobacco and alcohol during public receptions. The city's chief architect responded that the presidential decree made provisions for a museum, and it would therefore be built (Ivanicheva 1997b:4).

Despite the apparent loyalty of the Muslim clergy to the political regime, the authorities carefully measured out the level of influence the clergy could gain over such a symbolically important site as the Kazan Kremlin. According to the government decree, the use of the mosque for mass religious events was restricted to two festivals per year: *Uraza Bairam* and *Kurban Bairam*. During the rest of the year, the mosque would mainly be used as a museum (Kabinet Minisrov of Tatarstan 1995).

Figure 6.2. Blagoveshchenskii (Annunciation) Cathedral and Kul-Sharif Mosque in the Kazan Kremlin. The cathedral was built from 1556 to 1562, renovated in 1994–2005, except for the bell-tower demolished in 1928. Photo by the author, 2011.

On 24 July 2005 Blagoveshchenskii Cathedral was opened after a reconstruction that lasted nine years. Mintimer Shaimiev—then President of Tatarstan Republic—stated that the decision to work simultaneously on the two sacred sites, Russian Orthodox and Muslim, was a gesture of historic justice and harmony between two traditional for Tatarstan religions (Shaimiev 2005).

The way the authorities implemented the reconstruction of the Kazan Kremlin was not unanimously supported. Questions were raised as to whether the construction of a new huge Mosque inside the protected historic site of the Kremlin (although presented as the 'resurrection' of something previously in existence) could be justified: "the Mosque is being reconstructed despite the fact that the only thing known about it is the number of minarets. Why not restore the ancient Spasskii Cathedral from the 16th century, which has a perfectly preserved basement as well as all necessary archival data?" (Zhuravskii 1995).

The Russian community of Tatarstan expected that the reconstruction of the Kazan Kremlin in line with the presidential decree would have done more for the

Russian monuments—churches and monasteries—destroyed or damaged during the Communist period. For example, the reconstruction of Blagoveshchenskii Cathedral was only partial: while the interiors and facades were restored, its 50-meter tall bell-tower, which was demolished in 1928, was not reconstructed.

The Society of Russian Culture in Tatarstan Republic on numerous occasions approached the authorities in Tatarstan raising issues related to preservation of church buildings but have not received a satisfactory answer. At a conference titled *Russians in Modern Tatarstan: Status, Problems, and Search for Solutions* held in Kazan in 2011, Russian civil right activists complained about a "hostile decision" of the Tatarstani authorities to open the Museum of History of the Tatar Statehood inside one of the church buildings located in the Kremlin. The activists added, that it seems to be acceptable to have a Tatar museum in the former church building, but it would be unthinkable to use a mosque building to accommodate a museum of Russian history (Ordinsky 2011).

State–Religion Relations

Mintimer Shaimiev—then President of Tatarstan—stated that "the destiny of the mosque is the destiny of the people" (President of Tatarstan 2001). Not everyone regarded the active support for a mosque project by former communists as an unproblematic proposition. A chief research fellow at the Tatarstan Republic Academy of Sciences noted that Shaimiev supported the resurrection of the mosque for purely political reasons, "as a communist and post-communist political leader and an atheist at heart; as a symbol only, but without any religious or spiritual contents"4. A senior member of staff within the Tatarstani President Administration offered a more down-to-earth explanation of state involvement in the mosque project: "the context of the project was historical but the task was political"5.

During the 1990s, the main political task of the Tatarstani leadership was strengthening the special semi-sovereign status of Tatarstan within the Russian federation which created certain economic advantages not available to 'ordinary' regions. These advantages took the form of direct aid or fiscal privileges granted by the Russian government. Gaining these privileges could significantly affect regional economic prosperity (Valuev 2007). Competing for these privileges with other regions required the deployment of various techniques, including political bargaining and secessionist threats (Solnick 1998).

The mosque project helped to substantiate claims for larger political and eco-

4 Interview, January 2007, Kazan.

5 Interview, June 2007, Kazan.

nomic autonomy via its powerful image and location inside the predominantly Russian cultural landscape. One informant explained that:

The Mosque in the Kremlin was not about faith… It was selected as a symbol of threat—hostile threat… They exploited the weakness of the central state… Kazan used the possible disintegration of Russia as an opportunity to take advantage in the competition for federal financial flows… It was all about frightening and blackmailing a weak Russia…6.

The Tatarstani authorities only considered the nationalists useful when their claims were directed at the Russian authorities and not at the balance of power within the republic (Ponarin 2007). Once the special status of Tatarstan was established via a bilateral treaty in 1994, the Tatarstani authorities began to sideline nationalist leaders. While the authorities did everything to destroy the nationalist movement, they also made efforts "to organize the spiritual life of the wide Tatar masses on the basis of Islamic values… that is, linked to state support for the construction of mosques and the establishment of Russia's Islamic University" (Mukhametdinov 2006:84). The authorities considered mass mobilization around Islam to be more acceptable than that around the nationalist ideology because it was easier to establish political control over religious organizations than over the nationalists.

By getting involved in religious affairs, the authorities tried to 'kill two birds with one stone'. On one hand, they sought to contain the nationalist movement while on the other attempting to prevent the emergence of radical *Wahhabism* Islam in Tatarstan: In order to contain the threat of *Wahhabism*, the state offered the Muslin clergy of Tatarstan the approved version of Islam. The political advisor to the president actively theorized on the specifically Tatar version of Islam—*Djadidisme* or *Euroislam* (see Khakimov 2003, 2005). Euroislam was thought to be fundamentally important for securing inter-ethnic peace in the region where peoples of different nationalities and religious beliefs could peacefully coexist.

In Tatarstan, the Muslim clergy accepted such state involvement, resulting in "an unambiguously paternalistic" attitude of the Tatarstani authorities towards the clergy, and put the clergy in a dependent position in front of the state (Mukharyamov 2006:57). According to a Kazan-based journalist, in Tatarstan:

> Religion was used as an instrument of political marginalization of people and sacralization of the authorities. That is why the authorities were 'making advances' to the religious leaders. Long ago, religious leaders had been co-opted into the system of power. Both the Chair of the Muslim Religious Board of the Republic of Tatarstan (Gusman Hazrat) and the Archbishop of Kazan Anastasii were driven in cars with special registration plates issued only to top government officials.

6 Interview, January 2008, Kazan.

> They had been incorporated into the power structure and served that power. Effectively, they became government ministers—one for the Muslim religion, the one for the Russian Orthodox religion7.

In exchange for economic support, religious leaders offered loyalty to the political regime. According to Mukhametshin (2005), one of the leaders of the Tatar Muslim clergy officially opposed any involvement of Muslim religious organizations in politics, but at the same time urged believers to support the political authorities in their regions. He stated that political leaders, especially the presidents of Tatarstan and Bashkortostan, should be granted a lifelong term of office, and also called to prevent the alien ideas of democracy from penetrating public and political life (pp. 190–191).

The extent to which these strategies of creating a "state-authorized religion" worked remains an open question, especially in light of the terrorist attacks that shocked Tatarstan in 2012. Then, as a result of planned attacks, the Mufti of Tatarstan was injured and his deputy killed. Later, a special anti-terrorist unit met with armed response from a group of suspected Islamic terrorists after raiding their property in Kazan. The attacks showed that the authorities seriously miscalculated their level of influence over religion through the existing practices of co-optation and offering material stimulus in exchange for loyalty.

Creating the Post-Socialist Cultural Landscape

The choice to concentrate efforts on reconstruction of the Kazan Kremlin was not accidental. Kazan, once the capital of the Kazan Khanate, was conquered by the Russians in the 16th century, later rebuilt in the Russian architectural tradition, and became a symbol of colonization for many Tatars; conversely, among Russians, the Kazan Kremlin remains a symbol of national unity. This makes the Kremlin a symbolically important site for both dominant ethnic groups.

In order to reflect the region's multi-ethnic nature, the Tatarstani authorities adopted a comprehensive approach to reconstruction of the Kazan Kremlin, which implied resurrection of both the Kul-Sharif Mosque and also Russian monuments. A special administrative unit—the Museum-Reserve Kazan Kremlin—was created to oversee the reconstruction. The authorities mobilized financial resources from large government-controlled industries, the republic's oil production company, OAO 'Tatneft' that sponsored the resurrection of the Kul-Sharif Mosque and the OAO 'Kazan Helicopters' that paid for the reconstruction of Blagoveshchenskii Cathedral.

While there was no information on either the original location or appearance

7 Interview, June 2008, Kazan.

of the historical mosque, architects designed a new building in response to contemporary demands. The 'implanting' of the Mosque into the cultural landscape dominated by Russian Orthodox monuments helped to substantiate regional claims for sovereignty and strengthen ethnic and religious identities within the republic. The very close proximity of the resurrected mosque to Orthodox churches and monasteries acted to support the claims of harmonious coexistence of different peoples in the multiethnic Tatarstan, and promoted ethnic and religious tolerance as a fundamental component of Tatarstani national identity.

Despite the declared balanced approach, the Tatarstani authorities dedicated most effort to the completion of the Mosque project, doing as little as possible for the restoration of Russian heritage within the Kazan Kremlin: the Spaso-Preobrazhenskii (Savior-Transfiguration) Monastery still lies in ruins; Blagoveshchenskii Cathedral was only partially reconstructed. Although then-President Shaimiev denied that the Tatarstani state offered Muslim religious organizations preferential treatment, a prominent Tatarstani cleric claimed that "with no doubt, President Shaimiev should be given credit for having so many mosques constructed during such a short period of time" (Yakupov 2006:97).

The preferential treatment of Muslim religious organizations was also visible in other areas. While the Muslim Religious Board of the Republic of Tatarstan was settled in a refurbished building in the center of the city, the offices of The Kazan Diocese of the Russian Orthodox Church were located in a remote area of the city (Ponarin 2007:214). The mechanism of 'voluntary donations' also worked in a specific way. As the deputy chair of the Russian Cultural Society explained, the Society approached several businessmen asking for charitable donations to support its cultural and educational projects. Although businesses would not refuse, in principle, to support a Russian charity, they had been ordered by the authorities to support numerous Tatar cultural activities and could not afford to support both Tatar and Russian projects. The businessmen said that if there had been an order from the authorities to also support Russian charities, they would have done so[8].

Conclusions

Efforts by Tatarstani authorities to add more 'religious flavor' to the city's cultural landscape have revealed some important aspects of state–religion interaction during the post-socialist period. The rebuilding of the Kazan Kremlin took place after the communist ideology collapsed and Russia faced an 'ideological vacuum'. The return to "traditional values" based on ethnic, linguistic, and religious identities was

8 Interview, May 2008, Kazan.

by no means predefined or inevitable. The evidence from Kazan suggests that the process was far from being a 'natural' transition from communism to nationalism. The restoration of religious symbols was part of nationalist leaders' strategic choice to employ religion to create a new political-identity hegemony required for the successful implementation of the state sovereignty project.

The political leadership of Tatarstan used religion to strengthen their claims for secession from Russia. These claims were used to extend the economic, fiscal, and political privileges of Tatarstan *vis-à-vis* the central authorities. Claims for cultural revival were always accompanied by those for economic and political autonomy. The leaders also used symbolic architectural projects to strengthen their legitimacy with the central state and the population of Tatarstan. The transformations of the cultural landscape delivered a clear message to the central government in Moscow: that Tatarstan was different from the rest of Russia and was seeking greater autonomy. The resurrection of the mosque was one of the symbolic attributes of a nation—along with the declaration of state sovereignty, the constitution, the presidency, and monumental art and architecture. The simultaneous reconstruction of the Russian Orthodox Cathedral showed that the political leaders of Tatarstan were also prepared to respect the rights of Tatarstan's Russian population.

The transformations of the cultural landscape contributed to debates on the relationship between religion and state. The political authorities clearly took the lead, whereas religious authorities were generally compliant and subsumed into the structure of political power and economic relations. The resurrection of the mosque did not mean that the Muslim clergy were permitted to exercise any degree of power within the Kremlin: the group for whom the mosque was ostensibly provided was only allowed to use it by permission of the landlord—the government-controlled Museum-Preserve Kazan Kremlin.

The Kul-Sharif Mosque became a symbol of Tatarstan's 'official version' of Islam: insulated from local politics, loyal to the authorities and supported by the regional government. The authorities carefully nourished the state-sponsored religion trying to contain popular nationalism and prevent the spread of radical Islam within the region. Terrorist attacks in Kazan during 2012, in which two moderate Muslim clerics were attacked and one of them killed, raised concerns about whether the Tatarstani authorities managed to 'kill two birds with one stone' or, indeed, missed both. The publicly-acknowledged failure of the authorities to recognize and contain the threat of emergence of radical Islam in Tatarstan has rendered the previous claims of religious peace and harmony less credible.

References

Adams J (2008) Monumentality in urban design: The case of Russia. Eurasian Geography and Economics 49(3):280–303

Aidarov S, Khalikov, N (1994) The concept of reconstruction, development and use of the ensemble of Kazan Kremlin. Unpublished document, Kazan

Castells M, Kiselyova E (2000) Russian federalism and Siberian regionalism. City 4(2):175–198

Davies H, Hammond P, Nizamova L (2000) Media, language policy and cultural change in Tatarstan: Historic vs. pragmatic claims to nationhood. Nations and Nationalism 6(2):203–226

Dowley K (1998) Striking the federal bargain in Russia: comparative regional government strategies. Communist and Post-Communist Studies 31(4):359–380

Frierson C (2010) Dilemmas of post-soviet identity in Vologda. A sacred landscape in Moscow's shadow. In: Bassin M, Ely C, Stockdale M (eds) Space, place and power in modern Russia. Northern Illinois University Press, Dekalb, pp 218–242

Gill G (2005) Changing symbols: the renovation of Moscow place names. The Russian Review 64 (July):480–503

Graham B, Howard P (2008) Introduction. Heritage and identity. In: Graham B, Howard P (eds) The Ashgate research companion to heritage and identity. Ashgate, Aldershot, pp 1–18

Graney K (2007) Making Russia multicultural. Kazan at its millennium and beyond. Problems of Post-Communism 54(6):17–27

Graney K (2009) Of Khans and Kremlins. Lexington Books, Lanham

Harrison R (ed) (2010) Understanding the politics of heritage. Manchester University Press, Manchester

Hughes C (2007) The influence of ethnicity and nationalism on soviet and post-soviet urbanization in Tallinn, Estonia and Kazan, Russia (Geography Department, Macalester College). http://digitalcommons.macalester.edu/ cgi/viewcontent.cgi?article=1011&context=geography_honors. Accessed 24 Sept 2008

Ivanicheva O (1997a) Ch'ya Doroga Vedet k Khramu? Kazanskie Vedomosti, 24 May

Ivanicheva O (1997b) Mechet′ Kul-Sharif: Okonchatel′nyi Vybor Sdelan, Kazanskie Vedomosti, 31 May

Johnson J (2005) Religion after communism: belief, identity, and the soviet legacy in Russia. In: Johnson J, Stepaniants M, Forest B (eds) Religion and identity in modern Russia. Ashgate, Aldershot, pp 1–25

Kabinet Minisrov of Tatarstan (1995) O kontseptsii sokhranenia, razvitiya i ispolzovaniya ansambliya Kazanskogo Kremliya, Tatarstan Republic Government, Decree No. 927, 19 December 1995
Khakimov R (2003) Where is our Mecca? Manifest of Euroislam. Institute of History at the Academy of Sciences of Tatarstan Republic, Kazan
Khakimov R (2004) Euro Islam in the Volga region. Journal of South Asian and Middle Eastern Studies 27(2):1–13
Khalitov NH (1997) Polemika Vokrug Rekonstruktsii Mecheti Kul-Sharifa v Kazanskom Kremle. In: Islam v Tatarskom Mire: Istoriya i Sovremennost'. Kazan, The Institute of History of the Tatarstan Republic Academy of Science, 29 April–1 May 1996, pp 233–250
Leach N (2002) Erasing the traces. The 'denazification' of post-revolutionary Berlin and Bucharest. In: Leach N (ed) the hieroglyphics of space. reading and experiencing the modern metropolis. Routledge, London and New York, pp 80–91
Littler J, Naidoo R (eds) (2005) the politics of heritage. Routledge, London and New York
Mukhametdinov RF (2006) Ideino-Politicheskie Techeniya v Postsovetskom Tatarstane, 1991–2006 gg. (Kazan: Tamga)
Mukhametshin R (2005) Islam v Obshchestvennoi i Politicheskoi Zhizni Tatar i Tatarstana v XX Veke. Tatar Publishing House, Kazan
Mukharyamov N (2006) Islam v Povolzh'e: Politizatsiya Nesostoyavshchayasya ili Otlozhennaya? In: Matsoozato K (ed) Imperiology: from empirical knowledge to discussing the Russian empire, Sapporo: The Slavic Research Centre, Hokkaido University, pp 13–69
Ordinsky V (2011) Russians in modern Tatarstan: status, problems and search for solutions. http://www.apn.ru/publications/print25467.htm. Accessed 20 June 2013
Paasi A (1996) Territories, boundaries and consciousness. The changing geographies of the Finnish–Russian border. John Wiley & Sons, Chichester
Ponarin E (2007) Potentsial radikal'nogo Islama v Tatarstane. In: Iskhakov D (ed) Sovremennaya Tatarskaya Natsiya, Kazan: The Academy of Sciences of Tatarstan, pp 201–228
President of Tatarstan (1994) O Sozdanii Gosudarstvennogo Istoriko-architekturnogo i Khudozhestvennogo Muzeya-Zapovednika "Kazanskii Kreml", Decree No. 4, 22 January 1994 (Kazan)
President of Tatarstan (1995) O Kontseptsii Sokhraneniya, Razvitiya i Ispolzovaniya Ansamblya Kazanskogo Kremlya, Decree No. 764, 13 November 1995 (Kazan)
President of Tatarstan (2001) Polumesyatsy na Vsekh Minaretakh Kul-Sharif, President's Address, 5 October 2001, Kazan. http://president.tatar.ru/news/view/8409. Accessed 4 Sept 2009

Roeder PG (2007) Where nation-states come from: institutional change in the age of nationalism. Princeton University Press, Princeton and Oxford

Rolich A-A (1999) History, collective memory and identity: the Tatars of sovereign Tatarstan. Communist and Post-Communist Studies 32:379–396

Russian Orthodox Church (2012) Stenogramma vstrechi predsedatelia Pravitelstva FR VV Putina so Sviateishim Patriarhom Kirillom i liderami traditsionnih religiosnih obshin Rossii. htttp://www.patriarchia.ru/db/print/2005767.html. Accessed 17 Jan 2013

Shaimiev M (2005) Vistuplenie Presidenta RT na torzhestvennoy tseremonii po sluchaiu zavershenia restavratsionnih rabot v Blagoveshchenskom Sobore goroda Kazani. http://shaimiev.tatar.ru/pub/view/966. Accessed 21 June 2013

Sidorov D (2000) National monumentalization and the politics of scale: the resurrection of the Cathedral of Christ the Savior in Moscow. Annals of the Association of American Geographers 90(3):548–572

Sitdikov A (2006) Kazan'—khanskaia stolitsa. In: Siraev M, Akhmetzianov M, Khasanov A (eds) Navstrechu vechnosti—Seid Kul-Sharif. Idel-Press, Kazan pp 94–118

Smith L (2006) Uses of heritage. Routledge, Oxon

Solnick S (1998) Will Russia survive? Center and periphery in the Russian Federation. In: Rubin B, Snyder J (eds) Post-soviet political order. Routledge, London and New York, pp 58–80

Valuev V (2007) Resurs Etnichnosti v Pozitsionirovanii Regiona v Mire: Respublika Tatarstan, (Kazan, Kazan Institute of Federalism). http://www.kazanfed.ru/papers/1/. Accessed 31 Dec 2007

Verkhovnii Soviet RT (1990) Deklaratsia "O gosudarstvennom suverenitete Tatarskoi Sovetskoi Sotsialisticheskoi Respubliki". Supreme Soviet of Tatarstan Republic, Resolution No. 334-XII, 30 August

Yakupov V (2006) Minimer Shaimiev i Islamskoe Vosrozhdemie v Tatarstane. Iman, Kazan

Yuzeev, A (2005) Islam and the emergence of Tatar national identity. In: Johnson J, Stepaniants M, Forest B (eds) Religion and identity in modern Russia. Ashgate, Aldershot pp 91–105

Zhuravskii A (1995) O Tainakh Kremlevskogo Dvora, Vechernyaya Kazan, 13 December

Strong Emotions, Weak Subjects. On the Role of Hurt Feelings in the Trial against Pussy Riot

Inga Pylypchuk and Heike Winkel

On 17 August 2012, three members of the female activist collective 'Pussy Riot', Nadezhda Tolokonnikova, Maria Alyokhina, and Yekaterina Samutsevich, were found guilty of "hooliganism on the basis of religious hatred" under paragraph 213, part 2 of the Russian Criminal Code. They were each sentenced for two years in prison camps; Samutsevich was later released on probation. The defendants were judged for a performance they staged at the Cathedral of Christ the Savior on 21 February 2012. Wearing colored masks, four members of the group danced and sang at the ambo of Russia's most important Russian Orthodox Church. Immediately after the performance the material was used to compose a music video entitled "Punk Prayer—Mother of God, Chase Putin Away!" including some other scenes with one more group member that were filmed at the Epiphany Cathedral at Yelokhovo, also in Moscow. In the text of the "Punk Prayer", Pussy Riot criticized the close connection between the Russian Orthodox Church and the state, and Patriarch Kirill's support for Putin during the presidential election campaign.

In the very public and controversial trial that took place in August 2012, the issue of "hurt feelings" played a central role and was emphasized in every speech: The statements of the injured party in the court—the believers; the indictment, blaming the group members of religious hatred; and in the almost three-hour verdict of guilt.

The trial marked the culmination of a long, ongoing conflict between Russian Orthodoxy and secular subjects. Until this incident, it had mostly taken place within the sphere of art. The first remarkable event in this respect was Avdey Ter-Oganyan's performance "Поп-арт" (Pop-art), which took place during winter 1998 within the project "Юный безбожий" (Yunyy bezbozhiy—The Young Godless). At the International Art Fair 'ArtManezh' in Moscow, Ter-Oganyan had sold desecrations of copies of icons. This openly proclaimed blasphemy led to an indictment against the artist on grounds of violation of paragraph 282 of the Criminal Code of the Russian Federation. It was submitted by state authorities as a reaction to "multiple complaints of Orthodox believers". Here, for the first time, blunt blasphemy took place in the field of the art, and was persecuted on behalf of believers claiming that their religious feelings were hurt. Almost the same happened in 2000 when Oleg

Mavromati, in an action titled "Не верь глазам" (Ne ver' glazam—Don't Trust Your Eyes) allowed himself to be crucified in the courtyard of the Institute of Cultural Studies in Moscow, close to the Cathedral of Christ the Savior, with a notice on his back stating "Я не сын божий" (Ya ne syn bozhiy—I'm not the son of God). This inversion of the archetypal blasphemy in the history of Christianity, Jesus' claim of being God's son, was again prosecuted by the state. After some other minor incidents, in 2005 two of the curators of the exhibition "Осторожно, религия" (Ostorozhno, religiya—Beware, Religion) were convicted under paragraph 282. They were found guilty of inciting religious hatred, because the exhibition had been attacked by Orthodox radicals.

The persecution of blasphemous art reached a new peak in 2006, with the trial against the curators of the exhibition "Запретное искусство" (Zapretnoye iskusstvo—Forbidden Art). The exhibition gathered works of art that had been banned from public display during the course of 2006, which were then placed behind a large wooden fence with just a few peepholes to look at them. Again, the curators Yuri Samodurov and Andrei Yerofeyev were charged with incitement of hatred against church and state.

Public attention towards such religion-related events had continuously grown, but with the appearance of the punk performance video and the indictment against the members of Pussy Riot, it reached a new peak. What Pussy Riot had done was to bring the conflict between art and religion from the sphere of the art into the very heart of religious life in Russia. No other place in the whole country is more symbolic for the Russian Orthodox tradition than the Cathedral of Christ the Savior. Built 1883 and destroyed just forty years later on Stalin's command, the Cathedral was finally reconstructed in 1997. It immediately became a very visible symbol of Russia's imperial strength, Orthodoxy's post-Soviet revival, and Moscow's special place in the spiritual life, and recently has become a quite controversial building[1].

Our article wishes to contribute to the understanding of the significance of the performance—and especially the subsequent trial that was held against the band members—by exploring the subject of "hurt feelings", that was central in this trial. It will pursue the question of the relationship between obvious and hidden meanings and functions within the discourse on emotions, as well its intended and unintended effects. By doing so, we hope to contribute to a deeper understanding of the present-day role of the Russian Orthodox Church (ROC) in Russia's political and social life. We suggest that, by virtue of its potential to address and express

1 Zoe Knox has recently called the Cathedral of Christ the Savior a "testament to the intersection of church and state" (Knox 2004:121), and Alek Epshtein has given an in-depth-analysis of the cathedral's economic functionalization, which, as Pussy Riot members claim, became a central point of criticism in their performance (Epshtein 2012).

emotions, religion serves as an ideal craft to incite feelings. This potential is used extensively under the circumstances of the strong alliance between church and state that we are witnessing today. By analyzing how this is happening, we aim to provide an assessment of the politics of emotion in present-day Russia, and of how public discourses and politics in general become emotionally charged along with the aggravation of the political situation.

Blasphemy and the Law

To fully comprehend the fundamental role played by hurt feelings in the trial against Pussy Riot as well as in the other recent cases, one must consider their role in Russia's juridical system. There are three paragraphs relevant in such cases. The first is Article 5.26 (2) of the Russian Code of Administrative Offences (KoAP), dealing with the offence of "insulting the religious feelings of citizens or desecration of artifacts, symbols, and emblems of doctrinal significance". The second is Article 282 of the Criminal Code of the Russian Federation. This article sanctions "Actions aimed at the incitement of hatred or enmity, as well as abasement of dignity of a person or a group of persons on the basis of sex, race, nationality, language, origin, attitude to religion, as well as affiliation to any social group". These articles formed the basis for sentencing the curators of the 2005 exhibition "Осторожно, религия" (Ostorozhno, religiya—Beware, Religion) as well as artists in other infamous cases. It would also have been consistent to apply it in the trial against Pussy Riot; however, the court instead referred to Article 213 of the Criminal Code. In her consideration of the trial, Caroline von Gall rightly points out that this is to be understood as an even more rigorous handling of the case, because this article bears close reference to the Soviet-era crime of "hooliganism". This adds a strong political note to the case, as "in the Soviet Union, the article was used as a catch-all clause for any type of opposition to the regime" (von Gall 2013:2). According to von Gall, the post-Soviet Criminal Code of 1996 "expressly raised the requirements for convictions of hooliganism due to the problematic history of that article, but reduced them again in the course of the fight against extremism in 2007. Since then, hooliganism consists, amongst other things, of the motivation to political, ideological, racist, nationalist, or religious hatred" (von Gall 2013:3). Observers agree that the differences between the crimes defined in Articles 282 and 213 are quite blurred, and that by applying the latter the court used an opportunity to hand out a more severe punishment aimed at villainizing the band members[2].

2 Among the first Russian lawyers to give a critical assessment of the trial and to comment on the efforts being made to turn an administrative offence into a crime, was Genri Reznik, president

A brief comparison between the legal situation we find in Russia and those in other countries illustrates its specific nature. In other countries 'religious feelings' are only rarely legally protected by the state anymore. Mostly, they are not considered an entity qualifying as a legally protected good (e.g., Koch 2009:40). In Germany, to name just one example, Article 166 of the Criminal Code does not protect religions themselves or religious feelings, but rather the public peace (Berkmann 2009:19), whereas previous versions of this article both in the German Empire and in the Federal Republic of Germany had still dealt with the crime of a personal offence. This represents a remarkable distinction: an offence against a religious individual subject is not considered a crime nowadays, whereas an offense against the state order by using religion is. From an historical perspective, the shift away from the religious individual to the abstract state order marks the final point of a development that in the literature has been characterized as a secularization of criminal law (Koch 2009:39). Before the Enlightenment, blasphemy had predominantly been understood as an offence against God, the Virgin Mary, or the saints, by either abusing their names or speaking wicked words against them. Therefore, legal codes in countries all over Europe dealt with this crime to protect the Sacred. During the course of the Enlightenment, an alternative understanding of blasphemy became more important, namely the aforementioned attack on believers as citizens. Legal scholars as well as theologists both in Western and Eastern Europe have acknowledged this fact. Sebastian Koch cites German legal scholar Friedrich Carl von Savigny, who in 1848 deduced the importance of blasphemy as an *actus reus* for state policy from the fact that it could cause a severe violation of the religious feelings of a huge part of the nation (Koch 2009:35). This statement serves to underline the interdependence of the emergence of an understanding of blasphemy aimed at individual feelings and the idea of the nation-state[3].

In Russia, the same shift took place considerably later. Criminal Codes from 1845, as well as succeeding prerevolutionary codes, referred extensively to blasphemy, defining it in the traditional sense as an offense against God, the saints or the Church (Ulozhenie 1845:83 ff.). Soviet law, naturally, did not deal with the crime of blasphemy, and only in the 1990s was the offence included in legal codes—this time in the more believer-orientated versions already mentioned above.

---

of the Moscow Chamber of Lawyers (e.g., Reznik 2012).

3 One reason for the changing discourse on blasphemy was, of course, the idea of freedom of religion. In his 'History of Blasphemy in the Christian World', David Nash points out that in the West, blasphemy for a very long time only protected Christianity and has almost never been fundamentally scrutinized, whereas in the globalized multicultural present, numerous religions and faiths make a claim to equality before the law, while liberals wish to abolish blasphemy laws to protect the freedom of speech (Nash 2007:6, 24 f.).

The "Hurt Believer" as a New Legal and Cultural Subject

The 'hurt believer' as an individual citizen is therefore a very new phenomenon in Russian legal history that, nevertheless, has very rapidly entered the center of public attention. To properly assess the implications of this development, one should take into account that hurt religious feelings are a highly controversial philosophical, theological, and legal entity. This becomes evident on several levels. First, there is a very fundamental dispute about the meaning that they are ascribed within philosophical and theological discourse since the Enlightenment, especially amongst Protestants. Some, like Immanuel Kant, Baruch Spinoza, Friedrich Wilhelm Hegel, and others, argue for religion as a rational practice and deny that feelings can play a fundamental role in it. Others, like Friedrich Schleiermacher, considered feelings the essence of religion. Secondly, there is a long-running debate over the existence of 'religious feelings' as a distinct category, as well as their specifics. Those who claim the existence of religious feelings in the philosophical and theological discourse often discuss their meaning in the context of 'religious experience'. Referring to Christian mysticism, these concepts aim to deconstruct the dichotomy of reason and emotion. According to Rudolf Otto, for example, feelings are not to be misunderstood as pure reactions to stimulants. Instead, they are to be seen as a medium of cognition, namely the cognition of the numinous. Due to of their unique reference, there can be proposed a qualitative difference between natural and religious feelings.

Others, like American philosopher and psychologist William James, deny the existence of such a qualitative difference, claiming that there is no abstract "religious emotion" that exists as a distinct mental affection by itself: "There is religious fear, religious love, religious awe, religious joy, and so forth. But religious love is only man's natural emotion of love directed to a religious object" (James 1982:27). Naturally, the question of the existence of Orthodox feelings is currently a highly controversial issue amongst Orthodox theologists. In an effort to demonstrate the existence of religious feelings, the ROC has recently made frequent reference to scholars who engage a natural scientific point of view, such as Fedor Kondratev, a physician and psychiatrist. In his "Мы рождаемся с чувством бога" (My rozhdaemsya s chuvstvom boga—We are born with a sense of God), Kondratev gives a psychiatric explanation for the phenomenon, going back to the history of psychiatry and citing 19th century Russian psychiatrist Sergey Korsakov, who claimed that religious feelings are among basic anthropological feelings. From his psychological perspective, even atheism is to be considered an expression of religious feelings, namely a manifestation of repressed religious feelings (Kondratev 2012). Opponents like Jakov Krotov, liberal nonconformist priest of the Ukrainian Independent Orthodox Church, consider religious feelings an invention from people who are far from religion (выдумка далёких от религии людей—vydumka dalokikh ot religii lyudey)[4]. He states: "A religious person has exactly the same emotions as a non-religious one—the same mechanisms of perceptions; the same motivations. The encounter with God, the belief in Him does not produce any new emotions, but liberates the normal emotions, gives them the opportunity to endless growth. (…) What is usually understood by the expression 'hurt religious feelings' is the normal feeling (emotion) of anxiety"[5].

Given the controversial views on the existence of religious feelings, it seems even more difficult to define the characteristics of 'hurt religious feelings'. When reflecting on this topic, Viktor W. Weichbold suggests that religious education to a large part serves the development and cultivation of emotions. Religious narratives, rituals, beliefs, and ideals are highly charged emotionally[6]. When those values and traditions are suddenly treated without respect and/or without the usual emotional attitude, this can be understood as an offense, causing a negative emotional reaction towards persons who downgrade religious symbols or items (Weichbold 2007:6 ff.).

This means that there are two aspects of 'hurt religious feelings'. First, they occur when, for example, during the performance of a religious ritual the feelings that are experienced in this moment, such as awe or humility, are deformed by unwanted disruptions. Secondly, those disruptions, when regarded as an offence, cause negative emotions directed against the offender. Those two phenomena find their reflection in the wording of the law, which names the insult of religious feelings (Article 5.26 (2) of the Russian Code of Administrative Offences, see above) as well as the incitement of hatred or enmity (Article 282 of the Criminal Code of the Russian Federation, see above). As will be described later, this double meaning becomes quite important during the Pussy Riot trial.

The latest trials have served to greatly establish a subject identified by its hurt

---

4 An invention made by people who are far from religion.

5 У религиозного человека все те же чувства, что у 'обычного'. Те же механизмы восприятия, те же эмоции, те же мотивации. Встреча с Богом, вера в Бога не порождает никакого нового чувства, а лишь высвобождает обычные чувства, открывает им возможность для бесконечного роста. (…) То, что обычно подразумевают под ‚оскорблённым религиозным чувством' есть обычное чувство (эмоция) тревожности.

6 It may be mentioned in this context, that this is a core argument in the discussion evolving around the existence and specifics of religious feelings: Religious feelings representing a specific state of mind, emerging in a specific religious setting. This adds an understanding of a specific intensity of religious feelings, often believed to be higher than the average of natural feelings. As Friedrich Schleiermacher puts it in his "Über die Religion. Reden an die Gebildeten unter ihren Verächtern", asserting that the original task of religion is to stir up emotions in the highest direction (Schleiermacher 1995:132 note 4, 64).

religious feelings in the public spirit. To focus on this aspect means to add another perspective to the assessment of those events, because: in the past, trials of artists and curators on the grounds of violation of Article 282 have mostly been regarded as efforts to restrain the freedom of artistic expression or, to put it in more general terms, the freedom of speech; and as a sign of an ongoing aggravation of the political climate (e.g., Frimmel 2013). In this context, observers have frequently referred to such events as 'show trails'. Sandra Frimmel placed the trial of the curators of the show 'Forbidden Art', that took place in 2006, within the context of the Soviet tradition of staged trials, considering both the early Soviet tradition of 'agitsudy' and the infamous political show trials against various 'enemies within' during the Stalinist era, rightly stating that present-day trials serve the same function: to model an "inner enemy", supposedly acting against the Russian People and state (Frimmel 2013:257)[7]. In this context, the theatricality of those trials is of special significance. As performative spectacles, they serve two functions: first, to produce certain types by means of judicial performative speech acts; and secondly, to present those types to the public. In this context it is important to note that the morally corrupt or depraved inner enemy (of an artist in the former trials; and of liberal, feminist, Western-orientated women in the case against Pussy Riot) is not the only type that is being canonized. The trial deals not only with the offender, but also with the offended. Legal scholars have repeatedly pointed out that the extent to which the court referred to the witnesses' accounts in the trial against Pussy Riot as well as in other trials is quite remarkable and contradicts established judicial standards. Nevertheless, beyond legal considerations, this fact bears a broader significance: hurt believers are more than a medium in the line of juridical argumentation, but a self-contained model for identity-building.

As already mentioned, this type obtained a sort of tradition during recent years. It made a very strong entrance in the trial against the curators of "Осторожно, религия" (Ostorozhno, religiya—Beware, Religion) in 2005. That trial marked the first climax of the ongoing conflict between the ideal of freedom of artistic expression and the rights and interests of the ROC and Orthodox believers. Various expert assessments gave interpretations of the art works that aimed to reveal their shocking and demeaning estrangement of religious motifs and symbols, and

7 Considering the popularity of the analogy it is, however, important to point out a significant difference between the contemporary trials and the Stalinist show-trials. While in Stalinist times, the focus was on the presentation of the figure of the enemy and the performance of his repentance and subjugation under Soviet rule, contemporary trials can not be designed on this premise. Here, the accused usually remain resistant, and no confessions or self-abnegations can be expected. Therefore, the staging of victims becomes an even more important strategy to prove the danger presented by the inner enemy.

numerous witness accounts that where cited at length during the verdict placed a strong emphasis on the shocking impression made on them by the confrontation with the artistic works both in the press and in the gallery. In his account of the trial, Mikhail Ryklin has impressively described the heated atmosphere in the court room, where Orthodox believers constituted a majority of the audience, supporting the witnesses who made their statements (Ryklin 2006). In those statements, the master-plot of hurt feelings was established and extensively repeated, consisting mainly of accounts of the overwhelming effects of perceived or manifest insult or offence. We will return to similar statements discussing the trial of Pussy Riot.

As soon as the 'hurt believer' emerged as a legal subject, critics began to raise questions and doubts regarding its authenticity—and those doubts turned out to be credible. In this context, the remarkable campaign conducted during the trial of the curators of "Forbidden Art" is very revealing. During the examination trial, the civic organization "Гражданская оборона" (Grazhdanskaya oborona—Civic Defense) launched an appeal on its website calling all compassionates to participate as witnesses to the offence, and supplying a specimen letter of complaint to the public prosecution office. This specimen, containing a type of a 'master-plot' for the self-expression of a believer whose religious feelings were hurt, could easily be adopted by individuals. Remarkably, having visited the exhibition was not a condition for qualifying as a witness; it was deemed sufficient to be outraged simply by the show's existence.

Sandra Frimmel gives a description of how representatives of the organization "Civic Defense" helped volunteers to prepare their testimonies by providing notepads to be used while giving their testimonies, pointing out that this resulted in numerous entirely identical testimonies that were obviously not autonomous, authentic accounts but appropriated ones (Frimmel 2013:152 ff.).

This obviously very much resembles the Soviet method of systematically encouraging and demanding statements from the population on all kinds of topics, and subsequently using these to stage political discussions. Back then it was an important propaganda tool, serving to mobilize the population, and a means to legitimate hegemonic policies by suggesting that they were nothing but the execution of public political intent[8]. From the perspective of a political analysis this is, of course, a characteristic of authoritarian politics. However, when understanding court trials as a "generator of autobiographies" (Autobiographiegenerator) (Hahn 1987:12), an institution that engages in encouraging and controlling the emergence and production of identity-building, these discourses and utterances can also be read

8 In the Putin–Medvedev era, this tradition was revived, manifested, among other things, in staged TV press consultations given by the president.

as an attempt to launch a specific pattern of identity. This pattern of an emotionally charged, hurt, and outraged believer has become highly productive in the last couple of years. It is now to be considered a core element in the contribution of the ROC to the discourse on Russian national identity.

It is obvious that in the trial against Pussy Riot as in the previous trials, the hurt believer occupies the center stage. Throughout the trial, the judge systematically ruled out any reference to politics, refused to listen to arguments demonstrating the performance's political character, and dismissed questions by advocates during questioning that related to politics, e.g., about the political content of the lyrics of the Punk Prayer (which, incidentally, was not admitted as a piece of evidence). Legal scholars have pointed out that in its verdict, the court placed remarkable reliance on expert opinions, and the testimonies of the offended and witnesses for the prosecution. The same is true for the indictment, which bears a stunning resemblance to the verdict in the passages citing the testimonies. Obviously, this is not explained by any increased obligation to demonstrate the significance and depth of the offence in the light of a very liberal context, which emphasizes the importance of protecting free speech[9]. Instead, the aim is to produce a performance, and later a text, consisting of recurrent, serial expressions of hurt feelings[10].

Emotions and the Idea of the Nation-State

The reinvention of a coherent and hegemonic Russian national identity after the demise of the Soviet Union became a fundamental project of Russian politics in the Putin–Medvedev era. It is a well-known and widely discussed fact that the ROC plays a leading role in this process of national resurrection, as the Orthodox belief is considered to be a core element of Russian national identity. Numerous scholars have examined how the ROC benefits from this situation, in which it has been ascribed an absolutely dominant position in the nominally secular Russian

---

9 See Nash (2007:24), who notes that the level of need to justify accusation of blasphemy underlies change and depends on the importance given to the issue of tolerance of speech.

10 The authenticity of those testimonies has been repeatedly contested, as were those given during other religion-related trials (see above). Advocates for the defense tried to prove that one of the witnesses, named Istomin, a member of the extremely traditionalist citizens' movement Народный собор (People's Assembly), had already been a witness for the prosecution in the trial against Yuri Samodurov and Andrei Yerofeyev as curators of 'Forbidden Art', and was some kind of 'professional', hired witness. Their objections where dismissed, as was an objection in which the advocate suspected that the witnesses' statements where actually not written by themselves, but by some other person, which was indicated by identical spelling mistakes occurring in every statement (Morgan 2012:47).

Federation (e.g., Krindatch 2006). The same can be said about the long Russian tradition of a tight symbiosis between church and state, including a sacralization of power and the byzantine model of "symphony", a harmonious relationship between the emperor and the patriarch, granting both their specific sphere of influence in the state, thereby virtually eliminating the significance of society as a third, independent sphere (van der Zweerde 2009; Tsypin: Part IV)[11]. It is this very strong alliance that, according to Pussy Riot themselves as well as many observers, was the target of critique of their performance. It is not the aim of this article to comment on this topic any further. However, there is one aspect worth mentioning with reference to the role of religion in national identity-building: that is the conceptualization of states and nations as "affective communities" (Suny 2009:8 ff.; Suny 2010:94)[12]. Under this premise, religion as a cultural institution offering highly emotionally charged rituals and practices serves largely to create emotional ties that can be also used in national identity-building. This adds an additional aspect to the question of religious feeling: not only does the attitude towards a sacred sphere or entity stir emotions, but certain collective beliefs and practices also strengthen feelings of emotional belonging. Thus, the emergence of a social function of emotions as described by constructivist sociology comes into focus, and this inevitably implies questions of hierarchy building and power relations. With reference to William Reddy, it can be assumed that the staging of the trial against Pussy Riot as well as the previous court trials are an attempt to establish a specific "emotional regime", a "set of normative emotions and the official rituals, practices, and 'emotives' that express and inculcate them; a necessary underpinning of any stable political regime" (Reddy 2001:129). Reddy's concept, which—as commentators have noted—is designed

11 It is worth mentioning here that, besides the political ambition of the ROC arising from this situation, there is a broad subculture of politicized Orthodox Christianity in Russia today, political movements based on their own interpretations of the Orthodox doctrine, and not always guided by the ROC. For a detailed assessment of those subcultures, see Mitrofanova, Umland: (2005).

12 Suny derives this concept from Benedict Anderson's 'Imagined Communities: Reflections on the Origin and Spread of Nationalism' (London /New York: Verso, 1991), citing his argument that "with whom one feels a special bond, a tie of some kind of 'kinship' and affection distinct from the feelings one has toward those of other nations. Beyond the actual or fictive kinship of ethnic groups, nations are grounded in imaginative relations of various kinds—common origins and ancestors, common history and destiny, blood or culture, belief in the spiritual unity of a people or commitment to shared political principles that constitute a powerful cultural synthesis. The signs of commonality are also varied, selective, shifting, and often contested: language, religion, somatic features, foods, fashions, patterns of child-raising, appropriate expression of emotion, etc." (Suny 2009: 8). Jan Plamper, in his survey of the role of feelings in Russian History, suggests that the idea of the nation as an emotionally cohesive community is characteristic of 19th century historical thinking (Plamper 2010:14).

with regard to the nation-state (Plamper 2010:242), is based on the assumption that there are always conflicts between a dominant emotional regime, enforced at the center of power or authority and other, conflicting regimes; and of course, the public demonstration of enforcement serves to underline a hegemonic position. According to Reddy, particularly strict political regimes offer "strong emotional management tools" (Reddy 2001:126), serving to navigate ones feelings according to the rules.

In this sense, the trials can be regarded as show trials, serving two functions: firstly, they are a performance of the dominant emotional regime as they present "feeling rules" (Hochschild 1979:563), and secondly, they utilize the performative potential of the expression of emotions ("emotives", to put it in Reddy's terminology) to mobilize the public. The increasing number of Orthodox activists claiming the need to protect religious places and monuments, as well as the increasing sensitivities in general, might serve as an indication of the success these measures have.

Who Feels How? Pretentions and Inquiries on Emotions and Subjects

The ambiguity of hurt religious feelings discussed above, which brings together insult and hatred, becomes highly productive in the trial of Pussy Riot. Although the leitmotif of the hurt believer emphasizes insult, the trial is as much about hatred, as it is about insult. In her analysis of the cultural organization of hate, Sarah Ahmed explores speeches on asylum seekers by members of the Conservative Party in the UK during the early 2000s, suggesting that their rhetoric aimed to generate an imagined subject of the nation (the white man, housewife, and son) who is endangered by imagined others (asylum seekers). Those others then become the object of hate: "Hate generates its objects as a defence against injury" (Ahmed 2004:42). This appears to describe exactly what occurred during the trial of Pussy Riot: It served the organization of religiously motivated hatred via a discourse on emotions. Therefore, naturally, during the trial as well as in the course of the discussion that evolved around it, one central controversial question regarded the nature and types of emotions of those involved in or affected by the performance. In court, the prosecution aimed to demonstrate that the performance was motivated by religious hatred, that religious feelings had been hurt, and religious hatred incited. The defense council initially attempted to state that the performance was not designed as an attack on religion or religious feelings, but as an act of radical political criticism; and secondly contested the witnesses' credibility, thereby also calling into question the existence of hurt religious feelings and, to some extent, even the existence of religious feelings per se. This results in a highly complex and multilayered rhetoric discourse about the nature of emotions with explicit and implicit religious and political intentions and effects.

As the trial also serves as a cultural institution of subject formation, this discourse on emotions is at the same time a discourse on the Russian citizen as a subject. Therefore, naturally, the legal dispute creates affirmative und negative verbal images of state citizens by ways of the emotions they feel (or pretend to feel), express, or are being ascribed.

So, how are those subjects shown? Although at first glance the members of Pussy Riot seem to be the central figures of this trial, the victims occupy a huge space.

The cross-examination of victims and witnesses takes up much space in the course of the trial and in the trial's paratexts, such as in the indictment, the trial record, and the verdict. This is done in order to ensure that the display of offense becomes evident and picturesque. Therefore the most obvious rhetorical strategy to constitute a picture of subjects offended by blasphemous words and deeds is amplification in its most basic form via serial repetition. This is particularly noteworthy, as it has aroused suspicions regarding the authenticity of the emotions articulated. This happens because of the obvious similarities between the texts aforementioned, but also because we somehow expect an authentic expression of a strong emotion to be individualized, particularly in terms of narrative. When considering the complexity of emotions and their narrative expression, this anticipation is absolutely understandable[13]. The victims' statements as we can read them in the trial record are quite contradictory in this respect: they are apparently simple and redundant, and at the same time highly cohesive and effective in presenting the notion of serious offense. The cross-examinations of all victims and witnesses of the defense follow a standardized form: They start with questions whose purpose is to emphasize the religious faith of the person interrogated. Some of the interrogated respond simply by stating that they try to attend church on a regular basis, pray, and follow all canonical rituals. Afterwards, the cross-examinations continue with questions about the circumstances of the performance in the cathedral. Here, not only do the interrogated recall the course of events, but also make statements about the emotional effect these events had on them. This is where the offense becomes apparent. Of course, the descriptions are to a high degree intentionally predetermined by the lawyers' questions, as they are part of a cross-examination. The cross-examined witnesses follow a specific script of questions and answers that has been prepared during questioning before the trial, rather than unfold their story in the trial situation. Therefore, there are virtually no mimetic representations of the offense. Instead,

13 See Christiane Voss for an analysis of the complexity of (narrated) emotions. Voss suggests that emotions consist of various components, which have to be synthesized with regard to a specific intention serving as a superstructure. She calls this process a mental "narrative conjunction", and points out that narration becomes relevant on two different levels: Firstly in the mental processing of an emotion, and secondly in the stories we tell about them (Voss 2004:184 ff.).

we find generalizing accounts devoid of any rhetoric elaboration or, conversely, disruptions of a prepared speech like stuttering, stagnation, confused speech, etc.; or by outbursts of emotion (like tears that are being suppressed), which would seem appropriate for an expressive representation of emotions in other contexts and genres, maybe even in the court room. When Lyubov' Aleksandrovna Sokologorska, a then 52-year-old employee working in the Church of Christ the Savior, gives her assessment of the Pussy Riot members' actions and behavior in the cathedral, she states as follows:

> This impudent, profane behavior violated the visitor's right to turn to God in prayer. Me and the gatekeepers take care to ensure there is quiet in the church, so that everybody can pray (…) I tried to expel them. Tolokonnikova and the unrecognized person in the red dress clearly worked for the camera. For me as an Orthodox believer, this was very insulting; it hurt my emotions of faith, my ideals, myself as a person, and my choice; this is blasphemy (Khamovicheskiy raionniy sud 2012:78)[14].

After being asked by the prosecutor whether she had seen the internet video, she states:

> The first thing I was astonished about was that everything was combined. I want to point to the dynamics this had when those pieces were torn and repeated. I think it was one of their goals: to incite the believer's spite/rage. The defendants' actions were very insulting—they caused me huge moral pain; this pain is lasting and will not go away (Khamovicheskiy raionniy sud 2012:78)[15].

This statement is by no means accomplished by emotional distance towards the described matter. When asked what where the exact words of the piece Pussy Riot performed, she refuses to repeat them, assuring that this would mean to commit the sin of blasphemy herself, but instead repeatedly describes her affectionate relationship towards sanctuaries and sacred sites. In the low rhetoric of the accounts of both victims and witnesses, mentions of emotional turmoil and agitation sometimes appear strangely misplaced, more so because they appear in the form of concise

14 Такими дерзкими, кошунственными действиями было нарушено право прихожан обратитья с молитвой. Мы с охранником поддерживаем, чтобы в храме была тишина чтобы у всех была возможность помолиться. Все были в шоке. (...) Я пыталась их вытеснить. Толоконникова и неопознанная в красном платье работали четко на камеру. Для меня как православной верующей это очень оскорбительно, это осквернение моего чувства веры, идеалов, меня как личности и моего выбора, это кощунство.

15 Первое чему я удивилась, что все было представленно комбинированно. Я отмечу динамику, когда рвались и повторялись эти куски. Вызвать злость у верюущух, думаю, было одной из их целей. Действия подсудимых для меня оскорбительны, их действия мне причинили огромный моральный вред, эта боль непроходящая.

answers to very precise and obviously intentional questions. Sokologorskaya's statements may serve as an example for that, as do many others. Denis Istomin is one of the most infamous figures among the aggrieved parties, because defense lawyers demonstrated that he was obviously a professional, appointed witness, although the judge did not acknowledge this proof. Istomin states in his account: "A shock, I experienced a very severe emotional turmoil, and I do not consider myself a sentimental person"[16] (Khamovicheskiy raionniy sud 2012:84). Additionally, victim Vasiliy Tsyganyuk, a then 40-year-old employee at the church, when being asked if he had suffered mentally after the incident, answers: "My heart was in a heavy state"[17] (Khamovicheskiy raionniy sud 2012:90). There are only two victims, whose depictions of their perception of the situation and their assessment during questioning are slightly more elaborated. The first is given by Pavel Zhelezov, a graduate from the priest seminary who at the time of the incident worked in the Cathedral as an altar boy. His depiction, respectively the difference between his depiction and those of the others, illustrates the range of possible expressions under the given circumstances and underlines the passivity and conventionalism of those given by the other victims and witnesses. Apart from the fact that those victims choose some slightly more elaborate wordings and a rhetoric of amplification, the main effect of their rhetoric is that they succeed in condensing the 'master-plot' of offense:

> **State prosecutor Nikofonov**: Would you say that such a behavior can be considered blasphemy?
> **Offended**: Yes, you cannot do this. I was afraid that they might go to the altar, and the altar is the most sacred spot, the most sacred spot in the church; and even more so, I had to resist them so there would not be any worse harm. (…) After those incidents I was very concerned. Those actions touched my religious feelings to the depth of my soul, it was a pain in the soul, because all the innermost things which are holy for me in life, were trampled upon. Those actions clearly showed contempt for the Orthodox traditions and Orthodox believers; everything was very clear and understandable: it was obvious enmity and hostility. I remember particularly the movements of the hands, like fists frontwards. Later, I saw the video-clip on the internet, I don't remember when, but of course, I didn't watch it until the end: this was so dirty—the clip did not match what had happened in the church; (…). This insulted me and demeaned me. The sense of the song's lyrics insults the feelings of believers, because it used holy words, for example the Blessed Virgin, in a profane context. I heard something like that in church singing [but] this song was a parody on the service, but you cannot com-

16 Шок, я испытал сильнейшее эмоциональное потрясение, я не могу отнести себя к сентиментальным людям.

17 На душе было тяжелое состояние.

> pare this to the singing in a service. Those actions in the church instigate hate and enmity towards the Orthodox believers in the church, and no acquaintance of mine approved—some resented it (Khamovicheskiy raionniy sud 2012:99)[18].

This master-plot consists of several elements, representing the components of a complex emotional experience. This shows that the accounts, though very simple in terms of rhetoric, are very well constructed in terms of the semantics of representation of emotion. In her intentional theory of components of emotions, Christiane Voss defines four main components of any genuine emotion: 1) an intentional one (meaning cognitive, evaluative and imaginative representations; 2) a behavioral one, covering both physical expression and verbal or other acts; 3) a physical-perceptive component (meaning sensations, including sensations of physical changes); and 4) a hedonistic component (Voss 2004:184). The cross-examinations of the victims are organized in such a way that they can be summed up to a coherent verbal representation of offense. This becomes particularly apparent in the verdict. Here, every given victim account contains all of the aforementioned components defining emotions: Every account tells us that the victims have experienced certain physical sensations like a pain in the heart or some other inner pain, a shock, anxiety, and so on. They identified these sensations as being caused by an offense they suffered, by hatred with which they were confronted, and by hatred they felt towards their offenders. Furthermore, the victims' narratives contain explanations and evaluations of the offense (and the hatred) and depictions of the ways the incident made them react according to ruling conventions and circumstances. This includes an important hedonistic aspect: The victims consider their feelings and the expression of their feelings to be perfectly appropriate. One might even suggest that the victims derive

18 Государственный обвинитель Никифоров: Подобное поведение можно назвать кощунством? – Потерпевший: Да, такое непозволительно совершать. Я боялся, что они взайдут в алтарь, а алтарь это самое святое место, главное место в храме, тем более, чтобы не сотворилось худшего зла, я должен был этому воспрепятствовать. (...) После всех эти событий я сильно переживал. Эти действия затронули мои религиозные чувства до глубины души, была душевная боль, так как были растоптаны те сокровенные вещи, которые для меня являются святыми по жизни.Эти действия носили явное презрение к православным традициям и православным верующим, здесь все было открыто и понятно, явная вражда, неприязнь, особенно мне запомнились движения рук кулаками вперед. В последующем я видел видеоролик в интернете, не помню когда, но конечно я его даже не досмотрел, настолько это все грязно, ролик не соответствовал происходящему в храме, (....) Это меня оскорбило и унизило. Смысл слов песни оскорбляет чувства верующих , так как в ней используются святие слова, например Богородица, в кошунственном контексте. Я услышал похожее на церковное пение, это была пародия на церковную службу, но это не сопоставимо с пением богослужения. Эти действия в храме вызывают ненависть и вражду к православным верующим в храме, не один мой знакомый не одобрил, кто-то возмущался.

a sense of self-satisfaction from their own outrage at the perceived blasphemous insult to their faith.

The victims' narratives dealing with blasphemy are supposed to be factual statements acknowledging the presupposed crime of blasphemy rather than testimonies used in the juridical process of opinion making. Accordingly, the verbal representations of hurt feelings target the performative positing of self-evident emotions not open for debate. This strategy becomes particularly evident when the accused or the lawyers for the defense ask for more detailed descriptions of the nature of the offense or its effects on the offended. In many cases the judge dismisses such questions, as well as others regarding the victim's idea of faith, and questions related to their political and philosophical views. Sometimes, the questions are permitted and answered, but never do they contribute to a more detailed assessment of hurt feelings than that given in the initial assertion. One short example out of many is the cross-examination of Lyubov' Sokologorskaya:

> **Advocate Polozov**: Did you see a doctor or psychologist in respect to your psychological trauma?
> **Offended**: I felt the blessed energy of the Holy Spirit, and this is stronger;
> **Polozov**: Why didn't she heal you completely?
> **Chairman**: Question dismissed;
> **Polozov**: Why exactly was this parody of the sign of the cross?
> **Chairman**: Question dismissed;
> **Polozov**: What is your attitude towards feminism?
> **Chairman**: Question dismissed (Khamovicheskij raionnyj sud 2012:81)[19].

In addition, the cross-examination of Sergei Beloglazov includes the following dialogue:

> **Advocate Polozov**: Which emotions did you have when you saw what was going on in the church?
> **Offended**: It upset me very much;
> **Polozov**: You said that you could not enter the church for two months; could you describe your internal feelings and sufferings that were caused by these actions?
> **Chairman**: Question dismissed;
> **Polozov**: The fact, that the behavior of the defendants insulted you—those five months they have now already spent in jail: is this equal to your frustration?

---

19 Защитник адвокат Полозов: Вы обращались к врачам или психологам в связи с психологической травмой? – Потерпевшая: Я чувствовала благодатную энергию святого духа и это сильнее. – Защитник адвокат Полозов: Почему она вас не исцелила до конца? – Председательствующий: Вопрос снят. – Защитник адвокат Полозов: В чем было пародирование крестного знамения? Председательствующий: Вопрос снят – Защитник адвокат Полозов: Как в относитесь к феминизму? – Председательствующий: Вопрос снят.

> **Chairman**: Question dismissed;
> **Polozov**: Did you see a doctor or psychologist in respect to your sufferings?
> **Offended**: I see a priest (Khamovicheskiy raionniy sud 2012:108)[20].

As mentioned before, offense and hatred or enmity are closely connected in the case law on blasphemy. Article 282 addresses "actions directed at the incitement of hatred or enmity". In this trial, the application of this law is quite peculiar. A subject that is obviously full of hate or that instigates enmity among people evokes negative associations and presents a rather ambiguous role model. Such an image is incompatible with that of a liberal citizen, as it reminds us more of a fundamentalist zealot. In order to avoid any such impression, during the trial prosecutors do not emphasize the aspect of incitement, but concentrate much more on the figure of the hurt believer. Among the scenarios in which the believer's hatred is thematized is this one made by Lyubov' Sokologorskaya, as it marks the fine line between morally unimpeachable offense, that is 'felt', and a form of ethically more compromising hatred, that is only 'presumed':

> I think that it was one of their goals to instigate the believers' rage. The actions of the defendants insulted me; they caused me huge moral pain. This pain will last. This has stirred resonance amongst believers. It was the second week of preparation for the Great Feast, and here we have an attempt to blow up everything, to instigate rage and anger (Khamovicheskiy raionniy sud 2012:78)[21].

Instead of ascribing hatred to the believers, it is ascribed to the defendants. During the cross-examination of Vasily Tsyganyuk, Prosecutor Nikiforov asks him:

> Do the actions of the defendants show feelings of hatred and enmity towards Orthodox citizens?" (Khamovicheskiy raionniy sud 2012:91)[22].

---

20 Защитник адвокат Полозов: Какое чувство вы испытали, когда увидели то, что происходило в храме? –Потерпевший: Расстроило меня очень сильно. – Защитник адвокат Полозов: Вы сказали, что два месяца в храм войти не могли, вы можете описать свои переживания, страдания, которые были вызваны тем действием, что с вами происходило? Председательствующий: Вопрос снят – Защитник адвокат Полозов: То, что вас расстроило поведение наших подзащитных, те 5 месяцев, которые они находятся в заключении, равноценно вашему расстройству? Председательствующий: Снят вопрос – Вы обращались к врачу, психологу, в связи с вашими страданиями? – Потерпевший: Я хожу к священнику.

21 Вызвать злость у верующих, думаю, было одной из них целей. Действия подсудимых для меня оскорбительны, их действия мне причинили огромный моральный вред, это боль непроходящая. Это вызывало резонанс среди верующих, это была вторая неделя подготовки к Великому посту, а здесь стремление взорвать все и вся, вызвать гнев, раздражение.

22 Данные действия в храме и ролик показывают чувства ненависти и вражды к православным верующим?

This is a very short, but revealing question, as it documents the displacement of hatred from the believers to the members of Pussy Riot by using almost the exact words of Article 282 with just some slight changes in reference. This ascribing becomes established during the course of the trial, where it is constantly emphasized that the group members' actions were motivated by religious hatred and enmity. Finally, the verdict is full of repetitions of statements declaring that the facts of the case have been proven:

> The aforementioned actions where obviously targeted at the instigation of religious hatred and enmity, as well as the abasement of dignity of a person or a group of persons on the basis of attitude to religion[23].

When verbalizing their offence and their hatred, the overwhelming majority of the victims basically invoke the words of the law. By doing so, they are being represented or represent themselves as perfectly compliant citizens, allegiant to both the ROC and the Russian state, which defines the relevant jurisdiction in this trial. As a result, because of the prosecutor and judge's policies, those subjects seem rather one-dimensional. Most of them espouse narrow definitions and are obviously reliant on some form of diffuse common sense defined by religious and political authorities. The council for the defense systematically attempts to reveal these traits in order to undermine the victim's positive image and to discredit them. In this respect, the aforementioned cross-examination strategy is not only a means to try to establish that the members of Pussy Riot are no 'possessed women', but also to slightly question the victims' rationality. Or, to put it in other words, to confront the religious truth on rationality with a secular, evidence-based one. Beyond that, the defense also tries to reveal the bigotry of the image of a 'good Orthodox believer' by demonstrating to the judge and audience the believers' incapacity or unwillingness to forgive. Before and during the trial, Maria Alyokhina repeatedly gave her excuses to believers, as did the other members in various statements. Some believers accepted them, but most did not. Also during cross-examination, the defendants and their advocates emphasized that such lack of forgiveness was contrary to Christian virtues:

> **Advocate Polozov**: Is forgiveness a Christian virtue?
> **Offended**: Every faithful person should strive to be able to forgive;
> **Polozov**: Can you forgive?
> **Offended**: I'm not perfect (Khamovicheskiy raionniy sud 2012:102)[24].

---

23 Упомянутые действия были явно направлены на возбуждение религиозной ненависти и вражды, а также на унижение достоинства человека по признакам принадлежности к религии.

24 Защитник адвокат Полозов: Прощение – одна из христианских ценностей? – Потерпевший: Любой верующий человек, должен стараться уметь прощать. – Защитник

The offended believers' most obvious quality is their resemblance to other hurt believers. This is another quite important effect of the seriality of the numerous victims' statements. They represent themselves not as individuals (allegedly not even their petitions or opinions were authentically personal), but rather the abstract, ideal collective of Orthodox believers. This becomes apparent even in the statements made during cross-examination, where victims repeatedly refer not only to their own hurt feelings, but also to those of others: In the verdict, this rhetoric of the collective becomes emphasized even more. Pussy Riot were alleged to have hurt not only those present in the cathedral at the time the incident happened, but the Church collective. That is why the publication of the performance made partially with material filmed in the cathedral is considered an important part of the offence. Most of the offended are being questioned about the effect the video had on them, and all of them claimed that seeing the performance was as disturbing as witnessing the action in the cathedral. One witness was not even present in the cathedral at all but only saw the video clip. His more elaborate assessment of the events demonstrates perfectly how the incident is interpreted as an attack on the ROC and, on the other hand, as the formation of a dangerous "army of enemies" willing to break down the foundations of the Russian society, deeply rooted in Orthodoxy[25].

The relationship of individuality and collectivity is significant not only with respect to the hurt believers, but also with respect to the Pussy Riot members. The victims' statements can be regarded—and are designed—as a generic speech act of people symbolizing a collective, namely the collective of Orthodox believers, or, in broader terms, the collective of righteous Russian citizens, who are naturally of Orthodox faith. Therefore, they are not meant to express individuality, but exemplarity.

The image and speech of the members of Pussy Riot on the other hand are designed to express a different notion of collectivity. In his short comment on the trial against Pussy Riot, Slavoj Žižek has considered the Pussy Riot members to be global symbols of a simple but far-reaching message: "Their message is: IDEAS MATTER. They are conceptual artists in the noblest sense of the word: artists who embody an Idea. This is why they wear balaclavas: masks of de-individualization, of liberating anonymity. The message of their balaclavas is that it doesn't matter which of them got arrested—they're not individuals, they're an Idea. And this is why they are such a threat: it is easy to imprison individuals, but try to imprison an Idea!" (Žižek 2012)[26].

адвокат Волкова: Вы умеете прощать? –Потерпевший: Я не идеальный.

25 For the prosecutors, it is important to demonstrate the impression that the video has made, because the use of mass media is an important penalty, mentioned in the law.

26 Maria Chehonadskih, who has taken up this thought and asked, what exactly Pussy Riot's idea

Interestingly, in her commentary, Chehonadskih considers modes of speech as a central paradigm for the assessment of actionism. She claims that under the political and social circumstances of early 21st century Russia, to practice hysterical and obscene speech in artistic actionism was the most efficient way to distort the surface of a fake 'stability' established by the regime. Without doubt, the Pussy Riot performances fall into the category of this kind of actionism. Nevertheless, interestingly enough, during the court trial, particularly in their opening and closing statements, the Pussy Riot members attempted to convert this hysterical speech into a voice of reason of enlightened citizens, pulling out all the stops of pathetic rhetoric. This becomes apparent during the trial, when the defendants repeatedly interject during cross-examination to scrutinize the stereotypical questions and answers, in an attempt to obtain more differentiated, authentic comments on the nature of the emotions that are predicated and ascribed during the trial. Therefore, they ask how the victims can tell that the defendants acted out of religious hatred ("Почему из нарушения правил вы выводите, что у нас наличествует религиозная ненависть и вражда?"[27] (Khamovicheskiy raionniy sud 2012:83); about their understanding of blasphemy; and the exact ways in which their feelings had been hurt. They also try to contest implicit allegations that they are some sort of possessed demons or witches that could be concluded from the witness accounts describing them as carrying out wild and diabolical dances at the ambo. The group's lawyers assist them in establishing their sanity and questioning the victim's alleged expertise on insanity:

> **Advocate Polozov**: Have you met possessed persons?
> **Offended**: Yes;
> **Polozov**: How did they behave?
> **Offended**: In different ways, some screamed, some hit their heads, some fell. I've never seen them dancing;
> **Polozov**: Do you think that the possessed can dance?
> **Offended**: Usually they don't;
> **Polozov**: And can they run to the altar?
> **Offended**: They can try;
> **Polozov**: Are those women possessed?

was, rightly disagrees with Žižek, claiming that the de-individualizing effect had passed the moment the masks where taken off. The trial marks the beginning of a new phase in the history of the group's activity, when Pussy Riot rapidly became a global brand promoted by young political technologists, primarily via social media technologies like Facebook. In this campaign, establishing Pussy Riot as a voice of the universal category of the discontented, an 'extreme individualism' becomes apparent (Chehonadskih 2012:4). But still, in court, they stand for the idea of a collective identity opposed to that prompted by church and state.

27 Why from our infringement of rules do you draw the conclusion that we feel religious hatred and enmity?

Chairman: Question dismissed (Khamovicheskiy raionniy sud 2012:94)[28].

The members of Pussy Riot emphatically claim to have acted out of political reasons and as civil rights activists and feminists. In an effort to expose the hidden political motivations of the trial, such as the suppression of feminist activities or liberal thought, they ask about the victims' political attitudes and, in particular, their attitude towards feminism, but typically those and most other insistent questions are dismissed by the judge.

However, the most significant texts with regard to the establishment of an image of enlightened, non-conformist state subjects are the speeches given by the Pussy Riot members themselves, particularly the closing statements, which gained quite huge popularity. Interestingly, in those statements, the motif of speech plays a central role. In her statement, Nadezhda Tolokonnikova refers to herself and her fellow group members as being deprived of their voices, which she claims to be voices of reason:

> The medieval Inquisition methods that reign in the law enforcement and judicial systems of our country, the Russian Federation, are enough to make you weep. But from the moment of our arrest, we have stopped weeping. We have lost our ability to cry. We had desperately shouted at our punk concerts. With all our might, we decried the lawlessness of the authorities, the governing bodies. But now, our voices have been taken away. During the entire trial, people have refused to hear us. Hearing us would mean being receptive to what we say, being thoughtful, striving toward wisdom, being philosophers (Bozovic, Hanukai, Senderovich 2012) [29],[30].

---

28 Защитник адвокат Полозов: Вы встречали бесноватых? – Потерпевший: Да – Защитник адвокат Полозов: Как они себя вели? – Потерпевший: По-разному, кто-то орет, бьется головой, кто-то падает. Танцующих не бывало. – Защитник адвокат Полозов: Бесноватые могут танцевать? – Потерпевший: Обычно не танцуют. – Защитник адвокат Полозов: А в алтарь могут пробегать? – Потерпевший: Могут попытаться. – Защитник адвокат Полозов: Эти женщины бесноватые? - Председательствующий: Вопрос снят.

29 Хочется рыдать, глядя на то, как приемы средневековой инквизиции воцаряются в правоохранительной и судебной системах Российской Федерации, которая – наша страна. Но с момента ареста мы не можем больше рыдать, мы разучились плакать. Мы отчаянно кричали на наших панк-концертах, как могли и как умели, о беззакониях начальства и властей. Но вот у нас украли голос. Весь процесс нас отказываются слышать. Именно слышать. Слышать – это значит воспринимать, думать при этом, стремиться к мудрости, быть философами (Pussy Riot:2012a). Cited by the video recording of the statement, as the transcript of court proceedings differs slightly from this apparent original.

30 This argument appears in the other statements as well, with both Tolokonnikova and Yekaterina Samutsevich pleading for a culture of dialogue, and starting this dialogue by referring to all kinds of historical authorities.

Significantly, Tolokonnikova in her statement connects the motif of speechlessness with the motif of absent tears; of persecuted women. This is crucial, as it reveals a strategy of emotional charges pursued by Pussy Riot during the trial, which is intended to be more powerful and impressive than the discourse on feelings led by the law. This includes a deliberated reference to female gender stereotypes such as weakness, emotionality, etc. In addition, the group and their supporters put quite huge efforts into shaping a picture of beautiful, attractive women, two of whom are also mothers who are being brutally taken away from their children. The worldwide reception of the trial has shown how this staging of a conflict between weak but brave beauties and 'the beast' has developed. However, in their speeches, they aim to overcome this cliché and present themselves as enlightened feminists who act rationally and are very well aware of their place in the history of Russian political and cultural dissent. Therefore, they intend to create an ideal of a citizen, thereby fighting against the collectivism and anti-individualism they perceive to still be predominant in Russian society. Particularly Maria Alyokhina's closing statement is built around this argument:

> And right here, in this closing statement, I would like to describe my firsthand experience of running afoul of this system. Our schooling, which is where the personality begins to form in a social context, effectively ignores any particularities of the individual. There is no "individual approach," no study of culture, of philosophy, of basic knowledge about civic society. Officially, these subjects do exist, but they are still taught according to the Soviet model. And as a result, we see the marginalization of contemporary art in the public consciousness, a lack of motivation for philosophical thought, and gender stereotyping. The concept of the human being as a citizen gets swept away into a distant corner. (...) These people...this is yet another confirmation that people in our country have lost the sense that this country belongs to us, its citizens. They no longer have a sense of themselves as citizens. They have a sense of themselves simply as the automated masses. They don't feel that the forest belongs to them, even though the forest located right next to their houses. I doubt they even feel a sense of ownership over their own houses (Corrigan, Glazov-Corrigan 2012)[31].

31 И в этом последнем слове хочу вкратце описать мой непосредственный опыт столкновения с этой системой. Образование, из которого начинается становление личности в социуме, фактически игнорирует особенности этой личности. Отсутствует индивидуальный подход, отсутствует изучение культуры, философии, базовых знаний о гражданском обществе. Формально эти предметы есть. Но формы их преподавания наследует советский образец. И как итог, мы имеем маргинализацию современного искусства в сознании человека, отсутствие мотивации к философскому мышлению, гендерную стереотипизацию и отметание в дальний угол позицию человека как гражданина. (…) люди у нас в стране перестали ощущать принадлежность территорий нашей страны

Samutsevich, at the end of her statement, claims to have "mixed feelings" about the outcomes of the trial, which showed their defenselessness in the face of the institutions and yet raised awareness of political grievances in Russia. This expression can be considered a deliberate rhetorical displacement. In fact, Samutsevich's "mixed feelings" stand for the group's subversive "micropolitics of emotion" during this trial, in which they engaged in order to confront the politics of distinct, prescribed emotions evolving around blasphemy with the ambiguity and diversity of emotions connected to them as the symbol of resistance that they knew they were about to become. However, we must not forget that the 'hurt believer' has become a strong symbol as well, and quite a dubious one.

To sum up, it can be stated, that for the authorities, the Pussy Riot trial was a means to establish an emotional regime based on the concurrence of insult and hatred. This was ensured by the use of two opposing images: a positive collective portrait of honest, upright, and morally superior Orthodox believers— ideal Russian citizens on the one hand, versus a negative image of dangerous, pro-Western, feminist, anti-Orthodox individuals on the other. It focuses on the positive image of the Orthodox believer, who shall be insulted when his church and its sanctuaries are attacked and shall hate the offender. However, in order to ensure an unabated positive image of the hurt believer, his hatred gets moderated in the legal discourse and rather ascribed to the offender, who appears as the one threatening the community with his hatred. This strategy serves very effectively to establish a clear image of a citizen as a highly emotionally charged, but thereby vulnerable subject in need of protection. This protection, of course, is guaranteed by the strong alliance of church and state, which became apparent in this incident. Nevertheless, the effort to ensure a vivid image of hurt believers, as it was conducted by the prosecution, has quite contradictory effects. There is a very strong emphasis on the antagonism of good and evil and the fabrication of an idea of faith. This appears quite simple or naïve, because it is expressed mostly through insult; as a result, the Orthodox believer as a loyal citizen appears to be quite stereotyped. The Pussy Riot members and the defense, for their part, try to expose exactly this simplifying image, calling for a different notion of "the people" (народ) (Gapova 2012). Thereby, their performance in the courtroom is to be considered part of the performance for which they were

---

им самим, гражданам. Эти люди перестали чувствовать себя гражданами. Они себя чувствуют просто автоматическими массами. Они не чувствуют, что им принадлежит даже лес, находящийся непосредственно у них около дома. Я даже сомневаюсь в том, что они осознают принадлежность собственного дома им самим. (Pussy Riot 2012). Cited from the video recording of the statement, as the transcript of the court proceedings differs slightly from this apparent original.

eventually sentenced. Subsequent to the Pussy Riot trial, it is evident that the politics of emotion—which was so openly employed in that case—has continued as a means to both shape public attitudes and to define the role of Orthodoxy in the new Russia.

References

Ahmed S (2004) The cultural politics of emotions. Edinburgh University Press, Edinburgh

Berkmann BJ (2009) Von der Blasphemie zur "hate speech"? Die Wiederkehr der Religionsdelikte in einer religiös pluralen Welt. Frank und Timme, Berlin

Bozovic M, Hanukai M, Senderovich S (2012) Translation: Maria Alyokhina: Closing Statement. https://nplusonemag.com/online-only/online-only/pussy-riot-closing-statements. Accessed 28 August 2013

Bremer T (2012) Der Fall "Pussy Riot" und die Russische Orthodoxe Kirche. Russland-Analysen 246:6–8. http://www.laender-analysen.de/russland/pdf/Russlandanalysen246.pdf. Accessed 27 Feb 2013

Bremer T (2012) Der "Westen" als Feindbild im theologisch-philosophischen Diskurs der Orthodoxie. Europäische Geschichte Online (EGO). nbn:-de:0159-2012030774. Accessed 14 Mar 2013

Chehonadskih (2012) What is Pussy Riot's 'idea'? Radical Philosophy 176:2–7. http://www.radicalphilosophy.com/commentary/what-is-pussy-riots-idea

Epshtein AD (2012) Mobilizovannaya Bororoditsa: pank-moleben gruppy "Pussy Riot" v khrame Khrista Spasitelya. Neprikoznovennyj zapas 83. http://magazines.russ.ru/nz/2012/3/e10-pr.html. Accessed 14 April 2013

Frimmel S (2013) Nachwort. In: Lomasko W, Nikolajew A (eds) Verbotene Kunst. Eine Moskauer Ausstellung. Gerichtsreportage. Matthes and Seitz, Berlin

Gapova E (2012) Delo "Pussy Riot": Feministski protest v kontekste klassovoi bor'by. Novoe Literaturnoe Obozrenie 85 (5). http://www.nlobooks.ru/node/2794. Accessed 27 May 2013

Hahn A, Knapp V (eds) (1987) Selbstthematisierung und Selbstzeugnis: Bekenntnis und Geständnis. Suhrkamp Verlag, Frankfurt am Main

Hochschild AR (1979) Emotion work, feeling rules, and social structure. The American Journal of Sociology 85(3):551–575

James W (1982) The varieties of religious experience: a study in human nature. London and New York, Routledge

Khamovicheskiy raionniy sud (2012) Delo 177080 po obvineniyu In: Tolokonnikovoi NA, Alyokhina MV, Samutsevich ES po stat'yu 213 ch 2 u.k. Accessed 7 Aug 2013

Khamovicheskiy raionniy sud (2012) Delo 177080 po obvineniyu Tolokonnikovoi NA, Alyokhina MV, Samutsevich ES po stat'yu 213 ch 2 u.k. PF 7 Aug 2012 Prigovor imenem Rossiiskoi Federacii, 17 Aug. http://slon.ru/russia/prigovor_pussy_riot-821705.xhtml. Accessed 27 Jun 2013

Koch S (2009) Die strafbare Beschimpfung von Bekenntnissen, Religionsgesellschaften und Weltanschauungsvereinigungen. Kovač, Hamburg

Kondratev F (2012) My rozhdaemsya s chuvstom boga. Pravoslavie i sovremennost' 23(39). http://old.eparhia-saratov.ru/index.php?option=com_content&task=view&id=61587&Itemid=4. Accessed 28 May 2013

Krindatch A (2006) Changing relationships between religion, the state, and society in Russia. GeoJournal 67:267–282. doi: 10.1007/S10708-007-9066

Mitrofanova A, Umland A (eds.) (2005) The Politicization of Russian Orthodoxy: Actors and Ideas. Ibidem, Stuttgart

Nash C (2007) Blasphemy in the Christian world. Oxford University Press, Oxford

Corrigan M, Glazov-Corrigan E (2012) Translation: Nadezhda Tolokonnikova: Closing Statement. https://nplusonemag.com/online-only/online-only/pussy-riot-closing-statements. Accessed 28 August 2013.

Plamper J (2010) Emocii v Russkoi istorii. In: Plamper J, Shamma Shakhadat S, Eli M (eds) Rossiiskaya imperiya chuvstv. Podchody kul'turnoi istorii emocii, Novoe literaturnoe obozrenie, Moskau, pp 11–36

Plamper J (2010) The history of emotions: an interview with William Reddy, Barbara Rosenwein, and Peter Stearns. History and Theory 49:237–265

Pollack D (2009) Renaissance des Religiösen? Erkenntnisse der Sozialforschung. Osteuropa 59(6):29–45

Pravoslavnaya entsiklopediya. http://www.pravenc.ru/. Accessed 29 Apr 2013

Pussy Riot (2012a) Maria Alyokhina: Closing Statement. https://www.youtube.com/watch?v=wyAIpbea7G0. Accessed 1 September 2013

Pussy Riot (2012b) Nadezhda Tolokonnikova: Closing Statement. https://www.youtube.com/watch?v=pNQVJ_E1vzY. Accessed 1 September 2013

Reddy W (2001) The navigation of feeling. A framework for the history of emotions. Cambridge University Press, Cambridge

Reznik G (2012) Apofigei nepravosudnosti. Novaja Gazeta, 28.08. German edition: Osteuropa 62(6–8):225–228

Ryklin M (2006) Mit dem Recht des Stärkeren. Die russische Kultur in Zeiten der ‚gelenkten' Demokratie. Suhrkamp Verlag, Frankfurt am Main

Schleiermacher F (1995) Kritische Gesamtausgabe (KGA), vol. 1/12, 4th ed. De Gryter, Berlin

Suny RG (2009) The contradictions of identity: The legacies of being soviet and national in the USSR and post-soviet Eurasia. Paper presented at the conference Eurasianness and National Identities in the Post-Soviet Era. Asia-Pacific Research Center, Hanyang University, Seoul, Korea, June 18–19, 2009. http://www.hanyang.ac.kr/home_news/H5EAKB/0020/102/ 2009/%206/Suny.pdf. Accessed 28 Jun 2013

Suny RG (2010) Affektivnye soobshchestva: Struktura gosudarstva i nacii v Rossiiskoi Imperii. In: Plamper J, Shamma Shakhadat S, Eli M (eds) Rossiiskaya imperiya chuvstv. Podchody kul'turnoi istorii emocii, Novoe literaturnoe obozrenie, Moskau, p 78–114

Tsypin VA: Cerkovnoe pravo. http://lib.eparhia-saratov.ru/books/22c/cipin/eccllaw/contents.html. Accessed 07 May 2013

Ulozhenie o nakazaniyakh" ugolovnych" i ispravitel' nych" (1845)

van der Zweerde E (2009) Permanente Asymmetrie. Kirche und Staat, Staat und Kirche. Osteuropa 59(6):47–62.

von Gall C (2012) Vorerst gescheitert: "Pussy Riot" und der Rechtsstaat in Russland. Russland-Analysen 246:6–8. http://www.laender-analysen.de/russland/pdf/Russlandanalysen246.pdf. Accessed 27 Jun 2013

Voss C (2004) Narrative Emotionen. Eine Untersuchung über Möglichkeiten und Grenzen philosophischer Erkenntnistheorien. de Gruyter, Berlin, New York

Žižek S (2012) The true blasphemy, http://chtodelat.wordpress.com/2012/08/07/the-true-blasphemy-slavoj-zizek-on-pussy-riot/. Accessed 25 Jun 2013

4.

Conclusions

Conclusions

Julia Gerlach and Jochen Töpfer

More than two decades after the end of state socialism in Eastern Europe, attitudes towards religion and its roles in state and society have undergone profound changes. The atheist ideal of state socialism and the banning of religion from the public sphere have been overturned. While socialism clearly defined the relationship between politics and religion, the newly emerged forms of government tend to have more ambiguous perspectives—despite the fact that they all offer legal recognition of religion and religious organizations, and enshrine religious freedom.

In this volume, Sabine Riedel has discussed three models of church/state relations: *state church*, *cooperationist*, and *secular*. While an established state church enjoys (unlike non-established churches) support from the state, those close ties simultaneously expose it to the state's interference. The secular model professes to guarantee all churches the same freedom and autonomy, and the same rights and responsibilities: the political and the religious spheres are separated; church and state do not interfere in the public affairs of the other. The cooperationist relationship lies in the middle, as it provides a degree of autonomy yet also supports and subsides to some degree, which means interaction and interference between churches and the state. In reality, these ideal types rarely exist. Most states, not just those in Eastern Europe, fall between the three ideal types and display various elements of the different models.

Whereas the majority of contemporary constitutions in Eastern Europe are oriented towards the ideal of a secular and modern state, political reality differs—often significantly. In this respect, the case of the Russian Federation is especially interesting from various disciplinary perspectives. Legally, the secular state, guaranteed by the 1993 constitution, has been accompanied since 1997 by a law that defines a number of 'traditional religions' and its *primus inter pares*, the Russian Orthodox Church (ROC). The law assigns the ROC a 'special role'. This, and the perceived increasingly dense relationship between the ROC and the state, have recently been the source of controversy, especially in the context of the case against *Pussy Riot*. Heike Winkel and Inga Pylypchuk have analyzed that case, focusing on emotions released during the debate. The public discourse on the trial against the *Pussy Riot* activists involved in a critical performance in the Christ the Savior Cathedral in

Moscow in February 2012 has revealed deep cultural cleavages within Russian society, including between 'hurt believers' and 'pragmatic analysts'. In this respect, the actual relationship between state and church has been challenged, yet for the dimension in which the discourse diffused, political and legal arguments were often used to legitimate emotional reasoning. Damir Gainutdinov has developed this idea further. In his contribution, he concludes that the Russian legislature has been strategically responsive to the feelings of Russian believers by introducing a new law on blasphemy and conducting several sanctions such as blocking websites in the aftermath of the *Pussy Riot* case. All of these recent developments seem to be pre-emptive measures by the state not only to protect believers (favoring adherents of the ROC and, to a lesser extent, Muslim groups recognized by the state) but more in general, to protect the state from critical political activity and perceived 'threatening pluralism'.

Emotions (whether religiously motivated or not), their politically constructed violation, and the responsiveness of the state also play an important role for identity building. After the dissolution of the Soviet Union and the breakdown of Soviet identities, all of the successor states have undergone processes of state identity building. In the Russian Federation, these processes have been initiated almost entirely by political elites, hence from 'above', and occurred at both regional and federal levels. Whereas in many Russian ethnic republics, religion has been a distinct feature of state identity building from the early 1980s, the New Russia started to promote religion in state identity building only since the mid-2000s. Nadir Kinossian has analyzed the (imagined) resurrection of the Kul-Sharif Mosque in the Kremlin in Kazan, Tatarstan. For Tatar elites, the inclusion of Euro Islam, however defined, within Tatar nationalism is mostly a political and not a religious statement. Islam distinguishes the Tatar nation from mainly Orthodox Russia (not from all directly neighboring ethnic groups), and through its use of iconic architecture in Kazan, constructs heritage and identity. Yet, in contrast to decisive Chechen elites in the 1990s, Tatar elites have emphasized a 'tolerant Islam' and constructed Tatarstan's state identity as a bridge between a 'Christian West' and a 'Muslim East'. This approach complies with Russia's state identity, which Julia Gerlach has elaborated on. She concludes that the inclusion of religion, particularly Christian Orthodoxy, into the state identity constitutes a rational policy among political elites. Due to growing numbers of believers and corresponding trust in religious actors and religion rather than in political actors and politics, the increasingly close relationship between state and ROC must be understood as a responsive move that at the same time enhances the legitimacy and the performance of Putin's Russia today.

Following the theoretical approaches discussed by Jochen Töpfer, the role of religion within contemporary Russia, with respect to the church's relationship with the state, can be described as 'cultural state religion' (Fox), 'cooperation' (Minkenberg, Pollack), or 'politicized religion' (Linz). Religion and politics / church and state interact and intervene in a way that does not reflect the separation between religious and political spheres typical of secularism and hence the overall modernization of a society. Yet the ROC cannot be considered a state church. Rather, church and state seem to have established a form of symbiosis (or *symphonia*) in which each depends on—and thus supports—the other to a certain degree. In the first stance, both state and church derive mutual benefit from this symbiosis. The church enjoys state protection and state promotion. The state benefits from the church's endorsements and its spiritual (consequently emotionalizing) support, which enhances its legitimacy. The convergence of ideas is relatively wide, and ranges from basic values (protection of family, religious–patriotic education, etc.) to an abstract world-view that includes Russia's reach and status in the world. Here, a parallel development, intentional or not, is the political will of strengthening Russia's role in Eastern Europe, and recent efforts of the ROC to exert and widen its influence within the community of Orthodox Churches (see the relations to the Ecumenical Patriarchate of Constantinople as an example).

However, the relationship between religion and politics, and the role of religion in society has developed generally similar, yet different patterns were established in other sub-regions of Eastern Europe, as Jochen Töpfer and Sabine Riedel have shown. Similar to the Russian case, in the successor states to the former Yugoslavia, the relationships between state and church are mostly indistinct, neither strictly secular nor cooperationist nor based on a state church. 'Traditional religion' enjoys special state protection, for example in Slovenia, where the population is relatively homogeneous. For both state and society, religion plays a crucial role in identity building. Religion has been utilized for constructing distinct identities and mobilizing people in conflict. The cases of Bosnia-Herzegovina and Macedonia illustrate how different religious groups compete not only on the religious but also on the political market, through political parties that define their followers along ethnic–religious cleavages. In this respect, a number of cases in the region reflect a seemingly paradoxical development that can be observed globally: proceeding modernization and globalization, accompanied by a new search for identity that revitalizes religion as an important factor in identity building. It serves both to include people within a group, and to exclude others. In the cases discussed in this book, religious identities are used to support primordialist identity constructions, in line with the ethnic dimension. Especially for heterogeneous societies, this means walking a tightrope. Managing and balancing religious diversity is a major challenge at the top of the political agenda. What is often presented by media and academia as a 'pact' between religion and politics should also be seen as the consequence of a strategy of control. Some states have chosen to incorporate religion—or 'traditional faith'—not (only) for the sake of religious commitment and mutual support, but to ensure the state's influence over the church. If this is supported by religion and church both formally and informally, it serves the goal of protecting the state, respectively the state's identity.

Much has been discussed about changes in the relationship between religion and politics, and the role of religion in society in Eastern Europe after 1989/1991. The major change is the achievement of religious freedom, which has had a major impact on both relationship and role. The state serves as the guarantor of religious freedom, which—considering state socialist legacies—creates dependency and, in some cases, the state's expectation of support through religious organizations. Tensions between religion and politics remain, as does the imposed role over the field of religion. De facto, many of the cases analyzed are oriented towards cooperationist and state-church rather than secular models.

The reappearance of religion and church in the public sphere has promoted not only personal religiosity and religious affiliation, but also religious identification. Peoples' trust in religion and religious actors is significantly high in most East European countries, including those analyzed in this volume. The most convincing explanation is the loss of confidence in political institutions and actors during the initial post-socialist transition period, rather than the role that religion and religious actors played during that time. In fact, religion maintained its level of trust, whereas the political sphere lost reputation. Nevertheless, surveys indicate that a significant proportion of people in Eastern Europe and Russia want religion and politics to be separate spheres. However, religious matters have not only been widely discussed in the public sphere, they have led to developments in law. The question of whether, who, or what, is to be protected when religion is involved is not an issue specific to Eastern Europe. As Burkhard Breig has shown in his study on religiously motivated circumcision of minor boys in Germany, the balance between ensuring religious freedom and permitting bodily harm is disputed. An amendment to the German Criminal Code from 2012 defines the conditions under which parents are able to validly consent to elective circumcision of their minor child.

Summing up, religion in Eastern Europe today plays a crucial role beyond the dimension of belief, in both society and state identity building. In this respect, religion, when utilized by politics, unfolds both uniting and dividing effects, inclusion and exclusion. Religion has been employed to enhance consensus and coherence within one group, as well as to explain differences; create borders; and claim spiritual, emotional, and geographical territory. The relationship between state and church is often ambiguous. The states analyzed in this book tend to control, protect, and promote religion at the same time, while churches try to achieve influence, sometimes employing state support to do so. This approach causes tensions not only between state and church, but also within society. Besides the perspective of societal integration or exclusion, and conflict, social scientists analyzing the interplay between religion and politics today must be aware of those dimensions of societal culture that are affected by the newly established cooperation between state and church(es) in order to identify not only the associated means but also the overall political goals: shaping daily attitudes, political values, or constructing new collective identities. The conclusions of most contributions to this volume point to identity building as the key area of interaction between religion and politics in Eastern Europe. This development gives rise to the paradox of hybrid modernization, in which societies aim to modernize in technical and economic matters but 'preserve' what they construct as traditional, including by employing religion. This so-called social conservatism, which is rooted in the role that religion plays, seems to be typical of many Eastern European countries today.

Authors

Burkhard Breig, Prof. Dr., associate professor of Law at the Institute for East-European Studies at Freie Universität Berlin.

Damir Gainutdinov, PhD., lawyer, Agora Human Rights Association, St. Petersburg

Julia Gerlach, Dr. phil, research associate at the Institute for East-European Studies and the Center for Global Politics at Freie Universität Berlin.

Nadir Kinossian, PhD, postdoctoral researcher, Department for Culture and Literature, UiT—The Arctic University of Norway.

Sabine Riedel, Prof. Dr. habil., senior associate at the German Institute for International and Security Affairs (SWP), Berlin.

Inga Pylypchuk, journalist, Die Welt, Berliner Morgenpost.

Jochen Töpfer, Dr. rer. pol., Institute for Sociology, Otto-von-Guericke Universität Magdeburg.

Heike Winkel, research associate, Institute for East-European Studies, Freie Universität Berlin.

MIX
Papier aus verantwortungsvollen Quellen
Paper from responsible sources
FSC® C105338

If you have any concerns about our products,
you can contact us on
ProductSafety@springernature.com

In case Publisher is established outside the EU,
the EU authorized representative is:
Springer Nature Customer Service Center GmbH
Europaplatz 3, 69115 Heidelberg, Germany

Printed by Libri Plureos GmbH
in Hamburg, Germany